STECK-VAUGHN
GED Social Studies

D0764902

STECK-VAUGHN
C O M P A N Y
A Subsidiary of National Education Corporation

STAFF CREDITS

Supervising Editor: Ron Lemay
Editor: Melinda Veatch
Design Director: D. Childress
Design Coordinator: Sharon Golden
Editorial Consultant: Donna Amstutz

Contributing Writers/Editor: Virginia Lowe, Sharon Fear, Karen Davy

Design/Production: Fuller Dyal & Stamper Inc.
Cover Photograph: David Mackenzie

Editorial Development: McClanahan & Company, Inc.
Project Director: Mark Moscowitz

Photograph Credits: p. 26 AP / Wide World
p. 64 © Joe Sohm / Uniphoto
p. 128 © PhotoEdit
p. 168 © Michael Hayman / Stock, Boston
p. 218 © F B Grunzweig / Photo Researchers

ISBN 0-8114-4702-2

4 5 6 7 8 9 CP 97 96 95 94 93 92

Table of Contents

ECONOMICS

POLITICAL SCIENCE

BEHAVIORAL SCIENCE

POSTTEST

SIMULATED GED TEST

What You Should Know About the GED Test

What is the GED Test?

You are taking a very big step toward changing your life with your decision to take the GED test. By opening this book, you are taking your second important step: to prepare for the test. You may feel nervous about what is ahead, which is only natural. Relax and read the following pages to find out the answers to your questions.

The GED, the test of General Educational Development, is given by the GED Testing Service of the American Council on Education for adults who did not graduate from high school. When you pass the GED, you will receive a certificate that is the equivalent of a high school diploma. It is regarded as being the same as a high school diploma. Employers in private industry and government, as well as admissions officers in colleges and universities, accept the GED certificate as they would a high school diploma.

The GED tests cover the same subjects people study in high school. The five subject areas are: Writing Skills, Interpreting Literature and the Arts, Social Studies, Science, and Mathematics. In Writing Skills Part II, you will be asked to write a short essay on a specific subject. You will not be required to know all the information that is usually taught in high school. You will, however, be tested on your ability to read and process information. In some states you may be required to take a test on the U.S. Constitution or on your state government. Check with your local adult education center to see if your state requires this test.

Each year hundreds of thousands of adults take and pass the GED test. The *Steck-Vaughn GED Series* will help you to develop and refine your reading and thinking skills in order to pass the GED test.

What You Should Know About GED Scores

After you complete the GED test, you will get a score for each section and a total score. The total score is an average of all the other scores. The highest score possible on a single test is 80. The scores needed to pass the GED test vary, depending on where you live. The chart on page 2 shows the minimum state score requirements. A minimum score of *40 or 45* means that no test score can be less than 40, or if one or more scores is less than 40, an average of at least 45 is required. Scores of *35 and 45* mean that no test score can be less than 35, and an average of at least 45 is required.

GED Score Requirements

Area	Minimum Score on Each Test		Minimum Average on All Five Tests
UNITED STATES			
Alabama, Alaska, Arizona, Colorado, Connecticut, District of Columbia, Georgia, Hawaii, Idaho, Illinois, Indiana, Iowa, Kansas, Kentucky, Maine, Massachusetts, Michigan, Minnesota, Missouri, Montana, Nevada, New Hampshire, North Carolina, Ohio, Pennsylvania, Rhode Island, Tennessee, Vermont, Virginia, Wyoming	35	and	45
Arkansas, California, Delaware, Florida, Maryland, New York, Oklahoma, Oregon, South Dakota, Utah, Washington, West Virginia	40	and	45
Louisiana, Mississippi, Nebraska, Texas	40	or	45
New Jersey (42 is required on Test 1; 40 is required on Tests 2, 3, and 4; 45 is required on Test 5; and 225 is required as a minimum test score.)			
New Mexico, North Dakota	40	or	50
South Carolina	–		45
Wisconsin	40	and	50
CANADA			
Alberta, British Columbia, Manitoba, Northwest Territories, New Brunswick (35 and 45 for French), Nova Scotia, Prince Edward Island, Saskatchewan, Yukon Territory	45		–
Newfoundland	40	and	45
U.S. TERRITORIES & OTHERS			
Guam, Kwajalein, Puerto Rico, Virgin Islands	35	and	45
Canal Zone, Palau	40	and	45
Mariana Islands, Marshall Islands	40	or	45
American Samoa	40		–

The chart tells you what will be on each test. When you take the simulated GED test in this book, see how well you do within the time limit. In some states you do not have to take all sections of the test on the same day. If you take the test one section at a time, this chart can help you decide how much time you will need for each test. If you want to take all the test sections in one day, you will find that the GED test will last an entire day. Check with your local adult education center for the requirements in your area.

THE TESTS OF GENERAL EDUCATIONAL DEVELOPMENT

Test	Content Areas	Number of Items	Time Limit (minutes)
Writing Skills Part I	Sentence Structure Usage Mechanics	55	75
Writing Sample Part II	Essay	1	45
Social Studies	Geography U.S. History Economics Political Science Behavioral Science	64	85
Science	Life Science Earth Science Physics Chemistry	66	95
Interpreting Literature and the Arts	Popular Literature Classical Literature Commentary	45	65
Mathematics	Arithmetic Algebra Geometry	56	90

Where Do You Go to Take the GED Test?

The GED test is offered year-round throughout the United States, its possessions, U.S. military bases worldwide, and in Canada. To find out where and when a test is being held near you, contact one of the following institutions in your area:

- ◆ An adult education center
- ◆ A continuing education center
- ◆ A private business school or technical school
- ◆ A local community college
- ◆ The public board of education
- ◆ A library

In addition, these institutions can give you information regarding necessary identification, testing fees, and writing implements. Schedules vary: some testing centers are open several days a week; others are open only on weekends.

Why Should You Take the GED Test?

A GED certificate can help you in the following ways:

Employment
Employees without high school diplomas or GED certificates are having much greater difficulty changing jobs or moving up in their present companies. In many cases, employers will not consider hiring people who do not have a high school diploma or its equivalent.

Education
If you want to enroll in a college or university, a technical or vocational school, or even an apprenticeship program, you often must have a high school diploma or its equivalent.

Personal
The most important thing is how you feel about yourself. You have the unique opportunity to turn back the clock by making something happen that did not happen in the past. You can now attain a GED certificate that not only will help you in the future, but will help you feel better about yourself now.

How to Prepare for the GED Test

Classes for GED preparation are available to anyone who wants to take the GED. The choice of whether to take the class is entirely up to you; they are not required. If you prefer to study by yourself, the *Steck-Vaughn GED Series* has been prepared to guide your study. *Steck-Vaughn Exercise books* are also available to give you practice on all of the tests, including the writing sample.

Many people are taking classes to prepare for the GED test. Most programs offer individualized instruction and tutors who can help you identify areas in which you may need help. Most adult education centers offer free day or night classes. The classes are usually informal and allow you to work at your own pace and with other adults who also are studying for the GED. Attendance is usually not taken. In addition to working on specific skills, you will be able to take practice GED tests (like those in this book) in order to check your progress. For more information about classes available near you, call one of the institutions listed on page 3.

What You Need to Know to Pass Test Two: Social Studies

This test examines your ability to understand and use information. You will be asked to think about what you read. You will not be tested on any outside knowledge about the social sciences. The test takes 85 minutes and has 64 questions. The questions are divided into five categories of social sciences: geography, history, economics, political science, and behavioral science.

Geography

Fifteen percent of the test questions will cover geography. Geography is the study of the overall physical and cultural make-up of the world. The reading selections will focus on how the earth affects humanity and how humanity affects the earth.

History

Twenty-five percent of the test questions will cover the history of the United States. American history selections will be drawn from the events that began the country and from events that have occurred up to the present time.

Economics

Twenty percent of the test questions will cover economics. Economics selections focus on how goods and services are used by the government, businesses, and consumers.

Political Science

Twenty percent of the test questions will cover political science. Political science selections focus on the way government works and how citizens are involved in the way the country is run.

Behavioral Science

Twenty percent of the test questions will cover behavioral science. Selections are drawn from anthropology, psychology, and sociology; all study how and why people act as they do.

The Social Studies Test Questions

The test questions require you to think about the reading selections or graphics in several different ways. To answer the questions, you will be using four basic thinking skills. The *Steck-Vaughn GED Social Studies* text will train you in using these skills.

Comprehension

Twenty percent of the questions require you to understand the facts and unstated ideas of both written and graphic selections. You will need to understand the facts and the details supporting those facts. You may be asked to restate specific information so you can identify the general meaning of the entire selection. You will also have to understand what the author does not state directly. Sometimes an idea will be only suggested; you may need to turn to your own experiences to infer the author's meaning.

Analysis

Thirty percent of the questions ask you to analyze information or take it apart to see how it works. You will look at the relationship between one statement or idea and another to see how they fit together.

Application

Another thirty percent of the questions test your application skills. You will be asked to take the information you learned through comprehension and view it another way.

Evaluation

Twenty percent of the questions require you to evaluate, or make judgments about, the validity or accuracy of information.

Sample Paragraph and Questions

On the following two pages are a sample paragraph and four questions. These are similar to actual GED items. An explanation of the correct answer and the incorrect options follows each question. It is important to note that although many of the selections on the GED test will look like the example, some selections on the test come in shorter form followed by only one question.

Directions: Choose the <u>best answer</u> to each question.

Items 1 to 4 refer to the following paragraph.

The Great Depression of 1929 to 1939 began with Black Tuesday, October 29, 1929. On that day New York Stock Exchange prices fell drastically as 16 million shares were sold. Later the stock market rallied, but business activity in the United States continued to decline. Too few people held too much of the country's wealth. Many ordinary people were unable to buy products that were manufactured. As manufacturer inventories mounted, plants closed and workers were laid off. As the number of unemployed rose, demand dropped. Banks began to fail, and individuals lost their life savings, thus losing funds that might have gone into consumer spending. The industrial depression caused an agricultural depression since the unemployed could not even buy food. In California, orange crops were dumped in the ocean because the cost of transportation would not be covered by the sale of the oranges. The poor starved while food was wasted.

1. Which is the best summary of the paragraph?

(1) The Great Depression began with the stock market crash.
(2) The Great Depression was a time of economic loss and personal hardship.
(3) Many people starved during the Great Depression.
(4) The Great Depression was a time of waste.
(5) Wealthy people were responsible for the Great Depression.

Answer: **(2) The Great Depression was a time of economic loss and personal hardship.**

Explanation: This is an example of a comprehension item. You are asked to understand the intent of the entire paragraph. Options (1) and (3) are supporting details, while options (4) and (5) are unsupported generalizations.

2. Which statement shows a cause-and-effect relationship?

(1) Goods were available and people could not buy them.
(2) Banks failed and people lost their life savings.
(3) The poor starved and food was wasted.
(4) Prices fell and the stock market recovered.
(5) The stock market rallied and business activity declined.

Answer: **(2) Banks failed and people lost their life savings.**

Explanation: This is an analysis item. When you look for the result of an event, restate the options by beginning the idea with <u>because</u>: Because the banks failed, people lost their life savings. If you try that with the other options, the sentence does not make sense in terms of what you know about the world.

3. Which of the following are modern economists probably trying to predict by keeping an eye on the stock market and unemployment figures?

   (1) destruction of the orange crop
   (2) bank failure
   (3) the future of business activity
   (4) the kind of products that should be manufactured
   (5) how people will deal with waste

Answer: **(3) the future of business activity**
Explanation: This is an example of an application item. You must understand the specific information in the paragraph and apply it by reasoning that economists in general might pay attention to certain economic signals. Both the stock market and unemployment figures can indicate how much consumers are spending and will be able to spend. Consumer spending influences business activity. Options (1) and (2) were results of the Depression, but would not be primary concerns of modern economists. Options (4) and (5) have nothing to do with the stock market or unemployment.

4. Which statement is supported by information in the paragraph?

   (1) Ordinary people did not know how to deal with the Great Depression.
   (2) Poverty is a serious problem in America.
   (3) Overproduction by manufacturers was partially responsible for the Great Depression.
   (4) Farming is the only safe occupation during an economic depression.
   (5) Farmers can be negatively affected by what happens in other parts of the economy.

Answer: **(5) Farmers can be negatively affected by what happens in other parts of the economy.**
Explanation: This is an evaluation item. You must use several skills to arrive at the answer. You must understand the main idea and the meaning of the details. Next, you have to recognize the relationship between a specific detail and the main idea. Last, you need to decide which of the options given is accurate. Option (1) has no support in the paragraph. Option (2) is true, but is not discussed. Option (3) is incorrect because the problem was with purchasing power, not with overproduction. Option (4) is disproved by the paragraph.

Test-Taking Skills

Most people become nervous when they are faced with taking a test. Try to keep yourself as calm and relaxed as possible. Treat preparation for the GED as you would preparation for an important job interview. Feel good about yourself. Get plenty of sleep the night before the test, and have a good meal before you take the test. Wear something comfortable, because you will be sitting for a long time. Be sure to take important items, such as your watch or tissues, because you will not be allowed to leave your seat while the test is in progress.

Answering the Test Questions

The GED is not the kind of test you can "cram" for. You will be tested on your understanding of social studies skills, not on specific information that you can know about beforehand. There are, however, some ways you can improve your performance on the test. (It would be helpful to practice some of these as you work through this book.)

- Never skim the instructions. Read the directions carefully so that you know exactly what you are being asked to do. For example, you do not want to circle answers if you are supposed to be filling in the circles. If you are unsure, ask the test-giver if the directions can be explained.

- First skim the reading passage or visual to get a general idea of what it is about, and read the questions through once. Then go back and read the passage or look at the visual carefully before answering the questions.

- Be sure to read all the options closely, even if you think you know the right answer. Some answers may not necessarily seem wrong. However, one answer will be better than the others.

- Try to answer as many questions as you can. Wrong answers will not be subtracted from your score. If you cannot find one correct answer, eliminate all the answers you positively know are wrong. Now the number of possible correct answers is smaller. Then read the passage or look at the visual again to see if you can find the correct answer. If you still cannot find the correct answer, as a last resort, make your best guess.

- Remember that this is a timed test. Do not take a long time on each question. Answer each question as best you can and go on. If you finish before the time is up, go back to the questions you were unsure of and give them more thought.

Study Skills

Organize your time.

- If you can, set aside an hour every day to study. If you do not have time every day, set up a schedule of the days you can study and stick to that schedule. Be sure to pick a time when you will be the most relaxed and least likely to be bothered by outside distractions.

- Let others know your study time. Ask them to leave you alone for that period. It helps to explain to others why this is important.

- You should be relaxed when you study, so find an area that is comfortable and quiet. If this is not possible at home, go to a local library. Many libraries have areas for reading and studying. If there is a college or university near you, check the library there. Most college libraries have spaces set aside for studying.

Organize your study materials.

- Be sure to have sharp pencils, pens, and paper for any notes you might want to take.

- Keep all of your books together. If you are taking an adult education class, you probably will be able to borrow some books or other study material. Keep them separate from your own books so that there is no mix-up.

- Make a separate notebook or folder for each subject you are studying. A folder with pockets is useful for storing loose papers.

- If you can study at home, keep all of your material near your study area so you will not waste time looking for it each time you study.

Read!

- Read the newspaper, read magazines, read books. Read whatever appeals to you—but read! If it sounds as though this idea has been repeated a lot, you are right. Reading is the most important thing you can do to prepare for the tests.

- Go to your local library. If you are not familiar with the library, ask the librarian for help. If you are not sure what to read, ask the librarian to suggest something. Be sure to tell the librarian the kinds of things you are interested in. Ask for a library card if you do not have one.

- Try to read something new every day.

Take notes.

- Take notes on things that interest you or things that you think might be useful.

- When you take notes, do not simply copy the words directly from the book. Restate the information in your own words.

- You can take notes any way you want. You do not have to write in full sentences. Just be sure that you will be able to understand your notes later.

- Use outlines, charts, or diagrams to help you organize information and make it easier to learn.

- You may want to take notes in a question-and-answer form, such as: What is the main idea? The supporting details are . . .

Improve your vocabulary.

- As you read, do not skip over a word you do not know. Instead, try to figure out what the difficult word means. First, omit it from the sentence. Read the sentence without the word and try to put another word in its place. Is the meaning of the sentence the same?

- Make a list of unfamiliar words, look them up in the dictionary, and write down the meanings.

- Since a word may have several meanings, it is best to look up the word while you have the passage with you. You can then try out the different meanings in the sentence.

- When you read the definition of a word, restate it in your own words. Use the word in a sentence or two.

Make a list of subject areas that give you trouble.

- As you go through this book, make a note whenever you do not understand something.

- Go back and review the problem when you have time.

- If you are taking a class, ask the teacher for special help with the problem areas.

Use the glossary at the end of this book to review the meanings of the key terms.

- All of the words you see in boldface type are defined in the back of the book.

- In addition, definitions of other important words are included.

Self-Inventory of Study Skills

Ask yourself the following questions:

- Am I organized?
- Do I have a study schedule?
- Do I stick to my study schedule?
- Do I have a place to study?
- Do I have a place for my study material?
- Do I have a notebook and a pencil or pen?
- Do I read something at least once a day?
- Do I take notes on what I read?
- Do I review my notes later?
- Do I pay attention to words I don't know?
- Do I look up words in the dictionary and write down their meanings?
- Do I know where my local public library is?
- Do I have a library card so that I can check out books to read?
- Do I keep a list of things that give me trouble?
- Do I ask for help when I need it?

If you said yes to all the questions, good for you! If there were a few no's, why not give those areas a try?

PRETEST

Social Studies

Directions

The Social Studies Pretest is intended to measure your knowledge of general social studies concepts.

This pretest consists of multiple-choice questions that are based on short readings, graphs, maps, charts, and diagrams. Study the information given and then answer the questions that follow. Refer to the information as often as necessary in answering the questions.

You should spend no more than 45 minutes answering the questions on this test. Work carefully, but do not spend too much time on any one question.

Record your answers to the questions on the separate answer sheets provided on page 261 and 262. Be sure that all requested information is properly recorded on the answer sheet. You may make extra copies of the answer sheets. To record your answers, mark the numbered space on the answer sheet beside the number that corresponds to the question on the pretest.

Example:

Early pioneers of the western frontier looked to settle on land that had adequate access to game and fowl.

To ensure access to food, many early pioneers settled on land near

(1) rivers
(2) grasslands
(3) forests
(4) glaciers
(5) oceans   ① ② ● ④ ⑤

The correct answer is <u>forests</u>; therefore, answer space 3 should be marked on the answer sheet.

Do not make any stray or unnecessary marks on the answer sheet. If you change an answer, erase your first mark completely. Mark only one answer space for each question. Multiple answers will be scored as incorrect. Do not fold or crease your answer sheet.

Pretest

Directions: Choose the best answer to each item.

Items 1 to 3 refer to the following map.

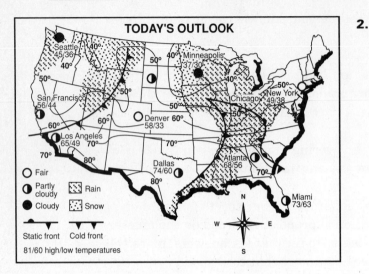

TODAY'S OUTLOOK

O Fair
◑ Partly cloudy
● Cloudy

▒ Rain
▒ Snow

Static front   Cold front

81/60 high/low temperatures

1. What is the most likely effect of today's weather?

(1) Snow delays flights at Minneapolis airports.
(2) The Denver school system announces a snow day.
(3) Pollution closes Los Angeles beaches.
(4) Smog disrupts air travel in New York.
(5) Hurricane Alice threatens Miami.

2. Which statement is supported by the information in the map?

(1) Temperatures in Denver will not reach the expected high of 58°F.
(2) There should be fair skies for several days throughout the southwestern U.S.
(3) Partly cloudy skies and highs in the 70s are expected in Dallas today.
(4) Rain-slick roads will cause traffic accidents in New York.
(5) Isolated flash-flood warnings are expected in the Chicago area.

3. Which statement below is best supported by information in the map?

(1) People practice dry farming in the arid regions of the United States.
(2) The higher a place's altitude, the colder its climate.
(3) Along cold fronts, where warm and cold air meet, precipitation often occurs.
(4) The eastern half of the U.S. has a larger population than the western half.
(5) Temperatures tend to be warmer in the northern half of the U.S.

Item 4 is based on the following paragraph.

Geography and history support each other. A knowledge of the history of a particular region requires an understanding of the region's geography. For this reason, studying the lay of the land, the routes available for easy travel, the location of population centers, and the region's economy and political direction provides a clear idea of the role of geography and history in the development of the region.

4. Which statement best summarizes the paragraph?

(1) A geographer must also be a historian.
(2) To understand the history of a place, one must understand its geography.
(3) Geography affects political development.
(4) Geography influences economic development.
(5) Geography affects travel routes and the locations of cities.

Item 5 refers to the following graph.

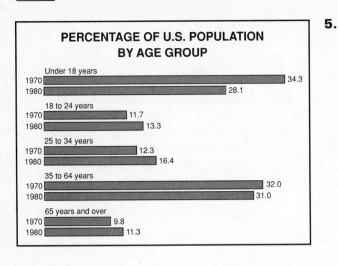

PERCENTAGE OF U.S. POPULATION
BY AGE GROUP

Under 18 years
1970 — 34.3
1980 — 28.1

18 to 24 years
1970 — 11.7
1980 — 13.3

25 to 34 years
1970 — 12.3
1980 — 16.4

35 to 64 years
1970 — 32.0
1980 — 31.0

65 years and over
1970 — 9.8
1980 — 11.3

5. Based on the graph, which issue probably became a concern to children and their parents between 1970 and 1980?

(1) civil rights
(2) foreign aid
(3) health care
(4) the environment
(5) election reform

Items 6 and 7 refer to the following paragraph.

Congress outlawed the manufacture and sale of liquor with the passage of the Eighteenth Amendment. It was quickly ratified by the states and became law in 1920. Support for Prohibition, as it was called, was strong among rural and small-town people, but weak in the cities. Widespread refusal to obey the law led to dishonesty among public officials, courts that did not function properly, and the rise of criminals who profited from illegal liquor sales. The law was repealed in 1933 by the passing of the Twenty-first Amendment.

6. The purpose of Prohibition was to

(1) prevent the making and selling of liquor
(2) prevent public officials from becoming dishonest
(3) ratify the Eighteenth Amendment
(4) repeal the Twenty-first Amendment
(5) keep liquor away from children

7. One effect of Prohibition was

(1) the corruption of small-town America
(2) a better court system
(3) the passage of the Eighteenth Amendment
(4) an increase in urban crime
(5) support among rural people

Item 8 refers to the following map.

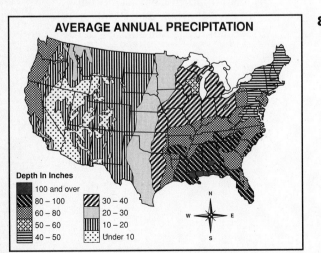

AVERAGE ANNUAL PRECIPITATION

Depth In Inches
100 and over
80 – 100
60 – 80
50 – 60
40 – 50
30 – 40
20 – 30
10 – 20
Under 10

8. Certain types of wheat are resistant to drought and use water economically. The map would suggest that this type of wheat is probably grown in the

(1) eastern United States
(2) western United States
(3) southeastern United States
(4) northeastern United States
(5) Great Lakes region

Item 9 refers to the following map.

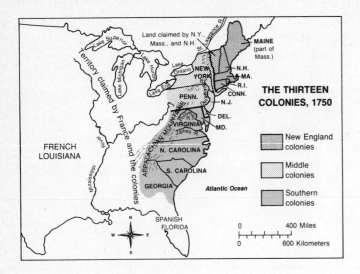

THE THIRTEEN COLONIES, 1750

New England colonies
Middle colonies
Southern colonies

9. Which event can be predicted from the information in the map?

(1) Land disputes would erupt between the colonists and the French.
(2) Fighting would occur between the colonists and the Indians.
(3) The colonists would fight the British for independence.
(4) Slavery would become common in the Southern colonies.
(5) France would sell the Louisiana Territory to the United States.

Items 10 to 12 refer to the following advertisement.

BOOKKEEPER / PAYROLL

North Shore firm seeks person to handle payroll and book-keeping. Ideal candidate is high school grad with 2 years bookkeeping and computer experience. Payroll experience a plus, but will train. We offer flexible hours and a competitive salary and benefits, including dental. Small, nonsmoking office. Send résumé with salary history to:

Barr & Co. 500 North Shore, Chicago, IL 60604

An Equal Opportunity Employer

10. Mike is applying for the job described in the ad. Which fact should he stress in an interview?

(1) He speaks two languages.
(2) He lives on the North Shore.
(3) His hobbies are reading and swimming.
(4) He has worked as a lifeguard.
(5) He got excellent grades in high school.

11. Which fact would not be included in your résumé of skills that are important to the job?

(1) You graduated from high school.
(2) You are married and have two children.
(3) You worked for three years as a bookkeeper.
(4) You worked in payroll for a year at a local hospital.
(5) You are taking a computer course.

12. Which statement about the job in the ad expresses an opinion rather than a fact?

(1) The firm is located on Chicago's North Shore.
(2) The job offers a dental plan.
(3) Flexible hours can be arranged.
(4) An applicant without experience in payroll probably will not be hired.
(5) Smoking is not allowed in the office.

Items 13 and 14 refer to the following paragraph.

The Industrial Revolution refers to the period of great economic and social change brought on by the use of machines. Beginning in the mid-1700s in England, the machine age then spread throughout western Europe and the United States in the eighteenth and nineteenth centuries. As people turned from making things by hand at home to making them by power-driven machines, often in huge factories, production increased a great deal. Mechanization brought great wealth to some and made others lose their jobs. The mechanical reaper, for example, displaced thousands of farm workers.

13. The author states that the Industrial Revolution caused social upheaval. Which evidence from the paragraph best supports this?

(1) The Industrial Revolution began in England.
(2) The Industrial Revolution spread throughout western Europe and the United States in the eighteenth and nineteenth centuries.
(3) People once made things by hand at home.
(4) Mechanization increased production.
(5) The mechanical reaper left thousands of farm workers without jobs.

14. According to the paragraph, what was the direct cause of increased production during the Industrial Revolution?

(1) making things by hand
(2) making things at home
(3) power-driven machines
(4) great wealth
(5) displaced farm workers

Item 15 refers to the following paragraph.

In one small city with no public transportation, the ABC Taxi Company is the only way to get around if you do not have a car.

15. Which of the following is most likely true of the ABC Taxi Company?

(1) Its service is good.
(2) The price of a taxi ride is high.
(3) The price of a taxi ride is low.
(4) The city will regulate the company.
(5) ABC will go out of business.

Item16 refers to the following paragraph.

During the Vietnam War, some American soldiers tortured and killed Vietnamese civilians. When this was first reported in the press, many Americans refused to believe the reports.

16. The paragraph suggests that, even in war, many Americans believe in

(1) individual liberty
(2) religious freedom
(3) free speech
(4) hard work
(5) protection of innocent people

Items 17 and 18 refer to the following map.

WESTERN HEMISPHERE TRADE WITH U.S.

CANADA

UNITED STATES

THE BAHAMAS
JAMAICA
HAITI
DOMINICAN REPUBLIC
VENEZUELA
TRINIDAD AND TOBAGO
GUYANA
SURINAME

MEXICO

GUATEMALA
EL SALVADOR
HONDURAS
NICARAGUA
COSTA RICA
PANAMA

COLOMBIA

BRAZIL

ECUADOR

PERU

PARAGUAY

BOLIVIA

URUGUAY

CHILE

ARGENTINA

60 +
51 – 60
41 – 50
31 – 40
21 – 30
10 – 20

(as percentage of each country's total, average for 1978 – 1980)

17. Which is not a fact that can be verified by information in the map?

(1) At least 60 percent of Mexico's total trade is with the U.S.
(2) More than half of Canada's total trade is with the U.S.
(3) Cultural similarity helps the U.S. and Canada maintain close trade relations.
(4) Brazil and the U.S. are not major trading partners.
(5) Panama, Honduras, and Venezuela trade goods with the U.S.

18. Which conclusion is best supported by evidence in the map?

(1) Political differences prevent trade between some countries.
(2) Geographic distances can influence trade between countries.
(3) The U.S. imports more goods than it exports.
(4) In the future, trade between the U.S. and Brazil will increase.
(5) The economies of countries in the Western Hemisphere are largely independent of one another.

Item 19 refers to the following graph.

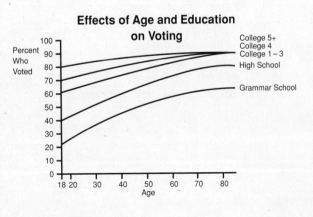

Effects of Age and Education on Voting

College 5+
College 4
College 1 – 3
High School
Grammar School

Percent Who Voted

100
90
80
70
60
50
40
30
20
10
0

18 20   30   40   50   60   70   80
Age

19. The graph shows that the group with the highest percentage of voters was the

(1) older with college education
(2) older with high school education
(3) younger people
(4) middle-aged
(5) college educated between 35 and 45 years of age

Items 20 and 21 refer to the following paragraph.

When Congress sends a proposed law, or bill, to the president, the president may veto it. The bill can still become law, however, if two thirds of the members of both houses of Congress vote to override the veto. The president can further influence the passing of legislation with what is called a pocket veto. If a bill is sent to the president within ten days of the time Congress adjourns, the president may simply hold the bill, neither signing it into law nor vetoing it and taking the chance that the veto will be overridden. If the president chooses to do this, the bill will automatically become law after ten days of congressional session. However, if Congress adjourns before the end of the ten days, the bill dies.

20. The most likely reason for the president to use the pocket veto a week before Congress adjourns is so that

(1) Congress will not adjourn
(2) a bill will be killed
(3) the proposed legislation will become law
(4) Congress can adjourn on time
(5) Congress will debate the bill further

21. Congress sends the president a bill nine days before adjournment. At this time, the president <u>cannot</u>

(1) sign the bill into law
(2) veto the bill and have the veto overridden
(3) veto the bill and have it fail to become law
(4) consider the bill's strengths and weaknesses for two weeks
(5) use the pocket veto

Items 22 and 23 are based on the following information.

Political scientists classify political systems according to the person or persons in a society who have the power to govern. Listed below are five types of political systems.
1. <u>dictatorship</u>—one person has total power
2. <u>monarchy</u>—a member of a royal family inherits the right to rule; today's monarchs usually have little real power
3. <u>oligarchy</u>—a small group, usually a wealthy or privileged class, holds power
4. <u>representative democracy</u>—all voters elect others to represent them in making laws
5. <u>pure democracy</u>—all citizens propose and make laws directly

22. Letters from voters in the senator's district persuade the senator to vote in favor of a law increasing the minimum wage. This type of political system is a(n)

(1) dictatorship
(2) monarchy
(3) oligarchy
(4) representative democracy
(5) pure democracy

23. The president orders foreign journalists to leave the country, arrests his political opponent, and declares himself "President-for-Life." This type of political system is a(n)

(1) dictatorship
(2) monarchy
(3) oligarchy
(4) representative democracy
(5) pure democracy

Items 24 and 25 refer to the following information.

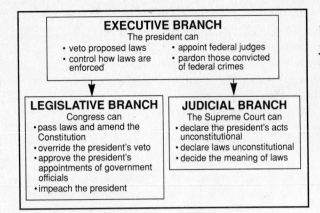

The federal government is divided into three branches: the executive, the legislative, and the judicial. Each branch has certain powers that only it can exercise. The powers of one branch can act as a check on the other two. The purpose of this system—called checks and balances—is to keep a balance of power among the three parts of government. The chart shows the specific powers of each branch of the federal government.

24. One check the president has on the powers of the judicial branch is the power to

- (1) pass laws
- (2) interpret the Constitution
- (3) rule laws unconstitutional
- (4) appoint federal judges
- (5) veto new laws

25. Congress proposes a law against burning the American flag. The president believes this interferes with the constitutional right to free speech. To prevent this law, the president can

- (1) veto the law
- (2) pass the law over Congress's veto
- (3) rule the law unconstitutional
- (4) interpret the law's meaning
- (5) grant a pardon

Item 26 refers to the following information.

The Fifth Amendment to the U.S. Constitution says in part that no one shall be forced in any criminal case to be a witness against himself or herself, nor be deprived of life, freedom, or possessions, without due process of law.

26. Which of the following ideas is behind this part of the Fifth Amendment?

- (1) Capital punishment is cruel and unusual.
- (2) Citizens have the right to have weapons.
- (3) A person is innocent until proven guilty.
- (4) A free press is necessary to a free society.
- (5) All citizens are free to criticize the government.

Items 27 and 28 refer to the following paragraphs.

The term hyperactivity has been loosely applied to children who are loud and misbehave. But the key sign of hyperactivity is not a high activity level. Instead, the primary signs are short attention span and poor impulse control. A minor malfunction in the central nervous system leaves these youngsters unable to focus on one task, so they race from one activity to another.

Experts today use the more accurate label ADD—attention deficit disorder—to describe this problem. ADD children almost always have trouble paying attention and completing assignments. As the child falls farther behind in school, the problem grows worse. If behavior problems were not there to begin with, they quickly develop.

Many ADD children can be helped through parent counseling, behavior modification, and special education. When the disorder is serious, medications are sometimes used.

27. Based on the paragraphs, all of the following are effects of ADD except

(1) a short attention span
(2) poor impulse control
(3) a minor malfunction of the central nervous system
(4) trouble completing assignments
(5) behavior problems

28. Which of the following is not a treatment for ADD?

(1) medication
(2) parent counseling
(3) special education
(4) hyperactivity
(5) behavior modification

Items 29 to 31 refer to the following information.

Learning in humans is a complex process, one that is not totally understood. Psychologists have, however, described some of the ways we use, or fail to use, old and new experiences. They note that earlier learning can make mastering new skills or material easier. A mother, for example, finds that her child-rearing skills help her cope with her students when she takes a teaching job. Psychologists call this use of earlier experience positive transfer. Sometimes, however, earlier learning can interfere with learning new skills or material. A person switching from one word processing system to another with a different keyboard may spend time constantly striking the wrong keys. Psychologists call this negative transfer.

29. Psychologists have noted that earlier learning

(1) is a rather simple process
(2) has helped them understand positive transfer
(3) is rarely related to later learning
(4) is never applied to later learning
(5) can help or hinder later learning

30. Which statement is best supported by examples in the article?

(1) Someday psychologists will completely understand the learning process.
(2) All learning occurs as a result of either positive or negative transfer.
(3) The learning process in humans is different from that in other animals.
(4) In each individual, learning can take place in more than one way.
(5) Negative transfer could be useful in teaching people to avoid unwanted behavior.

31. Which of the following is an example of negative transfer?

(1) A child learns to tie shoelaces.
(2) A doctor learns of a promising new treatment for arthritis.
(3) A Peace Corps worker finds that former work with labor unions helps in organizing fishermen into a cooperative.
(4) A person who is used to driving an automatic transmission has difficulty mastering a new car's standard shift.
(5) A person studies electronics at home.

Item 32 refers to the following graph.

POPULATION SHIFTS SINCE 1950

32. Which statement cannot be verified by information in the graph?

(1) Between 1950 and 1960, the urban population increased by about 25 percent.
(2) Between 1950 and 1960, the rural population increased by about 5 percent.
(3) During this period, the population grew in both rural and urban areas.
(4) Between 1950 and 1980, the trend was toward less growth in urban areas and increased growth in rural areas.
(5) In the next two decades, the population will continue to grow, but at a slower rate.

Answers and Explanations

1. (Analysis) **(1) Snow delays flights at Minneapolis airports.** The map shows snow in Minneapolis, making snow and flight delays possible. Options (2), (3), (4), and (5) are not supported by information in the map.

2. (Analysis) **(3) Partly cloudy skies and highs in the 70s are expected in Dallas today.** This statement is a fact based on a correct reading of the map's symbols. Only Dallas displays the symbols for partly cloudy skies combined with a high temperature in the 70s. Options (1), (2), (4), and (5) are not based on the information in the map.

3. (Evaluation) **(3) Along cold fronts, where warm and cold air meet, precipitation often occurs.** The map shows two fronts. Along both of them there is precipitation in the form of either rain or snow. This supports option (3). The map contains no information that supports options (1), (2), and (4). Option (5) is contradicted by information in the map.

4. (Comprehension) **(2) To understand the history of a place, one must understand its geography.** This is the best statement of the main idea of the paragraph. Option (1) is not a correct interpretation of the author's point. The author does <u>not</u> say that a geographer must know a place's history. Options (3), (4), and (5) are details that support the main idea.

5. (Application) **(3) health care** The graph shows that, in general, the population of the United States is getting older. Older people tend to have more health problems. This suggests that health care will become a major concern. The other issues may worry many Americans, but you cannot predict those based on the information given in the graph.

6. (Comprehension) **(1) prevent the making and selling of liquor** The first sentence of the paragraph states the purpose of Prohibition, which "outlawed the manufacture and sale of liquor." Option (2) is the opposite of what is stated in the paragraph. Options (3) and (4) are incorrect because the purpose of Prohibition was not to amend the Constitution. Option (5) is not supported by information in the paragraph.

7. (Analysis) **(4) an increase in urban crime** The paragraph says that many people in the cities disobeyed the law. This led to an increase in urban crime. The information in the paragraph gives no evidence to support that options (1), (2), and (5) resulted from, or were effects of, Prohibition. Option (3) refers to the action by Congress that made Prohibition law.

8. (Evaluation) **(2) western United States** Drought-resistant wheat is probably grown in areas with little rainfall. As the map shows, there is less rainfall in the western United States than in any of the other regions mentioned in options (1), (3), (4), or (5).

9. (Application) **(1) Land disputes would erupt between the colonists and the French.** The map shows territory between the Mississippi River and the Appalachian Mountains being claimed by both France and the colonies. Using this information, you could predict that there would be disputes. The other options describe real historic events, but they could not have been predicted from information in the map.

10. (Application) **(5) He got excellent grades in high school.** The employer wants a high school graduate, and success in school might indicate that an applicant can do well on the job. Options (1), (2), (3), and (4) are not requirements described in the ad.

11. (Application) **(2) You are married and have two children.** Being married and having children is not a skill needed to do the job described in the advertisement. Options (1), (3), (4), and (5) all relate directly to the requirements of the job; an applicant with these qualifications would probably want to include them in his or her résumé.

12. (Analysis) **(4) An applicant without experience in payroll probably will not be hired.** The word <u>probably</u> marks this as an opinion. Also, the advertisement indicates that payroll experience is helpful, but not required. Options (1), (2), (3), and (5) are facts that can be verified by reading the ad.

13. (Evaluation) **(5) The mechanical reaper left thousands of farm workers without jobs.** This is stated in the last sentence. Options (1), (2), (3), and (4) do not describe effects of the Industrial Revolution.

14. (Analysis) **(3) power-driven machines** The third sentence in the paragraph states that production increased when people started making things by power-driven machines. Options (1) and (2) are identified as the older, slower methods of production. Options (4) and (5) are two effects—not causes—of increased production.

15. (Comprehension) **(2) The price of a taxi ride is high.** The taxi company is a monopoly, a business with complete control over the selling of its service. Since there is no competition to take away business by offering lower prices and/or better service, ABC can, and probably does, keep its prices high in order to make more profit. Option (1) may be true, but there is no incentive for the company to provide good service. Options (3) and (5) are very unlikely. Option (4) may come about only if prices are high and service is poor.

16. (Evaluation) **(5) protection of innocent people** This shows a sense of right and wrong. Many Americans could not believe that American soldiers would harm innocent people. While Americans may believe in the values named in options (1), (2), (3), and (4), these values are not mentioned in the paragraph.

17. (Analysis) **(3) Cultural similarity helps the U.S. and Canada maintain close trade relations.** This statement is an opinion, not a fact. It cannot be verified, or proved, by anything in the map. Options (1), (2), (4), and (5) are clearly supported by information in the map.

18. (Evaluation) **(2) Geographic distances can influence trade between countries.** The two countries bordering the U.S. are shown as doing the most trade with the U.S. The five countries farthest from the U.S. are shown as doing the least trade with the U.S. Options (1), (3), and (4) may or may not be true, but no evidence is given that supports them. Option (5) is contradicted by information in the map.

19. (Comprehension) **(1) older with college education** The three lines showing the highest percentage of voters (between 60 and 80 percent) are those of the college educated. The lines tend upward, indicating an increase in percentage along the age line, reaching their highest point in the 70-80 age range. Options (2), (3), (4), and (5) are not supported by the map.

20. (Analysis) **(2) a bill will be killed** The paragraph states that if Congress adjourns before the end of the ten day limit, the bill dies. Based on the paragraph, you can conclude that the president uses the pocket veto as a way to kill legislation. Options (1) and (4) are incorrect because the paragraph does not indicate that the pocket veto influences the time when Congress will adjourn. Option (3) is unlikely since a bill automatically becomes a law if the president neither signs nor vetoes it and Congress stays in session for more than ten days after having sent the bill to the president. Option (5) is incorrect because Congress cannot debate if it is no longer in session.

21. (Application) **(4) consider the bill's strengths and weaknesses for two weeks** The president does not have two weeks to decide whether or not to sign the bill. In nine days, when Congress adjourns, the bill dies if the president has neither signed it nor vetoed it. According to the paragraph, options (1), (2), (3), and (5) are all actions that the president can take nine days before Congress adjourns.

22. (Application) **(4) representative democracy** A senator is elected by, and so represents, the people of his or her state. As a representative, a senator responds to an electorate in deciding on laws. This is characteristic of a representative democracy, ruling out options (1), (2), (3), and (5).

23. (Application) **(1) dictatorship** An individual, destroying the power and influence of the press and the political process, declares himself the only ruler. This is characteristic of a dictatorship, ruling out options (2), (3), (4), and (5).

24. (Comprehension) **(4) appoint federal judges** The president can influence the judicial branch, or the judiciary, by appointing judges with views similar to his or her own. Options (1), (2), and (3) are not powers that a president has. Option (5) is a power that the president has over the legislature, not over the judiciary.

25. (Application) **(1) veto the law** This is one check that the president has on Congress's lawmaking power. Option (2) is not a presidential power. Options (3) and (4) are powers of the judicial branch. Although option (5) is an executive, or presidential power, this action would not prevent the proposed law.

26. (Analysis) **(3) A person is innocent until proven guilty.** The amendment says that a person cannot be punished "without due process of law." In other words, a person must be treated as innocent until it is proven in a legal process, such as a trial, that he or she is guilty. Options (1), (2), (4), and (5) are not mentioned in the information.

27. (Analysis) **(3) a minor malfunction of the central nervous system** The paragraphs identify this as the cause of attention deficit disorder, or ADD. The other choices are identified as effects of ADD.

28. (Comprehension) **(4) hyperactivity** According to the information, hyperactivity describes the behavior of children who misbehave and make a lot of noise. In the second paragraph, the writer states that this problem has been given another name: ADD, or attention deficit disorder. Options (1), (2), (3), and (5) are identified in the last paragraph as treatments for ADD.

29. (Comprehension) **(5) can help or hinder later learning** The paragraph states that positive transfer involves using earlier learning to learn new skills more easily; negative transfer describes the interference of earlier learning with new learning. Option (1) is incorrect because the paragraph states that learning is a complex process. There is no information in the paragraph that indicates that option (2) is true. The examples given show that options (3) and (4) are not true.

30. (Evaluation) **(4) In each individual, learning can take place in more than one way.** The concrete examples in the paragraph describe the same person transferring earlier learning in two ways: once by positive transfer and once by negative transfer. This supports option (4). No evidence is given to support any of the other options.

31. (Application) **(4) A person who is used to driving an automatic transmission has difficulty mastering a new car's standard shift.** The person's earlier learning (driving with an automatic transmission) is interfering with later learning (driving with a standard shift). This is an example of negative transfer. Option (3) is an example of positive transfer. Options (1), (2), and (5) do not describe effects of earlier learning.

32. (Analysis) **(5) In the next two decades, the population will continue to grow, but at a slower rate.** This statement is an opinion, not a fact, and cannot be proved by information shown in the graph. Options (1), (2), (3), and (4) are facts based on the data.

PRETEST Correlation Chart

Social Studies

The chart below will help you determine your strengths and weaknesses in reading comprehension and in the content areas of geography, history, economics, political science, and behavioral science.

Directions

Circle the number of each item that you answered correctly on the Pretest. Count the number of items you answered correctly in each column. Write the amount in the Total Correct space for each column. (For example, if you answered 5 comprehension items correctly, place the number 5 in the blank before *out of 7*). Complete this process for the remaining columns.

Count the number of items you answered correctly in each row. Write that amount in the Total Correct space for each row. (For example, in the Geography row, write the number correct in the blank before *out of 5*). Complete this process for the remaining rows. Boldface items indicate that the question refers to a map, chart, table, or graph.

Cognitive Skills/Content	Comprehension	Analysis	Application	Evaluation	Total Correct
Geography *(pages 26-63)*	4	**1, 2, 32**		3	____ out of 5
History *(pages 64-127)*	6	7	9	**8,** 13	____ out of 4
Economics *(pages 128-167)*	15	12, 14, **17**	10, 11	16, **18**	____ out of 8
Political Science *(pages 168-217)*	**19,** 24	20, 26	21, 22, 23, 25		____ out of 8
Behavioral Science *(pages 218-247)*	28, 29	27	**5,** 31	30	____ out of 6
Total Correct	____ out of 7	____ out of 10	____ out of 9	____ out of 6	total correct:____out of 32 1-25: need more review 26-32: Congratulations! You're Ready

If you answered fewer than 26 questions correctly, determine which areas are hardest for you. Go back to the *Steck-Vaughn GED Social Studies* book and review the content in those areas. In the parentheses under the item type heading, the page numbers tell you where you can find specific instruction about that area of social studies in the *Steck-Vaughn Social Studies* book.

GEOGRAPHY

The Middle East has vast oil reserves.

- **ocean**
  a large body of salt water

- **continent**
  one of the seven major landmasses on the earth

- **culture**
  the knowledge, beliefs, morals, laws, arts, and customs of a society

- **region**
  a specific area of the earth

- **natural resources**
  materials we use that are supplied by nature

Geography is the study of three basic things:

1. the physical environment—the shape of the land, what grows on the land, what natural resources can be found on the land, and the climate of the land
2. the human environment—the population, migration, and cultural distribution of people on the earth
3. the earth and its people—how the physical environment affects people and how people affect the land, air, and water

The earth is a planet, a large ball covered by **oceans** and **continents**. Over the thousands of years of human history, the world's population has spread over all of the earth's usable land. Understanding the surface of the earth has always been important to people's survival. People need to know where water can be found, where there is land to grow food, and where the natural materials needed for shelter can be found. The study of geography helps us understand the form of the land and how we can use it. Because people have divided the world into nations and **cultures**, geography also covers some of the ways people use the earth.

- **map**
  a line drawing of a specific area

- **table**
  a way of arranging information about an area or group of people, using rows and columns

- **graph**
  a drawing that shows how one quantity depends on or changes with another

In Topic 1, you will learn about the physical and human geography of different parts of the world. You will see how people are grouped in **regions** and how the land has affected the way they live. You will also learn how to restate the information you read.

In Topic 2, you will take a closer look at the people on one continent and in one culture. The focus will be on North America and one of its major countries, the United States of America. In this topic, you will also learn how to summarize ideas.

Topic 3 explains how humans have affected the shape and **natural resources** of the land they live on. You will learn how people have, at times, abused the earth and what some people are trying to do to correct the problems. You also will learn how to make certain decisions based on the information you read.

In each topic, you will learn something about reading **maps**, **tables**, and **graphs**. These skills will help you understand more about the earth and its people.

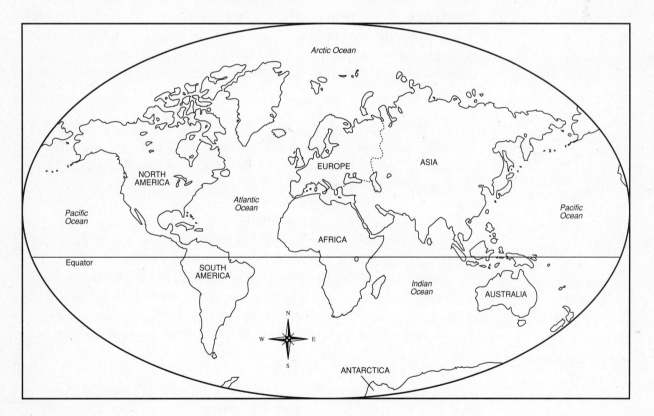

☞ *See also: GED Exercise Book Social Studies, pages 4-14*

LESSON 1 Comprehension Skill: Restating Information

This skill will help you understand the information that you read and that you see in maps and charts.

A **fact**, or **detail**, is a piece of information. When you put an idea into your own words, you are restating the information. When you restate what you have heard, do you include all the important details? Is your restatement accurate?

Imagine that you and a friend bought the same do-it-yourself kitchen cabinets. You have read the instruction booklet and are about to put together your cabinets. Your friend calls to say that his kit doesn't have an instruction booklet, so he hopes you can help by telling him how to put together the cabinets. Reading the instruction book to him won't be helpful because it has a lot of information he will not need. When you give your friend information, you will have to remember everything he should do. Otherwise, he may end up with parts left over and doors that don't close. If you give him the wrong information, he may end up putting the handles on the inside of the cabinet doors.

What you will have to do is pick out the facts needed to put together the cabinets. How are the pieces laid out? What tools are needed? Which kind of screw goes where? Be sure to find all the details for each part of the process.

In the situation above, you would have to read carefully and think carefully. This is true for everything you read if you really want to understand it. When you read, ask yourself the following questions: Who or what is being discussed? What is happening? Where is the action taking place? When is it happening? How is it happening? Sometimes you will find that you have to read a paragraph or a page two or three times before you can answer all these questions. Don't worry. All reading skills take some practice at first.

As you practice, remember that you will be asked to recognize a restated idea. A GED question will give you five options that could be restatements of an idea in a passage. First try to put the idea in your own words. Then match your own restatement with the restatements in the possible answers. Be sure that your choice covers all the information that was requested. Also be sure that your choice is the most accurate.

Practicing Comprehension

Read the following paragraph.

How many times have you heard the phrase "It's a small world"? Is the world really small or does it sometimes just seem that way? If you followed the equator, the imaginary line that goes around the middle of the earth, you would have to travel about 25,000 miles before you got back to where you started. For most of your journey, you would need a boat. Seventy percent of the earth is covered by water. However, you would have to get out of your boat several times and find a way to travel across the three major landmasses that extend over the equator. Each time you landed, you would need to know several different languages in order to communicate with people in the many countries in East Asia, South America, and Africa. By the time you reached the place where you began, you would know that our planet is not really small. It now sometimes seems that way because people have invented ways to travel over the large oceans and vast amounts of land. Also, our modern technology allows us to talk almost instantly to someone halfway around the world.

Questions 1 to 4 refer to the paragraph. Circle the best answer for each question.

1. According to the paragraph, our planet is

   (1) mainly covered by water
   (2) made up mostly of dry land
   (3) very small
   (4) smaller than the planet Jupiter
   (5) divided in two by a major landmass

2. According to the paragraph, one of the landmasses on the equator is

   (1) hard to travel over
   (2) a small country
   (3) Africa
   (4) 25,000 miles away from the other two
   (5) broken up into islands

3. The phrase "It's a small world" was coined because

   (1) the earth is shrinking
   (2) the earth is small when viewed from the moon
   (3) people can travel great distances quickly
   (4) many people have more money to spend
   (5) only thirty percent of the earth is covered by land

4. According to the paragraph, which two inventions make the world appear small?

   (1) the satellite and the computer
   (2) the airplane and the telephone
   (3) the video cassette recorder and the television set
   (4) the automobile and the boat
   (5) the facsimile machine (FAX) and the photocopier

To check your answers, turn to page 36.

Topic 1: Earth's Regions

A map of the earth shows that the land is divided into seven continents. A continent is a major landmass. North America is a continent. But a map of the physical land does not talk about the people who live there. The population of the world falls into nine major areas, often called **cultural regions**. The cultural regions of the world are divided according to physical, economic, historical, and political similarities. When we talk about these cultural regions, we are talking about the people who live there. This is called human geography.

The way people live often depends on the physical limits of the land they have settled in. People who live in a desert will probably wear clothing that protects them from heat, sand, and wind. People who live in a cold climate will probably place importance on ways of growing food and building structures that can keep them warm.

Map-Reading Skills

A map is a form of shorthand that tells you how and where to find things. Maps give information about location, distances, directions, the way the land is shaped, the size and shape of nearby objects, and even the climate and population of a place. Most maps give only some of this information. It is important to know how to read a map's **legend**. A legend is a list or chart of symbols that explain the information that can be found on a map. Distance measurements are given in a map **scale**. Directions of locations on a map are shown by a special sign called a **compass rose**. When you use a map, be sure to read both the heading, or title, and the legend.

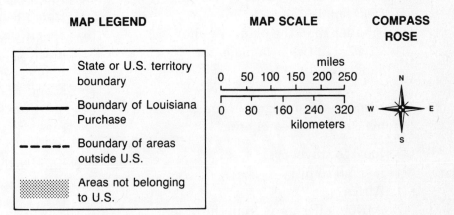

Exercises

Questions 1 and 2 refer to the previous information. Circle the best answer for each question.

1. According to the information, a cultural region can best be described as

   (1) a landmass
   (2) one of the continents
   (3) an area defined by its population
   (4) a political division
   (5) the way people behave

2. The study of geography includes

   (1) living in a desert
   (2) growing food
   (3) predicting the weather
   (4) studying people
   (5) wearing protective clothing

Look at the map.

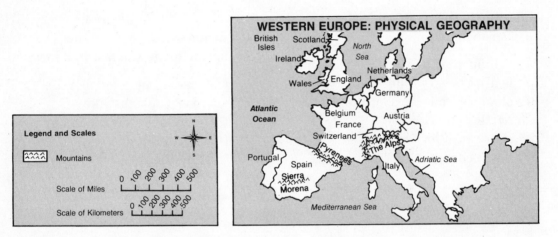

Questions 3 and 4 refer to the map. Circle the best answer for each question.

3. Which of the following can you learn from the map?

   (1) the location of rivers in Western Europe
   (2) the climate in Western European countries
   (3) the distance from Western Europe to North America
   (4) the location of mountain ranges in Western Europe
   (5) the time it takes to get from Spain to Italy

4. Which of the following countries is completely surrounded by water?

   (1) Italy
   (2) Portugal
   (3) England
   (4) Scotland
   (5) Ireland

To check your answers, turn to page 36.

Reviewing Lesson 1

Read the following paragraph.

> Many countries are made up of groups of islands. One of these countries is Japan. The climate of Japan varies. Hokkaido, the northernmost island, gets very cold in winter. On the other hand, the southern island of Kyushu has subtropical summers. All of the islands were formed by volcanoes erupting from the bottom of the ocean. Japan has many mountains but not much land for farming or for building sprawling cities like Los Angeles.

Questions 1 and 2 refer to the paragraph. Circle the best answer for each question.

1. According to the paragraph, the weather in Japan

  (1) is influenced by volcanic eruptions
  (2) is always very mild
  (3) changes from the south to the north
  (4) is not good for farming
  (5) never changes

2. Knowing that Japan has very little usable land, you can guess that <u>sprawling</u> in the last line means

  (1) taking up a lot of space
  (2) very businesslike
  (3) having a warm climate
  (4) mountainous
  (5) southern

Read the following paragraphs.

> On a map, a river looks as though it follows a set line. But a river can change its course. A riverboat captain of one hundred years ago would be quite surprised by how the Mississippi River looks today. The water pushing against the mud and trees has changed all the bends and small islands in the river. Humans can also change the course of a river by building dams and digging channels. The most extraordinary example is the Chicago River. For economic reasons, engineers made the Chicago River run backward.
>
> The changes in a river can affect the way people live. The Nile River in Egypt overflows its banks every summer. The people who first settled near the Nile realized that the rich soil the river left behind as the water went down could allow them several harvests a year. The extra harvests made the people rich in food and eventually led to profitable trade between Egypt and other countries.

Questions 3 and 4 refer to the paragraphs. Circle the best answer for each question.

3. What did the early Egyptians discover about the Nile River?

(1) It made travel and trade easy.
(2) They could turn it around.
(3) Its flooding created good farmland.
(4) Harvesting could be done only in the summer.
(5) The floods could destroy all the newly planted crops.

4. According to the paragraphs, the land around a river can be shifted and changed by

(1) people who travel on the river
(2) engineers
(3) Egyptians
(4) the action of the water
(5) nothing at all

Look at the map.

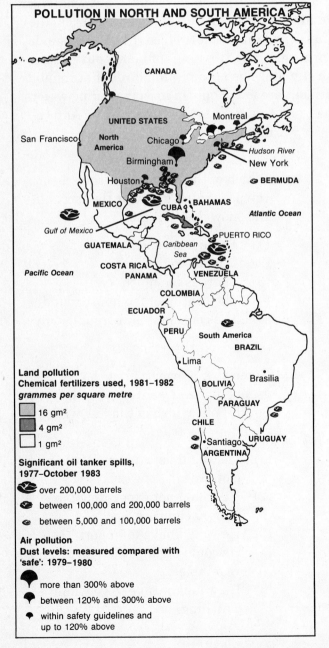

POLLUTION IN NORTH AND SOUTH AMERICA

CANADA

UNITED STATES
North America
San Francisco
Chicago
Montreal
Birmingham
Hudson River
New York
Houston
BERMUDA
MEXICO
CUBA
BAHAMAS
Gulf of Mexico
Atlantic Ocean
GUATEMALA
Caribbean Sea
PUERTO RICO
COSTA RICA
PANAMA
VENEZUELA
Pacific Ocean
COLOMBIA
ECUADOR
PERU
South America
BRAZIL
Lima
Brasilia
BOLIVIA
PARAGUAY
CHILE
Santiago
URUGUAY
ARGENTINA

Land pollution
Chemical fertilizers used, 1981–1982
grammes per square metre

☐ 16 gm²
☐ 4 gm²
☐ 1 gm²

Significant oil tanker spills, 1977–October 1983

🦪 over 200,000 barrels
🦪 between 100,000 and 200,000 barrels
🦪 between 5,000 and 100,000 barrels

Air pollution
Dust levels: measured compared with 'safe': 1979–1980

⬤ more than 300% above
⬤ between 120% and 300% above
⬤ within safety guidelines and up to 120% above

Questions 5 to 7 refer to the map. Circle the best answer for each question.

5. The map gives information about

(1) who is responsible for oil tanker spills
(2) three types of pollution in the Americas
(3) the effect of air pollution
(4) how far Colombia is from Mexico
(5) the climate of Brazil

6. In a six-year period, the most oil spills happened

(1) off the coast of Chile
(2) near Canada
(3) in the Pacific Ocean
(4) in the Gulf of Mexico
(5) near New York City

7. A person who suffered from dust allergies would <u>not</u> choose to live in

(1) San Francisco, California
(2) Birmingham, Alabama
(3) Brasilia, Brazil
(4) Lima, Peru
(5) Santiago, Chile

To check your answers, turn to pages 36 and 37.

GED Mini-Test

Directions: Choose the best answer to each item.

Items 1 to 4 refer to the following paragraph.

Of all the continents, only Antarctica has not attracted permanent settlers. Even though a part of the land is close to the tip of South America, it is probably the most difficult place in the world to live. The South Pole is at the very center of Antarctica. As can be expected, the weather is very cold. The average temperature is 56 degrees below zero. Even though the land is covered with snow and ice, Antarctica is considered to be a desert. This odd fact is the result of the extreme cold. Very little snow ever falls, but what snow does reach the ground almost never melts. Over the centuries, the light snowfalls have hardened into a sheet of ice that is thousands of feet thick. Not surprisingly, only two kinds of plants survive on the edges of the harsh climate. The animals and birds that inhabit this almost round continent are found only in its surrounding waters. Penguins, seals, whales, and fish seem to like the water off Antarctica's coast; this water is warmer than the land.

1. According to the paragraph, Antarctica has no

   (1) snowfall
   (2) plant life
   (3) human settlers
   (4) coastline
   (5) close neighbors

2. A surprising fact about Antarctica is that it is

   (1) very cold
   (2) covered with ice
   (3) the home of many land animals
   (4) a popular vacation spot
   (5) considered to be a desert

3. Which of the following is the reason the paragraph gives for the fact that the snow does not melt?

   (1) There is no sunshine.
   (2) It is too cold.
   (3) There is too much ice.
   (4) The continent is almost round.
   (5) The continent is surrounded by water.

4. Given the information in the paragraph, if a man wanted to settle at the South Pole, which of the following would not be true?

   (1) He would have to bring warm clothes.
   (2) He would not expect to have many neighbors.
   (3) He would have to import his pets.
   (4) He could dig a garden for fresh vegetables.
   (5) He would be able to go whale watching.

To check your answers, turn to page 37.

Items 5 and 6 refer to the map.

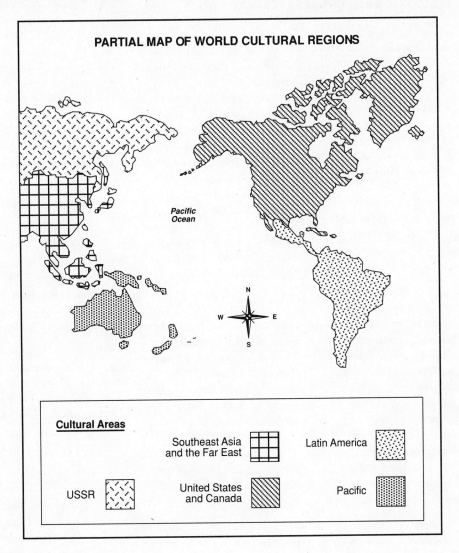

PARTIAL MAP OF WORLD CULTURAL REGIONS

Pacific Ocean

Cultural Areas

Southeast Asia and the Far East

USSR

United States and Canada

Latin America

Pacific

5. From the map you can tell that

(1) the Pacific area is north of Latin America
(2) Southeast Asia and the Far East are not near the USSR
(3) The USSR is south of the Pacific area
(4) more than one cultural region can be on one continent
(5) cultural regions are always separated from each other by water

6. The United States is often called the West. If you traveled directly east across the Pacific from the USSR, which of the following cultural regions would you most likely find?

(1) Latin America
(2) the Pacific area
(3) the United States and Canada
(4) the Far East and Southeast Asia
(5) the North Pole

To check your answers, turn to page 37.

Answers and Explanations

1. (Comprehension) **(1) mainly covered by water** Seventy percent of the earth, more than half, is covered by water. Options (2) and (3) are the opposite of what is stated. Option (4) is not mentioned. According to the paragraph, the only thing that divides the planet in two is the equator, which is not land; so option (5) is incorrect.

2. (Comprehension) **(3) Africa** The three landmasses are listed by name in the paragraph. There is no mention of travel conditions, so option (1) is incorrect. Option (2) is incorrect because the paragraph does not say that any of the landmasses make up only one country. Option (4) refers to the entire distance around the earth. There is no information in the paragraph to support option (5).

3. (Comprehension) **(3) people can travel great distances quickly** According to the paragraph, the planet seems small because of modern technology in travel and communication. There is no evidence to support option (1). Option (2) may be true but is not mentioned in the paragraph. Option (4) has nothing to do with the world seeming small. The same is true for option (5), even though the statement is supported by the paragraph.

4. (Comprehension) **(2) the airplane and the telephone** This is stated in the last two sentences of the paragraph. Although options (1) and (3) may be true, no mention is made of these inventions in the paragraph. The inventions in option (4) allow people to travel around the world, but the length of time to travel this way would make the world seem very large. No mention is made of option (5) in the paragraph, so it is incorrect.

Exercises (page 31)

1. (Comprehension) **(3) an area defined by its population** The first paragraph provides this information. Option (1) refers to a continent. Option (2) is incorrect because it is a physical feature, not a cultural one. Option (4) is only part of what makes up a cultural region. Option (5) is incorrect because behavior does not describe a region.

2. (Comprehension) **(4) studying people** This is a restatement of "human geography." Options (1), (2), (3), and (5) are human activities, but they are not part of studying geography.

3. (Comprehension) **(4) the location of mountain ranges in Western Europe** The legend gives a key for mountains, and this symbol can be found on the map. There is no key for rivers or climate in the legend or the map, so options (1) and (2) are incorrect. North America is not shown, so option (3) is incorrect. Option (5) is incorrect because even though mileage is given, there is no indication of how long it would take to travel any distance.

4. (Comprehension) **(5) Ireland** If you look carefully at the map, you can see that Ireland does not touch any other landmass. Options (1), (2), (3), and (4) refer to countries that border on at least one other country.

Reviewing Lesson 1 (pages 32 to 33)

1. (Comprehension) **(3) changes from the south to the north** The south is warm and the north is cold. There is no evidence of option (1). Options (2) and (5) are opposite of what is stated. There is no evidence of option (4).

2. (Comprehension) **(1) taking up a lot of space** The key is the contrast suggested by the words <u>not much</u> in the paragraph. The opposite would be <u>much</u>. There is no support for the meanings in options (2), (3), (4), or (5).

3. (Comprehension) **(3) Its flooding created good farmland.** Rich soil produces good crops. Option (1) is incorrect because there is no mention of travel. Option (2) refers to the Chicago River, not the Nile. Option (4) is incorrect because that is when the river flooded. There is no support for option (5).

4. (Comprehension) **(4) the action of the water** This is stated about both the Mississippi and the Nile. There is no mention of option (1). Option (2) refers to the course of the river, not the land. Option (3) might have been true in that single case, but it is not mentioned. Option (5) is opposite of what is stated.

5. (Comprehension) **(2) three types of pollution in the Americas** This information is found in the map legend. No information is given about options (1), (3), (4), or (5).

6. (Comprehension) **(4) in the Gulf of Mexico** The symbol for oil spills occurs most in the Gulf of Mexico. Option (1) is incorrect because only two symbols are there. No symbols are near Canada, so option (2) is incorrect. Only three symbols are in the Pacific, so option (3) is incorrect. Fewer symbols appear by New York than in the Gulf, so option (5) is incorrect.

7. (Application) **(2) Birmingham, Alabama** Find the legend code for dust levels. Check each choice against the code. Birmingham, Alabama, has the highest level of dust pollution in the code. There are no pollution symbols for options (1), (3), (4), or (5).

GED Mini-Test (pages 34 to 35)

1. (Comprehension) **(3) human settlers** This information is in the first sentence. Options (1) and (2) are not supported by the paragraph. Option (4) is not true; the last sentence refers to Antarctica's coast. Option (5) is incorrect because South America is nearby.

2. (Comprehension) **(5) considered to be a desert** This classification is called surprising because we usually think of deserts as extremely hot places. Since the continent is at the South Pole, options (1) and (2) are not surprising. Option (3) is opposite of what is stated in the paragraph. There is no evidence for option (4).

3. (Comprehension) **(2) It is too cold.** This information is given in the paragraph. Option (1) is partially true, but it is not mentioned in the paragraph. Option (3) is not given as a reason. Options (4) and (5) have nothing to do with the snow.

4. (Application) **(4) He could dig a garden for fresh vegetables.** A garden would not grow in Antarctica's weather. Also he would have a long way to dig through the ice. Option (1) is true because of the cold. Option (2) is true because Antarctica has no permanent residents. Option (3) is true because no animals naturally live there. Option (5) is true because whales live off the coast.

5. (Comprehension) **(4) more than one cultural area can be on one continent** The USSR, Southeast Asia, and the Far East are all on the same continent. Options (1) and (3) are not supported by the map. Option (2) is incorrect because they are next to each other. Option (5) is incorrect because the map shows at least three areas that are not separated by water.

6. (Comprehension) **(3) the United States and Canada** The U.S. and Canada are the only areas directly east of the USSR. Options (1), (2), and (4) would require travel in other directions. Option (5) is not a cultural area.

LESSON 2 Comprehension Skill: Summarizing Ideas

This skill will help you recognize the purpose of a reading passage or map.

Have you ever had a long conversation with one friend and then been asked to tell another friend about it? What you probably did with the second friend is talk about the main points made by the first friend. When you told the second friend about the first conversation, you were summarizing what the first friend said. A **summary** is a short, accurate account of the main points in a conversation or written work. Often a writer states the **main idea** of the work in a **topic sentence**. This one sentence tells the reader what the paragraph or article is about. All of the other sentences explain or give details about the main idea. Other times, there is no topic sentence; the main idea is made clear only through the **supporting details** you are told. These details give the reader extra facts that help explain the main idea.

If you were to summarize the preceding paragraph, you would probably say something like "The paragraph discusses a summary and supporting details." Instead of restating a specific detail, you are talking about the purpose of the passage. When you summarize a paragraph or a longer passage, use the following hints:

1. Look at the first or last sentence in a paragraph. Either of these may be the topic sentence.
2. Read the details. What do they tell you about the main idea?
3. State the main idea in your own words.

It may appear difficult to summarize a map. Actually, this skill is no different from working with a written passage. Read the title of the map first to understand its purpose. Look carefully at the map, then read all the other information. With a map, that information is usually given in the legend. Maps can tell you about the natural features of the land. You can find out the land's **elevation** and where rivers and mountains are. Some maps show weather patterns such as temperatures and rainfall. Many maps have symbols for man-made objects which you will find in the legends. For example, some common symbols on a road map are:

⊛ Capital city   IIIII Railroad

• or ○ City   —⑩— Road

Practicing Comprehension

Read the following paragraphs.

> North America's geography has been shaped partly by glaciers. A glacier is a snowfield of compressed ice. When a glacier reaches a depth of 100 feet, it becomes too heavy to stay in place. It moves down the slope it is on. As the glacier moves, it tears away masses of rock and land. Sometimes it leaves behind a lake or series of lakes. Most often, a glacier leaves behind a valley.
>
> New England and New York were once flat land covered by glaciers. When the ice began to melt and move, the land became the Adirondack Mountains, the Green Mountains, and the White Mountains. Now this northeastern area of the United States has many lakes and valleys surrounded by mountains.

Questions 1 and 2 refer to the paragraphs. Circle the best answer for each question.

1. Which best summarizes the second paragraph?

   (1) New England and New York's geography was affected by glaciers.

   (2) Mountains are made by glaciers.

   (3) New England is a flat area.

   (4) New York is covered by ice.

   (5) New England is a scenic region.

2. Which is the main idea of the passage?

   (1) Our land is always changing.

   (2) New York has many lakes.

   (3) Glaciers have helped to change the American landscape.

   (4) Glaciers are made of ice.

   (5) Once glaciers start moving, they cannot be stopped.

Look at the map.

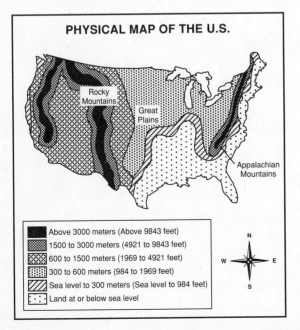

PHYSICAL MAP OF THE U.S.

Rocky Mountains

Great Plains

Appalachian Mountains

- ■ Above 3000 meters (Above 9843 feet)
- 1500 to 3000 meters (4921 to 9843 feet)
- 600 to 1500 meters (1969 to 4921 feet)
- 300 to 600 meters (984 to 1969 feet)
- Sea level to 300 meters (Sea level to 984 feet)
- Land at or below sea level

Question 3 refers to the map. Circle the best answer for the question.

3. Which best summarizes the map?

   (1) Mountains are found across the U.S.

   (2) Elevations in the U.S. change from place to place.

   (3) Part of the U.S. is at sea level.

   (4) Rainfall is evenly distributed across the U.S.

   (5) Mexico is far from the United States.

To check your answers, turn to page 46.

Topic 2: Earth's Regions II

The two largest countries on the North American continent are Canada and the United States. The line that divides them is a political border, not a physical one. Even though they are neighbors, the two countries are very different. Canada has two official languages: French and English. The United States' official language is English. Canada is larger than the United States, but the United States has more people. Their political systems, money, and laws are also different. The histories of both countries have been influenced by their geography.

The United States has a number of different geographic regions. It is divided by several mountain ranges, major rivers, desert areas, flat plains, and farmland. The physical features and natural resources of the land have affected where and how people live in different regions. People first settled in places that were easy to get to and that could provide what they needed to live. Areas with good farmland and fishing and mining resources attracted more people than did mountainous or desert areas. Towns that were at the center of trade routes became major cities. Much of the nation's population now lives or works in these urban areas.

Table-Reading Skills

A **table** is a way of arranging information. Tables use rows and columns to organize information about an area or group of people. Some tables compare and contrast the same kind of information about different areas or groups of people. The title will tell you the general subject of the table. One set of facts is listed on the side of the table and one set is listed at the top or the bottom. To get the information you need, find the point where the two sets meet. The table below tells you that Chicago, Illinois, is 344 miles from Des Moines, Iowa.

MILEAGE BETWEEN CITIES

	Albuquerque NM	Chicago IL	Des Moines IA	Las Vegas NV
Albuquerque, New Mexico	0	1312	974	586
Chicago, Illinois	1312	0	344	1780
Des Moines, Iowa	974	344	0	1430
Las Vegas, Nevada	586	1780	1430	0

Exercises

Questions 1 to 3 refer to the previous information. Circle the best answer for each question.

1. Which best summarizes the first paragraph?

   (1) The U.S. and Canada are separated by a political border.
   (2) There are two large countries in North America.
   (3) History can be influenced by geography.
   (4) The U.S. and Canada are neighboring countries, but they are not completely alike.
   (5) Some people in Canada speak French.

2. According to the second paragraph, the land in the U.S.

   (1) is all the same
   (2) is flat
   (3) is almost all farmland
   (4) is just like Canada's
   (5) has many different physical features

3. If you moved to the desert, which of the following would you expect to find?

   (1) good fishing
   (2) good farmland
   (3) large cities
   (4) mountains
   (5) very few towns

Look at the table.

U.S. POPULATION: 1950 TO 1980			
		Increase over preceding census	
Census Date	Population	Number	Percent
1950	151,325,798	19,161,229	14.5
1960	179,323,175	27,997,377	18.5
1970	203,302,031	23,978,856	13.4
1980	226,545,805	23,243,774	11.4

Questions 4 and 5 refer to the table. Circle the best answer for each question.

4. What is the main idea of the table?

   (1) The number of people who answer the census does not increase according to the increase in population.
   (2) The population is increasing.
   (3) People do not like to answer the census.
   (4) Fewer people answered the census in 1980 than in 1970.
   (5) The population decreased from 1970 to 1980.

5. The census is taken every 10 years. If this table had new information, it probably would be

   (1) different figures for 1950
   (2) the census figures for 1990
   (3) a lower percentage for 1960
   (4) a higher percentage for 1970
   (5) a different population count for 1980

To check your answers, turn to page 46.

Reviewing Lesson 2

Read the following paragraphs.

A small town can grow into a major city if it is located in the right place. Being near a waterway, a railroad, or a major land passage can make all the difference. These things all mean that transportation is easy. If transportation is available, trade can be carried on without trouble. People can travel to a town easily, perhaps settle in the area, and open new businesses. The urban areas of the United States exist today because it was easy for merchants, traders, and settlers to get to them.

Cities like New York and San Francisco attracted trade and residents because they had natural seaports. Ships from all over the world could find a place to dock. The Great Lakes and the canals formed a system of waterways that helped the growth of Buffalo, Detroit, and Chicago. Merchants and settlers could travel the inland waterways more quickly than they could travel over land. New Orleans became a great trade and cultural center because of its location at the mouth of the Mississippi River. The Mississippi is one of the most important waterways in the United States. Denver, located at the foot of the pass that cuts through the Rocky Mountains, became a gateway to the West. People and goods traveling west by land often went through Denver.

Questions 1 and 2 refer to the paragraphs. Circle the best answer for each question.

1. Which of the following best states the main idea of the paragraphs?

   (1) All cities have seaports.
   (2) Denver is the gateway to the West.
   (3) Cities grow where travel is easy.
   (4) People don't like to travel overland.
   (5) A town near a river always becomes a city.

2. According to the information, Denver grew as a city because it

   (1) is near a river
   (2) has a major seaport
   (3) is on top of a mountain
   (4) is located near the pass that cuts through the Rocky Mountains
   (5) developed a canal system

Read the following paragraph.

The wide range of geographical features in the United States provides a broad choice of beautiful vacation spots. Most of the beauty of the land can be enjoyed at little or no cost. A trip to Vermont in the winter can satisfy the person who wants crisp, cold air and white slopes for skiing. For nature lovers who prefer gently rounded mountains covered with wildflowers, good fishing, and the smell of pine trees, the Apache Tribal Enterprises allows camping in the White Mountains of Arizona. Sun-lovers might go to the sandy beaches in either southern California or Florida. The Black Hills of South Dakota are full of caves sparkling with the mineral deposits that brought men to Deadwood to find their fortunes. People who like adventure can travel down the white waters of the Colorado River. And for the backpacker, there is the long, long hike down to the bottom of the Grand Canyon.

Questions 3 and 4 refer to the paragraph. Circle the best answer for each question.

3. Which of the following is the best summary of the paragraph?

(1) The U.S. has many different types of landscapes.
(2) Outdoor vacations are the most enjoyable.
(3) Beaches and coastlines are geographic features.
(4) Vacations can be taken in the mountains.
(5) Going to the desert is not recommended for a vacation.

4. Which is not a geographic feature mentioned in the paragraph?

(1) mountains
(2) rivers
(3) hills
(4) islands
(5) canyons

Look at the map.

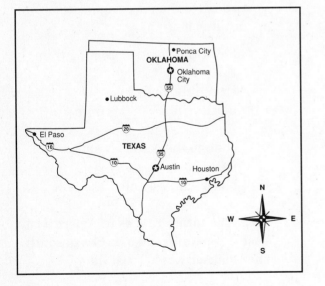

Questions 5 and 6 refer to the map. Circle the best answer for each question.

5. Which detail cannot be found in the map?

(1) the capital city of Oklahoma
(2) major highways
(3) cities in Texas
(4) the boundary between Texas and Oklahoma
(5) major railroads

6. If you went south on the highway that passes through Oklahoma City, you would eventually pass through

(1) Austin
(2) Houston
(3) Lubbock
(4) El Paso
(5) Ponca City

To check your answers, turn to pages 46 and 47.

GED Mini-Test

Directions: Choose the <u>best answer</u> to each item.

<u>Items 1 to 4</u> refer to the following paragraphs.

The weather in the United States is unlike the weather anywhere else in the world. Changing climates throughout the United States are the results of the special shape of the land.

At the eastern and western edges of the United States are the major mountain ranges. They run from north to south. The ranges form barriers that trap the weather from the Arctic and from Mexico over the lands between them. In winter the icy winds from the north are funneled down to the southern regions. When the warm air travels from the south, it reaches the far northern part of the United States. The weather covers a greater distance in the United States than it does anywhere in Europe.

The weather on the outer edges of the mountain ranges is much different from the weather between the ranges. The two coasts are not as affected by the north-south flow. Their weather is influenced more by the oceans that they border and how the ocean air changes as it struggles over the mountains. The weather is not just a matter of rain and snow and heat and cold. It is also influenced by the land itself.

1. The best summary of the paragraphs is that the weather in the U.S.

   (1) is unpredictable
   (2) varies because of land features
   (3) is always the same
   (4) depends on the ocean patterns
   (5) is like the weather in some European countries

2. According to the paragraphs, cold weather comes from

   (1) the north
   (2) the south
   (3) the east
   (4) the west
   (5) Europe

3. According to the paragraphs, the mountains help to

   (1) block the weather coming from the oceans
   (2) create the deserts
   (3) block winds coming from the Arctic
   (4) change the ocean's weather patterns
   (5) block winds coming from Mexico

4. If the mountain ranges in America ran east to west instead of north to south, the weather would most likely

   (1) remain the same
   (2) become hot and dry
   (3) be affected more by the ocean
   (4) be blocked off
   (5) become unbearable

To check your answers, turn to page 47.

Items 5 to 8 refer to the following table.

WEATHER BY DEGREES (°)			
State	**City**	**Yesterday**	**Today**
Ala.	Birmingham	89/69	85/68
	Mobile	93/71	91/72
Alaska	Anchorage	57/48	61/45
	Fairbanks	56/42	56/40
Ariz.	Flagstaff	70/33	74/42
	Phoenix	101/77	101/77
	Tucson	95/69	97/72
Ark.	Fort Smith	72/67	61/55
	Little Rock	78/66	71/61
Calif.	Fresno	100/61	95/56
	Los Angeles	85/62	85/66
	Sacramento	97/55	92/54
	San Diego	76/63	77/65
	San Francisco	73/54	81/56
Colo.	Aspen	55/37	67/37
	Denver	59/33	68/44

5. Which of the following types of information does this table contain?

(1) rainfall in different states
(2) high and low temperatures in different states
(3) humidity in different states
(4) the daily atmospheric pressure
(5) the daily smog measure

6. Based on the information in the table, the figures listed are most likely for a day in

(1) September
(2) November
(3) December
(4) January
(5) February

7. Which city was probably the least pleasant today?

(1) Flagstaff
(2) Phoenix
(3) Little Rock
(4) San Diego
(5) San Francisco

8. According to the table, the greatest difference in the weather is between which two cities?

(1) Mobile and Tucson
(2) Fort Smith and Little Rock
(3) Fresno and Aspen
(4) Los Angeles and Sacramento
(5) Fairbanks and Denver

To check your answers, turn to page 47.

Answers and Explanations

1. (Comprehension) **(1) New England and New York's geography was affected by glaciers.** The main idea can be understood by reading all the details of the paragraph. Not all mountains are discussed, so option (2) is incorrect. Option (3) is the opposite of what is stated. There is no support for option (4). Option (5) may be true, but it is not the main idea of the paragraph.

2. (Comprehension) **(3) Glaciers have helped to change the American landscape.** This is stated in the topic sentence of the first paragraph. Options (1) and (5) are true, but they are not discussed in the passage. Options (2) and (4) are only supporting details.

3. (Comprehension) **(2) Elevations in the U.S. change from place to place.** You can understand this by looking at both the legend and the map itself. Options (1), (4), and (5) are not supported by the map. Option (3) is true, but is only a detail. Option (4) is not the main idea of the map.

1. (Comprehension) **(4) The U.S. and Canada are neighboring countries, but they are not completely alike.** This is stated in the topic sentence, the fourth sentence of the first paragraph. Options (1), (2), (3), and (5) are details that support the main idea.

2. (Comprehension) **(5) has many different physical features** The topic sentence of the second paragraph states this. Options (1), (2), and (3) are the opposite of what is stated. Option (4) is incorrect because Canada's land is not described.

3. (Application) **(5) very few towns** Towns are usually built in areas that can provide people with what they need to live. The desert cannot easily support people. Options (1) and (2) would mean that the area was not a desert. Option (3) is the opposite of what is suggested. Option (4) is incorrect because mountains are not necessarily near deserts.

4. (Comprehension) **(2) The population is increasing.** The numbers in the table show that the population was larger every time the census was taken. There is no evidence for options (1) and (3). Options (4) and (5) are not true.

5. (Application) **(2) the census figures for 1990** The new census numbers would update the table. Options (1), (3), (4), and (5) are incorrect because numbers from past years would not change.

1. (Comprehension) **(3) Cities grow where travel is easy.** This is stated in the first paragraph. Options (1) and (5) are generalizations that have no support. Option (2) may be partly true, but it is only a detail. Option (4) is a misinterpretation of the idea that quick and easy travel occurs only on water.

2. (Comprehension) **(4) is located near the pass that cuts through the Rocky Mountains** It is easier to go through a pass than over a mountain. Options (1), (2), and (5) are incorrect because water is not mentioned. Option (3) is incorrect. The paragraph states that Denver is at the foot of the pass.

3. (Comprehension) **(1) The U.S. has many different types of landscapes.** This idea is stated in the first paragraph. Option (2) is not mentioned. Options (3) and (4) are supporting details. Option (5) is not mentioned.

4. (Comprehension) **(4) islands** Islands are the only geographic features from among the options that are not mentioned in the paragraph. Options (1), (2), (3), and (5) are discussed in the paragraph.

5. (Comprehension) **(5) major railroads** There are no railroad symbols on the map. Options (1), (2), (3), and (4) can all be found on the map.

6. (Comprehension) **(1) Austin** Austin is south of Oklahoma City on Highway 35. Options (2), (3), and (4) cannot be reached by Highway 35. Option (5) is incorrect because Ponca City is north of Oklahoma City.

GED Mini-Test (pages 44–45)

1. (Comprehension) **(2) varies because of land features** This is stated in the first and last paragraphs. Option (1) is not suggested. Options (3) and (5) are opposite of what is stated. Option (4) applies only to the coastal areas.

2. (Comprehension) **(1) the north** Icy winds indicate cold weather. There is no support for options (2), (3), (4), or (5).

3. (Comprehension) **(1) block the weather coming from the oceans** This is suggested in the last paragraph. Options (2) and (3) are the opposite of what is stated. There is no support for options (4) and (5).

4. (Application) **(3) be affected more by the ocean** The most likely answer is the one that describes the opposite of the actual situation. Option (1) is incorrect because the information given indicates that there would be a change. There is no support for options (2) and (5). Option (4) is impossible because although certain weather conditions are affected by the presence of mountains, weather itself cannot be stopped.

5. (Comprehension) **(2) high and low temperatures in different states** This can be understood from the title and the side information in the columns on the right. Options (1), (3), (4), and (5) are not included in the table.

6. (Application) **(1) September** The temperatures are all too warm to be winter months, so options (2), (3), (4), and (5) are incorrect.

7. (Comprehension) **(2) Phoenix** The table shows that the temperature in Phoenix went as high as 101 degrees—making it extremely hot. The temperatures in options (1), (3), (4), and (5) are more reasonable.

8. (Comprehension) **(3) Fresno and Aspen** There is a 45-degree difference in the maximum temperatures reached that day in the two cities. The differences in options (1), (2), (4), and (5) are of 12 degrees or less.

LESSON 3 Comprehension Skill: Drawing Conclusions

This skill will help you make decisions about information that is directly stated.

When you look at the facts about an idea and make a decision based on those facts, you are **drawing a conclusion.** Many times you will have to sort through a number of facts to figure out which ones are important. You will use your skills of restating information and identifying a main idea.

Drawing a conclusion is a logical process. A Little League game is scheduled for 4:00 P.M. on Friday, but if it rains, the game will be played on Saturday morning. At 3:00 P.M. on Friday, a heavy rain starts. The only logical conclusion that can be made is that the game may be played on Saturday morning.

When you draw a conclusion in a paragraph or a longer passage, find the facts that will help you make your decision. Imagine that the weekend weather forecast predicts a thunderstorm on Thursday. One morning you wake up to thunder, lightning, and heavy rain. You say, "Since there is a thunderstorm, today must be Thursday." In this case, the conclusion is wrong. Today is Wednesday. You know that a thunderstorm can occur on any day of the week. You must also use your common sense and experience. Always ask yourself if the facts clearly support your conclusion.

Conclusions can be drawn from graphs as well as from written information. Graphs compare one type of information with a similar type of information. To understand a graph, read the title to find out the topic or subject of the graph. For a line or bar graph, look at the numbers and information on the side (vertical line) and then on the top or bottom (horizontal line) of the graph. Facts about the topic are found at the points where the vertical and horizontal lines come together. These points are shown by a dot on a line graph and by the end of the bar on a bar graph. A line graph is most often used to show changes and trends over a period of time. A pie graph is a circle that is divided into wedges. The circle represents the total amount of something. The wedges stand for the ways that amount is divided up. In pie graphs, the information is usually given in percents. Examples of each type of graph are given on page 50.

Practicing Comprehension

Read the following paragraphs.

The environment we live in is not just air, water, and land. It also includes towns and cities. Much of the world's population now lives in cities. In the United States, almost 70 percent of the citizens have moved to urban areas. Unfortunately, most people have not been prepared for the rapid growth of the cities.

Even though the majority of the United States population lives in cities, the space occupied is only about 1 percent of the land. Cities are faced with problems that come from many people living in a small area: overcrowding, air pollution, trash disposal, water supply and treatment, inadequate housing, and more. If the environment of the urban areas does not get more attention, the problems will get worse.

Experts in the social sciences have been aware of the situation in American urban areas for over 30 years. Only recently has more of the general population come to know what faces the city dweller. Now even politicians are getting into the act and are starting to pass laws that will help to make cities better places in which to live.

Questions 1 and 2 refer to the paragraphs. Circle the best answer for each question.

1. Based on the information, one can conclude that the environment of American cities is

   (1) in serious trouble
   (2) very pleasant
   (3) quite livable
   (4) admired by social scientists
   (5) the model for cities all over the world

2. From the information in the paragraph, it can be concluded that the situation in American cities

   (1) will only get worse
   (2) is being ignored
   (3) may start to improve
   (4) cannot be changed
   (5) has gotten better in the last 30 years

To check your answers, turn to page 56.

Topic 3: Protecting the Environment

The word **ecology** is one that most people used to hear only in a science or social studies class. Today even many children have some idea of what it means. Ecology refers to the balance between humanity and nature. For much of human history, most people rarely gave this idea a thought. Natural resources were taken for granted.

As more and more countries became industrialized, people took more and more resources from the land. Labor-saving inventions required energy to run them. The overall standard of living rose, and people began to see comfortable lives as a basic right. But as the land was mined and stripped of its forests and minerals, and as water was rerouted to support growing cities, people began to realize an important fact. The earth could not renew its resources as quickly as they were being used. Some of the products that made life better for humans were actually poisoning plant and animal life. Some of the things that were designed to provide good living were also causing health problems for people.

As studies were made about these discoveries, a major question came up: Which is more important, a healthy economy or a healthy environment? This question is not easy to answer. People want to have jobs and to be able to take advantage of modern conveniences. But there is a cost for both. We now need to be aware of environmental problems and search for solutions that can restore the balance between the land and the people who live on it.

One way that information about the environment is presented is through graphs. Because graphs compare sets of information, they can help us to understand and make judgments about the problems we face. Look at the following types of graphs.

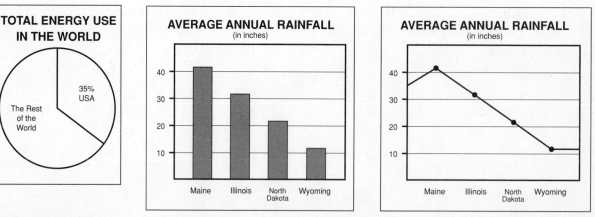

This **pie graph** shows that 35 percent of the world's energy is used by only one country.

The **bar graph** and the **line graph** give information about the average annual rainfall in certain states. These figures can help us understand why areas like North Dakota and Wyoming need to make special efforts to conserve water for their crops and animals.

Exercises

Questions 1 to 6 refer to the previous information. Circle the best answer for each question.

1. You can conclude from the information that the world's ecology

    (1) is still in balance
    (2) can take care of itself
    (3) is out of balance
    (4) makes everyone comfortable
    (5) is not an important issue

2. Which can be concluded from the information?

    (1) It will be easy to solve the earth's environmental problems.
    (2) Natural resources cannot be taken for granted.
    (3) America is a land of plenty.
    (4) No one understands much about ecology.
    (5) Industry has had little effect on the environment.

3. You can learn from the information that

    (1) things that make people comfortable can also cause problems
    (2) mining does not hurt the land
    (3) the earth renews its resources quickly
    (4) a healthy economy is more important than a healthy environment
    (5) a healthy environment is more important than a healthy economy

4. Which would be an example of people giving something back to the land?

    (1) rerouting a river
    (2) panning for gold
    (3) pulling weeds
    (4) using more electricity
    (5) planting trees

5. You can conclude from the information that Americans probably

    (1) use a lot of labor-saving devices
    (2) are not concerned about ecology
    (3) use very little energy
    (4) have well-educated children
    (5) use too much water

6. The main idea of the last paragraph is that graphs

    (1) have to be detailed to be useful
    (2) all give the same information
    (3) can restore the ecological balance
    (4) are good for conserving water
    (5) can help people learn about environmental issues

To check your answers, turn to page 56.

Reviewing Lesson 3

Look at the pie graph.

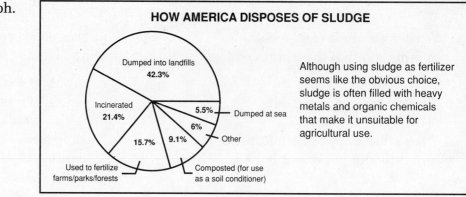

Questions 1 and 2 refer to the pie graph. Circle the best answer for each question.

1. From the graph, you can conclude that

(1) there is no one best way to dispose of sludge
(2) sludge makes an excellent fertilizer
(3) the landfills have a lot of room
(4) sludge is messy
(5) sludge is easy to get rid of

2. According to the graph, most of America's sludge

(1) is burned
(2) finds its way into the land
(3) is dumped at sea
(4) becomes compost
(5) is used as fertilizer

Look at the bar graph.

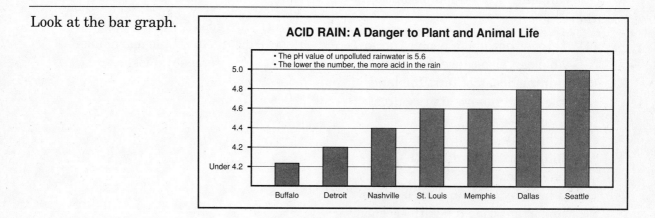

Questions 3 and 4 refer to the bar graph. Circle the best answer for each question.

3. From the graph, rainwater acidity

(1) is the same in all large cities
(2) cannot be measured
(3) is a serious problem in Texas
(4) changes from place to place
(5) is caused by factories

4. Which city would be the safest place to grow vegetables?

(1) Nashville
(2) Detroit
(3) Memphis
(4) St. Louis
(5) Dallas

Read the following passage.

Fossil fuels are the world's main source of energy. Underground deposits of coal, oil, and natural gas are located in all of the continents, with some areas having larger amounts than others. The economies of some Arab nations depend heavily on the profits from exporting oil out of what once seemed like bottomless wells. The world's increasing demand for energy, however, has begun to exhaust the fossil fuels.

In 1978, fossil fuels supplied 90 percent of the world's energy. Experts predict that by the year 2000, fossil fuels will supply 75 percent of the world's energy needs. The use of coal will have increased by then. By 2000, coal is expected to provide 24 percent of the energy used.

Questions 5 and 6 refer to the passage. Circle the best answer for each question.

5. Based on the passage, when oil reserves are gone, some Arab economies will be

(1) improved
(2) hurt
(3) unaffected
(4) based on natural gas production
(5) exporting more oil

6. It is predicted that by the year 2000

(1) coal will supply all of the world's energy
(2) there will be no more oil reserves
(3) natural gas reserves will be gone
(4) fossil fuels will produce a lower percentage of the world's energy
(5) oil prices will have increased

Look at the cartoon.

"Help"

from the *Herblock Gallery* (Simon & Schuster 1968)

Questions 7 and 8 refer to the cartoon. Circle the best answer for each question.

7. This cartoon is commenting on

(1) city governments
(2) the pleasures of city life
(3) serious problems in cities
(4) why people move to cities
(5) the increase in suburban population

8. From the cartoon you can conclude that the population of many cities is made up of

(1) criminals
(2) old people
(3) high-income groups
(4) low-income groups
(5) young people

To check your answers, turn to pages 56 and 57.

GED Mini-Test

Directions: Choose the best answer to each item.

Items 1 to 4 refer to the following passage.

The expression "Water, water everywhere, but not a drop to drink" refers to being in the middle of the ocean. People drink fresh water, not salt water. Today that expression has taken on a new meaning. Our most valuable natural resource, water, is a victim of pollution. Industrial waste has been slowly poisoning rivers and lakes. Also, the longtime use of pesticides has resulted in the contamination of rural groundwater.

Most water pollution cannot be seen. Only the effects of the pollution on plants and animals provide evidence of poor water quality. One example is Crab Orchard Lake in Illinois, a lovely and peaceful spot surrounded by trees. Thirty years ago, this lake was a favorite spot for fishing. Now fishers are warned against eating the catfish and larger game fish. Tests have shown that the fish are full of toxic chemicals from local industries.

Many people drink bottled water or use water filters because their tap water is no longer safe. Even the chlorine that is used by water treatment plants can give off a chemical that is hazardous to human health. Older homes often have lead pipes. Over the years, lead can seep into the drinking water. Studies have shown that high levels of lead can be harmful. Household water can be tested for the presence of lead contamination.

Water pollution is not limited to places where the contamination actually happens. In the cycle of nature, the water supply is used and reused. Surface water evaporates and later returns to the earth in the form of rain. The rain soaks down into the soil. Far under the surface of the earth, deposits of groundwater flow slowly through the rock. Eventually that water is tapped by wells or runs back into rivers and streams. So the pollution of any water becomes the pollution of all water.

1. From the passage, you can conclude that people in older homes

    (1) are safe from water pollution
    (2) are being poisoned by chlorine
    (3) should have their water tested
    (4) should use only tap water
    (5) cannot use water filters

2. You can conclude from the passage that water filters

    (1) are easy to use
    (2) increase the risk of pollution
    (3) help to purify drinking water
    (4) have no effect on water purity
    (5) produce chlorinated water

3. Which of the following is the best summary of the passage?

   (1) Lakes and rivers are being polluted.
   (2) Water pollution is hazardous to human health.
   (3) Water pollution is a widespread problem.
   (4) There is no solution for water pollution.
   (5) People should start drinking bottled water.

4. According to the passage, pollution in a lake

   (1) can be discovered just by looking at the water
   (2) cannot be discovered
   (3) immediately kills the fish
   (4) can be discovered by testing the fish
   (5) is good for fishing

Items 5 and 6 refer to the following graph.

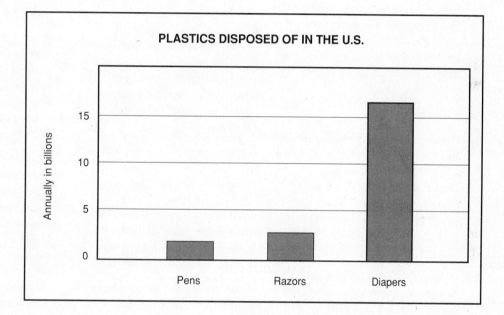

5. Based on the information in the graph, one can conclude that people in the United States

   (1) are having too many babies
   (2) do not waste anything
   (3) do a lot of writing
   (4) do not use anything made of plastic
   (5) buy a lot of disposable items

6. Which of the following would be the best title for the graph?

   (1) Evidence of a Throwaway Society
   (2) Too Many Diapers
   (3) To Shave or Not to Shave
   (4) How to Recycle Disposables
   (5) Why Plastic Should Not Be Used

To check your answers, turn to page 57.

Answers and Explanations

Practicing Comprehension (page 49)

1. (Comprehension) **(1) in serious trouble** The list of problems in the second paragraph indicates trouble. Options (2), (3), (4), and (5) are not conclusions that can be drawn from the information given.

2. (Comprehension) **(3) may start to improve** This is supported by the fact that people are now paying attention to the problems. Option (1) refers to what would happen if nothing were being done. Option (2) is the opposite of what is suggested. There is no evidence for options (4) or (5).

Exercises (page 51)

1. (Comprehension) **(3) is out of balance** Ecology is balance, and people are taking more than the earth can afford to give. Options (1) and (5) are the opposite of what is stated. Option (2) is not suggested. There is no support for option (4).

2. (Comprehension) **(2) Natural resources cannot be taken for granted.** The earth cannot supply all the natural resources that people have taken for granted. Options (1) and (5) are the opposite of what is suggested. Option (3) is incorrect because no one country is mentioned. There is no support for option (4).

3. (Comprehension) **(1) things that make people comfortable can also cause problems** This is stated in the text. Option (2) is incorrect because the effect of mining is not mentioned. Option (3) is the opposite of what is stated. Options (4) and (5) are incorrect because they are the two sides of an unanswered question given in the text.

4. (Application) **(5) planting trees** Tree planting helps to provide new growth. Options (1) and (2) are examples of taking from the land. Option (3) is not related to the question. Option (4) is incorrect because the energy for electricity is taken from natural resources.

5. (Comprehension) **(1) use a lot of labor-saving devices** This is based on the pie graph and the fact that labor-saving devices use energy. There is no other information about the United States, so options (2), (3), (4), and (5) are incorrect.

6. (Comprehension) **(5) can help people learn about environmental issues** This is stated in the paragraph. Options (1) and (2) refer to details that apply only to these two graphs. Options (3) and (4) are incorrect because graphs cannot do anything; they only give information.

Reviewing Lesson 3 (pages 52–53)

1. (Comprehension) **(1) there is no one best way to dispose of sludge** The number of ways sludge is disposed of leads to this conclusion. Option (2) is incorrect because the note next to the graph indicates there are problems in using sludge as a fertilizer. There is no mention of how large the landfills are, so option (3) is incorrect. There is no support for options (4) and (5).

2. (Comprehension) **(2) finds its way into the land** Over 73 percent of the sludge is disposed of in the earth in one way or another. The figures do not support options (1), (3), (4), or (5).

3. (Comprehension) **(4) changes from place to place** The levels of acid rain are different in different cities. Options (1) and (2) are the opposite of what is shown. There is not enough evidence for option (3). Option (5) is incorrect because the cause of acidity in rainwater is not indicated in the graph.

4. (Application) **(5) Dallas** Dallas has the highest pH value of the cities listed, so vegetables would be the least damaged there. Options (1), (2), (3), and (4) all have lower pH values.

5. (Comprehension) **(2) hurt** Oil-based economies would collapse. Options (1) and (5) are the opposite of the logical conclusion. There is no support for options (3) or (4).

6. (Comprehension) **(4) fossil fuels will produce a lower percentage of the world's energy** This is a restatement of the beginning of the second paragraph. Option (1) is not true according to the passage. There is no support for options (2), (3), and (5).

7. (Comprehension) **(3) serious problems in cities** The city is crying for help, and the problems are described. There is no mention of government, so option (1) is incorrect. There is no evidence of options (2) or (4). Only one reference is made to the suburbs, and it does not give figures, so option (5) is incorrect.

8. (Comprehension) **(4) low-income groups** If the high-wage industries and upper-income groups are leaving, these are what remain. Options (1), (2), and (5) refer to only certain segments of the population. Option (3) is incorrect because according to the cartoon, this is the group that is leaving.

GED Mini-Test (pages 54–55)

1. (Comprehension) **(3) should have their water tested** A test would reveal the level of lead. Options (1) and (4) are the opposite of what can be logically concluded. Option (2) is incorrect because the age of the house has nothing to do with the presence of chlorine. There is no support for option (5).

2. (Comprehension) **(3) help to purify drinking water** Water filters are used when the tap water is unsafe. There is no evidence for option (1). Options (2) and (4) are the opposite of what is suggested. Option (5) is incorrect because chlorinated water comes from treatment plants.

3. (Comprehension) **(3) Water pollution is a widespread problem.** Options (1), (2), and (5) are details, not the main idea. Option (4) is not suggested in the passage.

4. (Comprehension) **(4) can be discovered by testing the fish** The details in the second paragraph lead to this conclusion. Options (1) and (2) are the opposite of what is stated. Option (3) is not suggested. Option (5) is incorrect because most fishers will not go fishing if they cannot eat their catch.

5. (Comprehension) **(5) buy a lot of disposable items** If disposable items are thrown away by the billions, they are bought by the billions. Figures are given only for diapers, not for babies, so option (1) is incorrect. The graph suggests the opposite of option (2). Option (3) is incorrect because the graph does not give information about how the pens are used before they are thrown away. Option (4) is incorrect because all the items contain plastic.

6. (Comprehension) **(1) Evidence of a Throwaway Society** The purpose of the graph is to show the number of pens, razors, and diapers that are thrown away each year. Options (2) and (3) refer to only one item in the graph. Options (4) and (5) refer to information that is not given in the graph.

Review: Geography

In this unit, new map, table, and chart reading skills were introduced along with three types of comprehension skills. The review questions will help you to practice all these skills.

Directions: Choose the best answer to each item.

Items 1 and 2 are based on the following map.

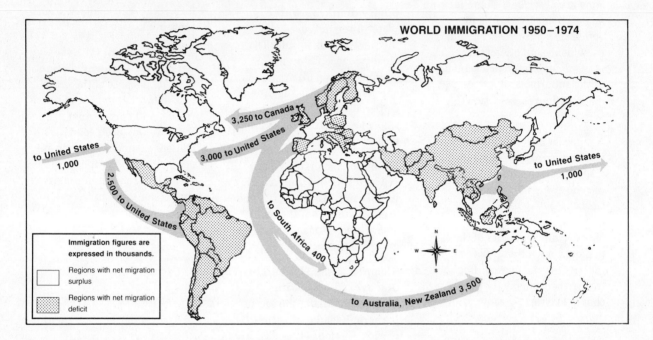

1. According to the map, which country has the fewest immigrants?

(1) Australia
(2) Canada
(3) South Africa
(4) New Zealand
(5) the United States

2. It can be concluded from the map that

(1) the United States has a special attraction for immigrants
(2) people emigrate to improve their lives
(3) Australia attracts people from the United States
(4) immigration figures went up between 1950 and 1974
(5) immigration stopped after 1974

Items 3 to 6 are based on the following paragraph.

Climates on the earth are determined by three things: latitude, elevation, and closeness to a large body of water. Latitude is the distance of a place from the equator. The heat of the sun is strongest at the equator and weakest at the poles. Elevation affects climate because the higher an area is, the cooler the temperature will be.

Closeness to water affects the climate because the winds are warmed or cooled by the water's temperature. In general, coastal areas have the least extreme temperatures.

3. Hot tropical climates would most likely be found

(1) in mountainous regions
(2) near the North and South poles
(3) close to the equator
(4) on sea coasts
(5) halfway between the equator and the poles

4. Which best summarizes the paragraph?

(1) Latitude least affects climate.
(2) The climate at the poles is similar to the climate at the equator.
(3) Climates are similar coast to coast.
(4) Islands have the best climates.
(5) Several factors affect climate.

5. Based on the paragraph, the latitude of an area

(1) tells how high the land is above sea level
(2) determines how hot the sun is there
(3) influences the amount of rainfall
(4) makes the temperature even
(5) shows how close the land is to water

6. Elevation affects climate by making the land

(1) wetter
(2) cooler
(3) hotter
(4) swampy
(5) drier

Item 7 refers to the following graph.

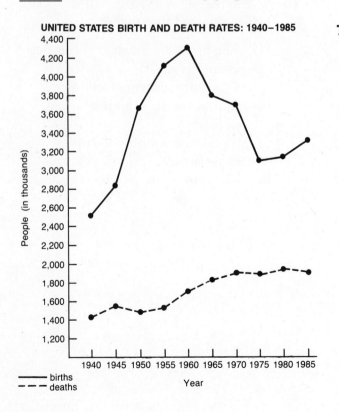

UNITED STATES BIRTH AND DEATH RATES: 1940–1985

births
deaths
Year

7. Which can be concluded from the graph?

(1) The death rate is lower than the birthrate.
(2) The birth and death rates are about the same.
(3) The death rate is higher than the birthrate.
(4) The birth and death rates are both decreasing.
(5) The birthrate is decreasing while the death rate is increasing.

To check your answers, turn to page 62.

Items 8 and 9 refer to the following paragraphs.

The Soviet population has changed since World War II. The birthrate has dropped from 31 births per thousand people in 1940 to 17 births per thousand people in 1970. Today at least 20 percent of the Soviet population is 55 years of age or older. Also, there is an increase in people moving to the cities. Less than 20 percent of the Soviet population lived in cities in 1920. Now only 20 percent of the people live in the rural areas. As a result, few people are available to work on the farms. As the older people leave the work force, there will not be enough young workers to replace them.

8. Compared to their parents, the Soviets born in 1940

   (1) are having more children
   (2) have more grandchildren
   (3) have fewer children
   (4) are retiring earlier
   (5) are living longer

9. What has changed in the Soviet Union over the past 80 years?

   (1) Twenty percent of the population lives in the cities.
   (2) Eighty percent of the population has gone to work on farms.
   (3) Most people now live in rural areas.
   (4) Most of the population now lives in the cities.
   (5) Unemployment has risen.

Item 10 refers to the following cartoon.

The built-in bomb

SLUMS

Copyright 1966. Herblock in the *Washington Post*

10. Which is the best conclusion that can be drawn from the cartoon?

   (1) The problem of urban slums has been solved.
   (2) Cities are growing rapidly.
   (3) Slums are an explosive urban problem.
   (4) Cities are building too many skyscrapers.
   (5) The crime rate in cities is rising.

To check your answers, turn to page 62.

Items 11 and 12 refer to the following paragraphs.

There is an old joke that someday San Francisco and Los Angeles will fall into the ocean. In October 1989, the people of San Francisco were not laughing. Within minutes, an earthquake had toppled buildings and bridges. Many people were injured or killed. Homes were destroyed by fires that broke out. But this was not the first time San Francisco had suffered a major earthquake. In 1906, a more powerful quake almost destroyed the city.

The San Francisco disasters happened because the city is built on a fault. A fault is a weakness in the earth's surface. Earthquakes occur because the rocks in the fault suddenly give way to stresses on the crust of the earth. There are faults in the Midwest and Eastern states that can cause serious earthquakes. In fact, the worst earthquake recorded in the United States happened in Missouri in 1812. The shock to the earth was so great that the Mississippi River changed its course. Scientists predict that more major earthquakes will occur in the next 50 years.

11. Which is the best summary of the paragraphs?

   (1) Earthquakes happen only in California.
   (2) San Franciscans laugh at earthquakes.
   (3) The Midwest has the worst quakes.
   (4) Earthquakes can happen all over the U. S.
   (5) San Francisco is going to fall into the ocean.

12. According to the paragraphs, earthquakes

   (1) are nothing to worry about
   (2) can cause a great deal of damage
   (3) do not happen often
   (4) can be prevented by scientists
   (5) affect only people

Items 13 and 14 are based on the following paragraph.

Mountains act as natural boundaries that slow the movement of people and the spread of their ideas. Societies that are separated by mountains are often very different from each other.

13. Based on the paragraph, mountains influence human geography because

   (1) they are easy to travel through
   (2) they make travel difficult
   (3) people dislike learning new things
   (4) they have a wild beauty
   (5) many people live in the mountains

14. According to the paragraph, mountain ranges are most like

   (1) people
   (2) enemies
   (3) walls
   (4) windows
   (5) rooms

To check your answers, turn to page 62.

Answers and Explanations

1. (Comprehension) **(3) South Africa** Four hundred thousand is the smallest number listed. Options (1), (2), (4), and (5) have larger numbers.

2. (Comprehension) **(1) the United States has a special attraction for immigrants** The map shows that the most immigration is to the U.S., so there must be a special attraction. There is no evidence for options (2) and (5). The map does not support option (3). Option (4) is incorrect because the figures do not show a comparison between these two dates.

3. (Comprehension) **(3) close to the equator** The hotter the sun, the warmer the climate. Options (1) and (2) would tend to be cooler. Option (4) has no support. Option (5) refers to an area that would have fairly mild temperatures.

4. (Comprehension) **(5) Several factors affect climate.** This is the main idea stated in the first sentence. There is no support for options (1), (3), or (4). Option (2) is the opposite of what is stated.

5. (Comprehension) **(2) determines how hot the sun is there** This is stated in the paragraph. Option (1) refers to elevation, not latitude. There is no support for options (3) and (5). Option (4) is incorrect because it is closeness to water that helps to even out temperatures.

6. (Comprehension) **(2) cooler** This is stated in the paragraph. There is no evidence for options (1) or (5). Option (3) is the opposite of what is stated. Option (4) is not mentioned or implied in the paragraph.

7. (Comprehension) **(1) The death rate is lower than the birthrate.** A comparison of the figures supports this conclusion. Options (2) and (3) are the opposite of what is shown by the figures. There is no support for options (4) and (5).

8. (Comprehension) **(3) have fewer children** Seventeen is less than thirty-one. Options (1) and (2) are the opposite of what is stated. No mention of retirement age is made, so option (4) is incorrect. There is no information about option (5).

9. (Comprehension) **(4) Most of the population now lives in the cities.** Eighty percent of the people live in the cities; twenty percent live in rural areas. Options (1) and (2) have the figures backwards. There is no evidence of option (3). No mention is made of unemployment, so option (5) is incorrect.

10. (Comprehension) **(3) Slums are an explosive urban problem.** The combination of the labeled bomb with the city setting leads to this conclusion. There is no evidence for option (1). Options (2) and (4) may be true, but they are not highlighted in the cartoon. There is no support for option (5).

11. (Comprehension) **(4) Earthquakes can happen all over the U. S.** The purpose of the paragraphs is to make this point; San Francisco is just a famous example. Option (1) is the opposite of what is stated. Option (2) has no support. Not enough evidence is provided for options (3) or (5).

12. (Comprehension) **(2) can cause a great deal of damage** The brief description of the San Francisco earthquakes is evidence of this. Option (1) is the opposite of what is stated in the paragraph. There is no discussion of how often earthquakes happen, so option (3) is incorrect. There is no support for option (4). Option (5) is incorrect according to the evidence in the passage.

13. (Comprehension) **(2) they make travel difficult** The information given, together with what people know about mountains, leads to this conclusion. Option (1) is the opposite of what is stated. There is no support for options (3), (4), or (5).

14. (Comprehension) **(3) walls** Like walls, mountains stand between things. There is no support for options (1) or (2). Option (4) is incorrect because it would allow communication of a sort. Option (5) has no support.

Use the chart below to identify your strengths and weaknesses in each reading skill in the geography unit.

Circle the number of each item that you answered correctly on the review.

Comprehension Skill	Question	Lesson(s) for Review
Restating Information	1, 3, 5, 8, 9, 12, 14	1
Summarizing Ideas	4, 6, 11	2
Drawing Conclusions	2, 7, 10, 13	3

If you answered 11 or more items correctly, congratulations! You are ready to go on to the next section. If you answered 10 or fewer items correctly, determine which areas are most difficult for you. Then go back and review the lessons for those areas.

HISTORY

Americans have faced many challenges and undergone many changes since our country began.

♦ **settle**
to move to a new place to live

America's history is very much its own, yet it is also closely linked to the history of other countries. The most important link is that all American people came from other countries. Even the people we call Native Americans actually came from Asia thousands of years ago across a land bridge that no longer exists. America's modern history began when European countries explored and **settled** the American continents. The English settled in what is now the United States, so our history is especially tied to England. But the people who built America came from all over the world; our nation has been formed because of their contributions. All of the people who have come to America are united by their belief in American ideals: the rights and freedoms guaranteed by the Constitution.

Topic 4 will discuss how European countries began to explore the New World during the sixteenth century. You will see how America was "discovered" and how it was explored and settled.

colonize
a country starts a settlement by bringing its own laws and customs to a new area

immigration
people moving from one country to permanently settle in another country

industrialization
the process of becoming developed by mechanized industry

Topic 5 will explain how England **colonized** the New World. You will see how settlers learned to deal with the wilderness and how the settlers' experiences taking care of themselves helped to shape the American ideal of independence. The American Revolution was the result of the colonists' experience being independent. When the United States won its war against England and became a separate nation, the ideals of the initial settlers became the ideals of the new country.

The new country grew rapidly and expanded westward into the apparently open country. Development and expansion made America rich, but they also created problems. In Topic 6 you will see how these problems led to the War Between the States, or the Civil War, fought between the North and the South. A major result of the war was that slavery became illegal. Another result was that industry came to the South, which before the war had been mainly a farming area.

In topic 7, you will see how the United States became a major industrial power. The economy of the country became based on factories and industry. **Immigration** and mechanical inventions played an important part. The process of **industrialization** brought problems along with benefits. Factory workers who worked and lived under terrible conditions protested. New laws and social reforms came from the problems. The government began to play an active role in regulating the economy and other areas that affected people's lives.

Eventually, the United States became a world power. Topic 8 explains how, over the course of two centuries, the nation became more and more powerful. The two world wars increased this country's involvement in world affairs. By the time World War II had ended, the United States and the Soviet Union had become the two most powerful nations in the world. The tension between the two countries led the United States to a more visible role in world politics. Now that the world powers are becoming more friendly, the United States is active in encouraging good relationships between nations.

☞ *See also: GED Exercise Book Social Studies, pages 15-25.*

LESSON 4 Application Skill: Using Given Ideas in Another Context

This skill involves taking information you already know and making it work for you in a new situation.

Once you learn an idea, you can apply it, or use it, in many other situations or contexts. When you were in school, you probably learned the rule "i before e except after c." Once you learned this rule and its exceptions, you were able to apply it to the spelling of many words—piece, receive, and so on. Often you learn difficult ideas and apply them to everyday situations. For example, addition and subtraction can be used in balancing a checkbook or counting change after you buy something. In your daily life, you are always learning ideas in one context and using them in other contexts. Imagine that you bought a couch at the first store you stopped in. The couch is just what you wanted, so you are happy with your purchase. Several days later, you see the same couch in the window of a discount store—for half the price you paid. You probably are angry with yourself for not having gone to other stores. When you decide that you need some new chairs, you apply the lesson you learned in buying the couch. Before you buy the chairs, you shop around.

In social studies, ideas are often applied in other contexts. As you read about history, try to understand why events were important at the time they happened. Then ask yourself what can be learned and if that idea can be applied to another period of history. Generals, for example, often study history so that they can see how to apply strategies that were used in earlier wars. Judges look at decisions made in other courts to help them come to rulings about new situations. When you read about the social sciences, you will have many opportunities to apply ideas you learn to new contexts.

Practicing Application

Read the following paragraphs.

> Throughout history, people from many countries colonized and settled new areas. There were several important reasons, or motives, for colonization and settlement. Five different motives are listed below.
>
> 1. economic—to gain wealth from the new area, either from its natural resources or through trade
> 2. religious—to spread one's own religion to other people
> 3. political—to make one's own country more powerful by gaining more land
> 4. scientific—to learn more about the world by exploring
> 5. social—to get away from one society's problems and to set up a better society
>
> People from Spain, Portugal, England, France, and Holland colonized and settled the Americas. People from each country made the long trip for many different reasons.
> Each of the following statements is an example of one of the reasons. Choose the reason for which each situation is an example.

Questions 1 to 3 refer to the passage. Circle the best answer for each question.

1. Spain sent many priests to the Americas to convert Native Americans to Catholicism. In this case, Spain's motive was

   (1) economic
   (2) religious
   (3) political
   (4) scientific
   (5) social

2. Spanish explorers and settlers found and mined gold in the Americas. This gold was sent to Spain. In this case, Spain's motive was

   (1) economic
   (2) religious
   (3) political
   (4) scientific
   (5) social

3. Groups called Puritans and Quakers were often persecuted in England. Many members of these groups settled in America so they could worship freely. The motive of these English settlers was

   (1) economic
   (2) religious
   (3) political
   (4) scientific
   (5) social

To check your answers, turn to page 74.

Topic 4: The Colonization of America

By the 1400s, Europe had started to trade with China and India for goods such as spices, silks, and gems. Italy controlled this trade. Other countries such as Spain and Portugal wanted to get a share of the wealth, so they sought new routes to the Orient. Christopher Columbus reasoned that since the world is round, he could get to the East by sailing west. He convinced Queen Isabella of Spain to finance this voyage. On October 12, 1492, Columbus and his crew sighted land. They naturally assumed they had reached India. They became sure of this when they were given gold by the natives of the land, whom the explorers called "Indians."

Further exploration convinced Spain and the other European nations that Columbus had in fact discovered a new land. They decided they could benefit by colonizing what they came to call the New World. **Colonization** happens when a country sends people to live in a new area and keeps political and economic control over the area and the people.

Spain had a head start on the colonization of the Americas. Many Spanish settlements were soon located in Central America, the islands of the Caribbean, and North and South America. In North America, they settled in the area we know as the states of Florida, New Mexico, Arizona, Texas, and California. The Spaniards had two specific motives for colonizing the New World. They wanted to gain wealth by finding gold and by planting crops that could not be grown in Europe. They also wanted to introduce Christianity to the Indians. As one explorer said, "We came here to serve God and also to get rich."

Colonization by Spain and other European countries brought tragic events to Native Americans. The Spanish and Portuguese sometimes forced Native Americans into near slavery. Colonists also took land from the Native Americans. In addition, many Native Americans died from diseases carried by the Europeans.

The Portuguese colonized the area of South America that is now Brazil. There they set up large plantations to grow sugar, a valuable crop.

The French colonized parts of North America in what is now eastern Canada and along the Mississippi River as far south as New Orleans. They traded with the Indians for furs that sold for high prices in Europe.

The Dutch settled mainly in what is now New York and New Jersey because of the profit that could come from the fur trade. Both the Dutch and the French eventually lost their North American colonies to England.

Like Spain, England sent many colonists to America. The English settled in what is now Canada and the eastern United States. The English had different motives from the Spanish. The Spaniards wanted to convert the Indians, but the English were more concerned simply with having the freedom to practice their own religion. Also, their economy depended on activities such as farming because the English had settled in an area without gold.

Exercises

Questions 1 to 4 refer to the previous information. Circle the best answer for each question.

1. A study of death rates among Native Americans following the arrival of Europeans would most likely show a steep rise in which of the following causes of death?

   (1) poison
   (2) drowning
   (3) smallpox and influenza
   (4) starvation
   (5) accidents and natural disasters

2. Columbus's motive for traveling to the New World was to

   (1) convert "heathens" to Christianity
   (2) take some of the trade with the Orient away from Italy
   (3) find new sources of gold
   (4) obtain scientific proof that the world is round
   (5) discover and colonize unknown lands

3. Based on the passage, the first to have extensive settlements in the New World were the

   (1) Dutch
   (2) English
   (3) French
   (4) Portuguese
   (5) Spanish

4. World history has many examples of colonization. One example is discussed in the passage. Which of the following would be another example?

   (1) The American Revolution, which began in 1776, ended England's control over its American colonies and began a new nation.
   (2) During the twentieth century, people from many different countries have settled in the United States.
   (3) In 1861, Southern states seceded from, or left, the United States.
   (4) Around 1800, England claimed the continent of Australia and sent settlers there.
   (5) During World War II, the United States sent troops to Italy and France in order to fight the Germans.

To check your answers, turn to page 74.

Reviewing Lesson 4

Read the following paragraph.

> The Pilgrims were persecuted in England because their beliefs differed from the teachings of the Church of England. To escape this situation, the Pilgrims decided to settle in the New World. Although they had planned to settle in Virginia, their ship, the *Mayflower*, was blown off course. They reached Massachusetts instead. Even before going ashore, the Pilgrims wrote and signed an agreement, the Mayflower Compact. The compact is now a key document in American history. In part, it reads as follows:

> "In the name of God Amen. We . . . the loyal subjects of our dread and sovereign Lord King James . . . having undertaken, for the glory of God, and advancements of the Christian faith and honour of our king and country, a voyage to plant the first colony in the Northern parts of Virginia, do . . . solemnly and mutually covenant and combine ourselves together into a civil body politic for our better ordering, and preservation of our ends, and by this virtue to enact, constitute and frame such just and equal laws, ordinances, acts, constitutions and offices, from time to time, as shall be thought convenient for the general good of the Colony to which we promise all due submission and obedience."

Questions 1 and 2 refer to the paragraph. Circle the best answer for each question.

1. Based on the quotation, the Mayflower Compact was probably written in order to

   (1) develop a plan for dealing with the Indians
   (2) establish religious rules
   (3) express rebellion against the king of England
   (4) divide the land among the colonists
   (5) establish plans for governing the new colony

2. The Mayflower Compact was an important influence in American history. Based on the quotation, how was the Mayflower Compact applied?

   (1) It helped establish the right to bear arms.
   (2) It provided a basis for treaties with Native Americans.
   (3) It helped establish the principles of self-government.
   (4) It set terms for trade with foreign countries.
   (5) It was used to argue against slavery.

To check your answers, turn to page 74.

Read the following paragraphs.

By the 1730s there were 13 colonies in what is now the United States. There were certain differences among these colonies. But there were also many things that united them all.

The colonies differed in their geography and in the way people earned their livings. There were three main groups of colonies. The New England colonies included New Hampshire, Massachusetts (including Maine), Rhode Island, and Connecticut. The middle colonies were New York, New Jersey, Pennsylvania, and Delaware. Maryland, Virginia, North and South Carolina, and Georgia formed the southern colonies. The New England colonies were cold and had poor soil. They did, however, have good harbors. The middle colonies had soil that was good for growing grains such as wheat. The southern colonies had warm weather and very rich soil. These conditions made it possible to raise crops grown in large areas, such as tobacco, cotton, and indigo, a dye.

The colonies were united by their English heritage. One important part of this heritage was the belief in democratic ideals such as self-government. This democratic English heritage indirectly led the colonists to rebel against England because the colonies were united by another factor. They increasingly saw themselves as Americans, separated from the English by their experience in the New World.

Questions 3 and 4 refer to the paragraphs. Circle the best answer for each question.

3. Which can be concluded from the paragraphs?

(1) People in the middle colonies suffered economic hardships.
(2) Plantations, or large farms, were most common in the southern colonies.
(3) The southern colonies had trouble attracting settlers.
(4) The three groups of colonies were often at war with one another.
(5) Settlers in New England usually came from countries other than England.

4. Based on the paragraphs, why did the colonists rebel against England?

(1) They came to reject their English heritage.
(2) The colonists came to feel they should be governed only from America.
(3) They were influenced by other groups in the New World.
(4) The colonists came to believe in freedom of religion.
(5) They came to feel that the English king was not ruling them with a strong enough hand.

To check your answers, turn to page 75.

GED Mini-Test

Directions: Choose the best answer to each item.

Items 1 to 3 refer to the following map.

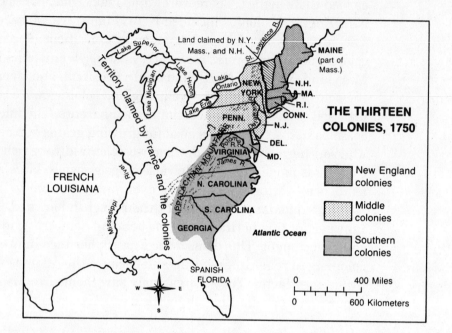

1. According to the map, which colonies made up the New England colonies?

   (1) colonies to the east of the Appalachian Mountains
   (2) colonies closest to Lake Erie and Lake Ontario
   (3) the five northeastern colonies
   (4) colonies west of the St. Lawrence River
   (5) territories claimed by France

2. In order to transport goods from New York to Delaware, an important trade route might have been the

   (1) Potomac River
   (2) James River
   (3) St. Lawrence River
   (4) Delaware River
   (5) Mississippi River

3. Which of the following conclusions can be drawn from the map?

   (1) Florida was one of the original colonies.
   (2) The original colonies did not extend much past the Appalachian Mountains.
   (3) The coastline of the colonies along the Atlantic was about 800 miles.
   (4) The land that is now Canada was once part of the colonies.
   (5) Lake Michigan and the other Great Lakes provided easy transportation among the colonies.

To check your answers, turn to page 75.

Items 4 and 5 refer to the following paragraphs.

Democracy means that the people rule themselves. The greater the voice of the people, the more democratic the system. In a true democratic system, all people have a voice in the government. Systems of government can be democratic in different ways. The thirteen colonies developed three basic systems of government that applied democratic principles in different ways.

In self-governing colonies, the colonists themselves elected the governor and all members of the legislature. Connecticut and Rhode Island were self-governing colonies. In proprietary colonies, the proprietor, or owner, of the colony selected the governor. The colonists elected all members of the legislature. Maryland, Pennsylvania, and Delaware were proprietary colonies. The other eight colonies were royal colonies. In royal colonies, the governor was selected by the king of England. The legislature was divided into two branches. The colonists elected the members of one branch, but the king chose the members of the other.

4. Given the definition of democracy and of a true democratic system, which of the following lists the types of colonial government from most democratic to least democratic?

(1) self-governing, proprietary, royal
(2) proprietary, royal, self-governing
(3) royal, self-governing, proprietary
(4) proprietary, royal, self-governing
(5) self-governing, royal, proprietary

5. Some parts of colonial government were democratic; others were not. Which of the following parts was democratic?

(1) In the southern colonies, local officials were appointed by the governor, rather than elected by the people.
(2) In all colonies, people had to own land in order to vote.
(3) In the proprietary colonies, governors could veto, or reject, laws that the elected legislature had passed.
(4) In the New England colonies, people ran their own towns through meetings in which they discussed and voted on issues.
(5) The king of England had final say about laws passed in the colonies.

To check your answers, turn to page 75.

Answers and Explanations

1. (Application) **(2) religious**
    Wanting to convert other people is a religious reason. Since the priests had no economic, social, political, or scientific motives, options (1), (3), (4), and (5) are incorrect.

2. (Application) **(1) economic**
    Getting gold means gaining wealth. Gold has nothing to do with options (2), (3), (4), or (5).

3. (Application) **(2) religious**
    People who want to worship as they choose have a religious motive. Options (1), (3), (4), and (5) are not based on religion.

1. (Application) **(3) smallpox and influenza** These are diseases, and the passage states that many Native Americans died from diseases carried by the Europeans. Options (1), (2), (4), and (5) do not refer to disease.

2. (Comprehension) **(2) take some of the trade with the Orient away from Italy** This is stated in the text. The passage gives no evidence that Columbus had any interest in options (1), (3), (4), or (5).

3. (Comprehension) **(5) Spanish** The passage states that the Spanish had a head start. Options (1), (3), and (4) are not supported by the passage. Option (2) is incorrect because even though the English had many colonies, these came later than the Spanish colonies.

4. (Application) **(4) Around 1800, England claimed the continent of Australia and sent settlers there.** Colonization is defined as sending people to a new area to settle there. Option (1) is about the end of a colony. Option (2) is incorrect because it does not involve one country taking control of another. Option (3) has nothing to do with colonization. Option (5) refers to only a temporary movement of people.

1. (Comprehension) **(5) establish plans for governing the new colony** According to the compact, the Pilgrims agreed to set up laws needed for government. There is no mention of options (1), (2), and (4). Option (3) is incorrect because there is no suggestion of rebellion.

2. (Application) **(3) It helped establish the principles of self-government.** The statements in the compact focus on a group of people making their own laws, even when supervised by a higher authority. Nothing in the quotation relates to options (1), (2), (4), or (5).

3. (Comprehension) (2) **Plantations, or large farms, were most common in the southern colonies.** This is suggested by the text. Option (1) is the opposite of what is suggested. There is no support for options (3), (4), or (5).

4. (Comprehension) (2) **The colonists came to feel they should be governed only from America.** The colonists began to see self-government as a reality. As people living in America, not England, they felt they should not be ruled by England. Option (1) is too general. There is no support for option (3). There is no connection between option (4) and rebellion. Option (5) is the opposite of what the colonists felt.

GED Mini-Test (pages 72–73)

1. (Comprehension) (3) **the five northeastern colonies** The New England colonies are in what is now the northeastern part of the United States. Option (1) refers to the southern colonies. Option (2) refers to the middle colonies. There are no colonies on the map in the areas mentioned in options (4) and (5).

2. (Application) (4) **Delaware River** The Delaware reaches from New York to Pennsylvania. The rivers in options (1), (2), (3), and (5) were in other colonies or territories.

3. (Comprehension) (2) **The original colonies did not extend much past the Appalachian Mountains.** There is no evidence in the map for options (1), (3), (4), or (5).

4. (Application) (1) **self-governing, proprietary, royal** A self-governing colony is the most democratic, and one that is ruled mainly by a king is the least democratic. Options (2), (3), (4), and (5) are not correct according to the definitions.

5. (Application) (4) **In the New England colonies, people ran their own towns through meetings in which they discussed and voted on issues.** Democracy is based on involvement of the people. Options (1), (2), (3), and (5) are not concerned with the citizens' involvement in government.

LESSON 5 Comprehension Skill: Making Inferences

This skill can help you make decisions based on what is directly stated, what is only suggested, and what you already know.

An **inference** is a kind of decision. In Lesson 3, you learned how to make a decision based on the facts you were given in order to arrive at a conclusion. Making an inference is very similar, but you also will be thinking about what the author is suggesting. Often an author does not state an idea directly. It is important to remember that what a writer or a speaker suggests is an **implication**. When you figure out what the author is getting at, you are **inferring** what was meant.

This skill may sound complicated, but actually you make inferences every day. If your best friend calls and says he wants to come over to talk but he won't say why, you infer that he has something important on his mind. Because of your experiences in life, you know that people usually feel more comfortable talking about difficult things face to face than over the telephone. Or you may call someone you met recently. The person is polite but does not seem interested in talking to you. You can infer that the person is not interested in getting to know you better. In both examples, you were not told directly what the person's attitude was. What you did was make a judgment based on what you know about the world combined with what you heard and what you did not hear. Sometimes what is **not** said is as important as what is said.

When you read, you have to be sure to understand all the facts before you make an inference. Look for words that suggest emotions and attitudes. If an author says that the President gritted his teeth before making a decision, the implication is that the President was unhappy about having to make that decision. We know that people often grit their teeth when they are unhappy. Also, pay attention to the author's choice of words. Read the following example: The President, a skinny man, got to his feet with a start. Now read the next sentence: The President, a slender man, rose quickly to his feet. The first sentence is less flattering. The second sentence makes the President sound more graceful and self-assured. You can infer from the first sentence that the author does not have a high opinion of the President. The second sentence implies more respect.

Practicing Comprehension

Read the following information.

> In 1763, Britain won the Seven Years War, known in the colonies as the French and Indian War. The cost of the battles had been so high that Britain decided to tax its colonists in order to raise money to pay the debts. This move led to a major debate about the nature of government. The first question was whether the mother country had the right to tax a colony without its consent. This became a broader question about who the colonists really were. Were they the king's subjects or were they independent Americans? Many essays were written about this important conflict. The following are excerpts by two famous writers of the times:

> "The colonists are the descendants of men who either had no vote in elections, or who voluntarily resigned them for something, in their opinion, of more estimation. They have therefore exactly what their ancestors left them, not a vote in making laws, or in constituting legislators, but the happiness of being protected by law and the duty of obeying it."
>
> —Samuel Johnson

> "But, admitting that we were all of English descent, what does it amount to? Nothing? Britain, being now an open enemy, extinguishes every other name and title; and to say that reconciliation is our duty is truly farcical. The first king of England of the present line (William the Conqueror) was a Frenchman, and half the peers of England are descendants from the same country; wherefore by the same line of reasoning, England ought to be governed by France."
>
> —Thomas Paine

Questions 1 and 2 refer to the information. Circle the best answer for each question.

1. It can be inferred that Samuel Johnson

   (1) was a famous colonial writer
   (2) believed the colonists should not be taxed
   (3) supported the British position
   (4) admired the American colonists' spirit of independence
   (5) believed in the right of rebellion

2. Thomas Paine implied that the American colonists should

   (1) be ruled by France
   (2) not be ruled by England
   (3) accept British rule
   (4) be proud of having British ancestors
   (5) have objected to the French and Indian War

To check your answers, turn to page 84.

Topic 5: The American Revolution

As Britain's colonial empire in America grew, the English government began to have trouble controlling the settlers across the ocean. The king of England continued to treat these distant people as if they still lived in England.

Life in America required the colonists to adjust to many new challenges. The customs and traditions they brought from England were not always suited to the harsh climate and nonagricultural land of New England. A new way of life had to be developed in order to survive. Because the goods that were easily available in England could be bought only at high prices with long waits for delivery, what had been common often became a luxury. The settlers became more and more used to producing the necessities by themselves. American colonists came to be self-reliant.

When King George III passed laws such as the Stamp Act and the Townsend Act, which imposed heavy taxes, the colonists refused to obey the laws. At first, the Americans hoped to force England to give in to their demands, but when the Second Continental Congress met in 1775, the king rejected their petitions and called them rebels. Eventually the colonists decided to fight, not for their rights as Englishmen, but for complete freedom from England. The discontent was no longer limited to the issue of taxes. On July 4, 1776, representatives from all the colonies signed the Declaration of Independence. This document, written mainly by Thomas Jefferson, declared the colonies to be an independent nation. It also set out the basic principles of democratic government. The foundation of many American laws can be found in the beliefs that "All men are created equal" and that people have "certain unalienable rights" including "life, liberty, and the pursuit of happiness."

The War of Independence took seven hard years to win. It is important to remember that this small group of colonists was fighting the most powerful country in the world. Also, most Americans had close relatives in England and had to take sides against them. It took brave and determined people to continue the long war. It also took help from France. The French contributed money and soldiers, and perhaps more importantly, ships.

After Cornwallis surrendered to Washington following the battle at Yorktown, the British House of Commons voted for ending the war. Peace negotiations took over a year, but the Treaty of Paris was finally signed in September 1783. The thirteen American states were recognized as an independent nation.

Exercises

Questions 1 to 4 refer to the previous information. Circle the best answer for each question.

1. It can be inferred from the passage that the prices of some common goods were high because

    (1) the colonists had not developed good trading skills
    (2) goods had to be imported all the way from England
    (3) pirates were attacking many of the trade routes
    (4) the colonists would accept only the best
    (5) these goods were really luxury items

2. It can be inferred from the passage that the colonies' first reaction to King George III's taxes was to

    (1) declare their freedom from England
    (2) demand their rights as English subjects
    (3) agree to pay the taxes
    (4) ask for help from France
    (5) form a democratic government

3. According to the information, King George III

    (1) was very old
    (2) passed fair laws
    (3) understood the colonists' problems
    (4) did not understand the attitude in the colonies
    (5) was a cruel and uncaring man

4. It can be concluded from the information that the colonists might not have won the war if

    (1) their British relatives had not supported them
    (2) Britain had had a better navy
    (3) Jefferson had not been such a good writer
    (4) they had listened to the French advisors
    (5) they had not received help from France

To check your answers, turn to page 84.

Reviewing Lesson 5

Read the following paragraphs.

After the Revolutionary War, the first thing the people of the new country had to do was form a national government. The thirteen American colonies had become thirteen independent states loosely held together by an agreement called the Articles of Confederation. Each new state wrote its own constitution that described its form of government and the basic rights of the people. These rights included freedom of speech, freedom of the press, freedom of religion, and the right to trial by jury.

Each state also allowed new freedoms in trade, manufacturing, and settlement of arguments about land ownership. The American belief in free enterprise and self-government was put into practice. Free from British rule, the young American states encouraged shipping, manufacturing, and the westward migration of settlers. Also, large colonial estates that had been held by royal grants were broken up, which resulted in an increase in small, independent farms in the South.

But these newfound freedoms brought unexpected problems in finances, political agreements, and trade. The states did not have uniform laws about coining money. Standards of measurement could vary from state to state. And each state even had the power to declare war with another country that was trading with its neighboring state. Another major problem was that the large territories had few good roads and inadequate methods of transportation. The Congress under the Articles was not really a national government. By 1787 many Americans felt they were ready for a more perfect union.

Questions 1 and 2 refer to the paragraphs. Circle the best answer for each question.

1. It can be inferred from the paragraphs that under British rule, the colonies

   (1) had many freedoms
   (2) had limited freedoms
   (3) had absolute control over their properties
   (4) had already formed a working government
   (5) were self-governing

2. It can be concluded from the paragraphs that the young nation was concerned with

   (1) developing trade relations with Europe
   (2) being left alone
   (3) becoming as powerful as England
   (4) specifying basic human rights
   (5) building roads

To check your answers, turn to page 84.

Look at the following map.

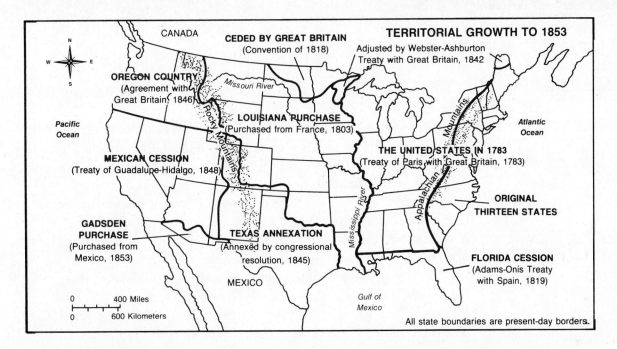

Questions 3 to 6 refer to the map. Circle the best answer for each question.

3. To which major geographic boundary had the original thirteen states expanded by 1783?

   (1) the Missouri River
   (2) the Mississippi River
   (3) the Appalachian Mountains
   (4) the Rocky Mountains
   (5) the Gulf of Mexico

4. From 1846 to 1848, the United States fought a border war with Mexico that resulted in acquiring from Mexico much of the present Southwest and California. This was known as the

   (1) Texas Annexation
   (2) Louisiana Purchase
   (3) Florida Cession
   (4) Mexican Cession
   (5) Gadsden Purchase

5. According to the map, much of the land acquired by the United States had been

   (1) uninhabited
   (2) fought over in previous years
   (3) owned by other countries
   (4) unexplored
   (5) heavily settled

6. Only a territory that is independent of another nation can be annexed. You can infer from the map that the Texas area had been

   (1) owned by Mexico
   (2) taken from Mexico by force
   (3) a free territory
   (4) purchased from France
   (5) obtained by treaty

To check your answers, turn to pages 84 and 85.

GED Mini-Test

Directions: Choose the best answer to each item.

Items 1 and 2 refer to the following paragraphs.

The original Articles of Confederation were quickly replaced by what is now known as the Constitution of the United States. The states' delegates who met in Philadelphia agreed that the new nation needed a strong federal, or central, government. The country faced many problems because of the differences among the states. Some had more power than others, some were larger, some were richer, and some had slaves while others did not. Sorting out these problems and coming to a compromise took weeks.

Eventually the Constitution was written and most of the problems were ironed out. America's system of government had been established. It was decided that Congress should have two parts. One was the Senate, where every state would have two senators. The other was the House of Representatives, where each state would be represented according to the size of its population. The one point that was not resolved was that of slavery. The convention did not outlaw slavery because that might have ended the possibility of getting the Constitution approved by all the states.

1. Which of the following best states the main idea of these paragraphs?

   (1) Writing the Constitution was difficult because of all the differences that had to be settled.
   (2) The Constitution is better than the Articles of Confederation.
   (3) The Constitution was written by states' delegates.
   (4) Politics always involves arguments.
   (5) All is well that ends well.

2. You can infer from the paragraphs that some states refused to

   (1) agree on the number of senators
   (2) agree on how representatives should be elected
   (3) divide the Congress into two sections
   (4) give up their slaves
   (5) finish writing the Constitution

To check your answers, turn to page 85.

Items 3 and 4 refer to the following paragraph.

Andrew Jackson, known as Old Hickory, was President of the United States from 1829 to 1837. He had grown up a poor orphan and was the first President not from a powerful Eastern family. Jackson, born in South Carolina, called himself the President of the "Common Man." He was elected shortly after many of the states had changed their voting laws. Voting had often been limited to landowners, but after 1820 most states permitted all adult white males to vote. The people voted to elect Old Hickory, a national hero and a competent lawyer.

3. You can infer that ordinary people voted for Jackson because

    (1) they disliked Easterners
    (2) they wanted a President much like themselves
    (3) he promised them all jobs
    (4) he would keep them out of war
    (5) he had a catchy nickname

4. Jackson's election being a departure from the norm is most similar to

    (1) Kennedy being the first Irish-Catholic president
    (2) Reagan being a persuasive speaker
    (3) Eisenhower having a reputation as a general
    (4) Dan Quayle being from Indiana
    (5) Lincoln being a lawyer

Items 5 and 6 refer to the following cartoon.

BORN LOSER® by Art and Chip Sansom

5. What is the cartoonist implying?

    (1) No one enjoys studying history.
    (2) The Declaration of Independence was written before Columbus discovered America.
    (3) Dates are not really important.
    (4) Some people know little about the history of their own country.
    (5) Children should be seen and not heard.

6. The cartoon is set in

    (1) an elementary geography class
    (2) an elementary history class
    (3) a college history class
    (4) a high school English class
    (5) a kindergarten

To check your answers, turn to page 85.

Answers and Explanations

1. (Comprehension) **(3) supported the British position** Johnson clearly believed that the colonists had no right to vote or to object to the king's laws. His description of the colonists is not flattering. Option (1) is incorrect because although Johnson is referred to as a writer, there is no evidence that he was from the colonies. Options (2), (4), and (5) are the opposite of what is suggested.

2. (Comprehension) **(2) not be ruled by England** Paine was indirectly comparing English ancestry to American ancestry. By making his statement about England, he was implying that the same was true for America. There is no support for options (1), (4), or (5). Option (3) is the opposite of what is implied.

1. (Comprehension) **(2) goods had to be imported all the way from England** Goods that could not be produced with the resources of the New World had to come from England. Shipping them took a long time and was expensive. There is no support for options (1) or (3). The quality and the types of goods are not specified, so options (4) and (5) are incorrect.

2. (Comprehension) **(2) demand their rights as English subjects** The Continental Congress had sent petitions asking to be heard about the problem. Options (1), (4), and (5) all followed after the petitions were denied. Option (3) is the opposite of what is stated in the passage.

3. (Comprehension) **(4) did not understand the attitude in the colonies** The king expected the colonies to act like regular English citizens. He forgot they lived under different circumstances. Option (1) might be true, but it is not suggested in the passage. Options (2) and (3) are the opposite of what is suggested. There is no support for option (5).

4. (Comprehension) **(5) they had not received help from France** France supplied some much-needed things that could help to offset the power of England. Option (1) is not suggested. Option (2) has no support. Option (3) has nothing to do with winning or losing the war. If there were French advisers, it is likely their advice was taken, so option (4) is incorrect.

1. (Comprehension) **(2) had limited freedoms** The clue here is the word <u>new</u> in the first sentence of the first paragraph, which suggests that these freedoms had not been available before. Option (1) is opposite to what is suggested. Option (3) is incorrect because some land had been held by royal grants. Option (4) is incorrect because a new government had to be formed. There is no evidence of option (5).

2. (Comprehension) **(4) specifying basic human rights** The long list of freedoms in the first paragraph supports this conclusion. There is no support for options (1), (2), (3), or (5).

3. (Comprehension) **(2) the Mississippi River** According to the map, the Mississippi River provided the westernmost geographic boundary of the United States by 1783. This new area extended past the Appalachian Mountains, option (3), but not as far west as the Missouri River, option (1), or the Rocky Mountains, option (4). The Gulf of Mexico was not a boundary for this land area at that time, so option (5) is incorrect.

4. (Comprehension) **(4) Mexican Cession** According to the map, the Mexican Cession added territory to the Southwest, including what is now the state of California. Option (1) refers to southwestern land acquisition but does not include California. Option (2) added territory from about the northwest to the southeast of the U.S. Options (3) and (5) refer to territories that are too far southeast or too small in the southwest to be correct.

5. (Comprehension) **(3) owned by other countries** There is enough information in the map to support this conclusion. There is no support for options (1), (2), (4), or (5).

6. (Comprehension) **(3) a free territory** The Texas territory was annexed and so must have been independent. Although options (1) and (2) are true, they are not referred to in the map. There is no support for options (4) or (5).

GED Mini-Test (pages 82–83)

1. (Comprehension) **(1) Writing the Constitution was difficult because of all the differences that had to be settled.** This is emphasized in the first paragraph and suggested in the second. Options (2) and (3) are supporting details. Options (4) and (5) are broad generalizations that could apply to many situations, not just to this one.

2. (Comprehension) **(4) give up their slaves** This inference is based on the fact that this is the only issue on which a compromise was not reached. Options (1), (2), (3), and (5) are incorrect because agreements and decisions were made and the Constitution was finally written.

3. (Comprehension) **(2) they wanted a President much like themselves** Jackson was one of the people who would not have been able to vote before 1820. He would understand ordinary people's problems. Options (1), (3), and (4) are not suggested in the paragraph. There is no evidence that his nickname had any influence, so option (5) is incorrect.

4. (Application) **(1) Kennedy being the first Irish-Catholic president** Religion, like wealth, is an important political tool. Kennedy's and Jackson's elections opened the door for others. Options (2), (3), and (4) are not revolutionary qualities. Option (5) is incorrect because several presidents have been lawyers, including Jackson.

5. (Comprehension) **(4) Some people know little about the history of their own country.** There is no support for options (1) or (2). Option (3) is the attitude of the girl, not the cartoonist. Option (5) has nothing to do with the cartoon.

6. (Comprehension) **(2) an elementary history class** The children are young, and there is a history book on the teacher's desk. Options (1), (3), and (4) do not match the evidence. Option (5) is unlikely because kindergarten children probably would not be having a history lesson.

LESSON 6 Analysis Skill: Fact and Opinion

This skill will help you to tell a fact from an opinion.

When you read, you often find that the writer is trying to convince you of something. Because authors often do not give only the bare facts about a subject, you need to be able to tell a fact from an opinion.

A **fact** is a statement about something that has actually happened or actually exists. A fact can be proven. The statement "that is a true fact" is misleading because it implies, or suggests, that a fact can be false. A false statement is a lie, not a fact. A fact does not change.

An **opinion** is one person's thoughts about a fact or group of facts. People make judgments about what they see, hear, taste, and touch. Those judgments are opinions. Opinions are interpretations of facts. Some opinions are more closely based on facts than others, so you need to look for facts that support an opinion. When you find facts that seem to support a person's opinion, first form your own opinion about them, and then compare your opinion to the other person's judgment.

You form opinions every day. For example, if you own a car, it is a fact that there is a car in your driveway. You can see and touch the car. You think the car works well. It starts every morning and needs few repairs. However, your teenage children think the car should be replaced because it does not have a stereo, an air conditioner, plush seats, and of all things, the car is gray, not red! To you, none of those facts are important. In the teenagers' opinion, they are. You are all basing your opinions on different facts about the car.

Opinions, unlike facts, can change fairly easily. Your son—who wanted a fancy red car—may change his mind when what he really needs is a car that starts in bad weather. You need to decide if an opinion is **valid**. Do not be fooled by an opinion that is stated as if it were a fact. In the early 1950s, many people stated as a fact that rock and roll music was just a fad. Actually this was only opinion. The fact is that rock and roll music is with us today, whether we like it or not.

When you look for opinions, watch for words that suggest emotion or judgment, such as good, bad, ugly, lovely, think, believe, might, and probably.

Practicing Analysis

Read the following paragraphs.

The Battle of Gettysburg was one of the most important, and one of the most horrifying, battles of the Civil War. On July 1, 1863, Confederate Army troops led by General Lee accidentally met Union soldiers led by General George Meade. Coming to Gettysburg, Pennsylvania from the north, the Southern soldiers were looking for supplies of shoes. Approaching from the south, the Northern forces were hunting for Lee. The Confederates were unlucky. They never found shoes, and they lost the battle.

At first it looked as if Lee was going to win the battle. The two armies had settled on ridges about half a mile apart, with the Southerners on Seminary Ridge and the Northerners on Cemetery Ridge. Lee had almost broken through the enemy's lines by attacking the edge of Meade's forces.

On the third day, Lee attacked again, but this time he sent 15,000 brave Confederate soldiers directly across the open field between the ridges. Meade's forces opened fire again and again on the helpless men in gray. Of the 100 Virginians who made it to the ridge, most were either killed or captured. The attack had lasted only about an hour. Lee waited for an answering charge, but Meade decided not to imitate the other side. Finally, Lee withdrew with his saddened troops back across the Potomac River to Virginia. The North was victorious, the Battle of Gettysburg was over, but the cost to both sides was staggering. Over 10,000 men were dead, wounded, or missing. This horrifying event was probably a turning point in the Civil War.

Questions 1 and 2 refer to the paragraphs. Circle the best answer for each question.

1. A fact about the Southern army is that they were

   (1) brave in battle
   (2) lucky in war
   (3) helpless against the Union forces
   (4) looking for shoes before the battle
   (5) very sad after their defeat

2. Which fact supports the opinion that the battle was horrifying?

   (1) The Southern army retreated.
   (2) The Northern army won.
   (3) Ten thousand men lost their lives or were injured.
   (4) Meade did not return the attack.
   (5) The Northern army was camped on a cemetery.

To check your answers, turn to page 94.

Topic 6: The Civil War and Reconstruction

The United States was almost split in two because of disagreements about issues important to the North and the South. When the Civil War was over, the task of rebuilding the nation was very difficult.

By the mid-1800s, economic tensions between the North and the South had come to the breaking point. The Southern states relied mainly on agriculture for their financial stability, and the Northern states were mainly industrial. Because of this, the North had more actual wealth and was better able to use its natural resources. These primary economic differences also had moral and emotional overtones.

The institution of **slavery** had been an issue for many years. Even the admission of states to the Union had been restricted to maintain a balance between slaveholding and free states. Although many Southerners did not own slaves, the large plantations depended on this inexpensive labor to produce their crops. Slaveholders did not want to see their investments go down the drain with the outlawing of slavery. They were finding themselves having to argue with **abolitionists**, people who wanted to do away with slavery throughout the nation. Northern abolitionists had even set up "underground railroads," safe houses across the country for runaway slaves.

The slavery question became an issue in the presidential election of 1860. The new Republican party tended to be antislavery, while the Democratic party was supported by Southern slave states and more moderate Northerners. Although newly elected Republican Abraham Lincoln did not support slavery, he did pass an amendment that would guarantee slavery in the states where it already existed. But the Southern states felt that Lincoln would do little else to support them.

In February 1861, seven Southern states seceded from the Union and founded the **Confederate States of America,** with Jefferson Davis as the president. War began when the Confederate government demanded the surrender of Union soldiers at Fort Sumter, South Carolina. The hastily organized Southern forces fired on a supply ship sent by President Lincoln. Six more Southern states immediately left the Union. During the next four bloody years, friends and families had to choose which side of the divided nation they would support.

Reconstruction is the term for the years from 1865 to 1877. After the Southern states had been brought back into the Union, the South needed help rebuilding cities, farms, railroads, and schools that had been destroyed during the War Between the States. Southerners also needed to learn how to live without slavery, and newly freed blacks needed help in finding a place in the new society.

Exercises

Questions 1 to 6 refer to the previous information. Circle the best answer for each question.

1. Following Lincoln's presidential election, seven Southern states seceded from the Union. This event was based on their belief that

   (1) the Constitution became invalid
   (2) Lincoln would not represent their interests
   (3) Jefferson Davis was a Southerner
   (4) the South was not part of the Union
   (5) Southern states had to rebel

2. Which is a valid opinion based on the facts in the information?

   (1) The South was right to secede.
   (2) Abolitionists should not have helped runaway slaves.
   (3) Slaveholders were right to protect their investments.
   (4) The South probably resented the North even after the war.
   (5) Lincoln should have supported the South.

3. It can be concluded from the information that slavery was

   (1) becoming unpopular in the South
   (2) needed to keep landowners wealthy
   (3) supported by abolitionists
   (4) the only cause of the Civil War
   (5) morally wrong

4. You can infer that the last six Southern states left the Union because

   (1) they felt they had to support the Confederacy after the Fort Sumter incident
   (2) Lincoln made them feel unwelcome
   (3) too many of their slaves were running away
   (4) they wanted to do away with slavery
   (5) they were afraid of the abolitionists

5. The information is mainly about

   (1) the evils of slavery
   (2) economic recovery
   (3) the rebuilding of the nation
   (4) Lincoln's position on secession
   (5) what led to the Civil War

6. The situation that many families of both the North and the South had to face when the war began is most similar to that of the families of American soldiers in

   (1) the Vietnam War
   (2) today's Army
   (3) the American Revolution
   (4) the French and Indian War
   (5) the Korean War

To check your answers, turn to page 94.

Reviewing Lesson 6

Read the following paragraph.

> General Grant of the Union and General Lee of the Confederacy continued to engage in battle until April of 1865. On April 9, facing encirclement and cut off from lines of supply, Lee sent a white flag of truce to arrange for a conference with General Grant. Grant suggested that Lee's retreating and dissolving army should surrender. Lee, after great consideration, asked for terms. Grant generously suggested and Lee gladly accepted these terms of surrender:
>
> > "officers and men paroled . . . arms and materials surrendered. . . officers to keep their side arms, and let all the men who claim to own a horse or mule take the animals home with them to work their little farms."

Questions 1 and 2 refer to the paragraph. Circle the best answer for each question.

1. Which best states a fact that supports the opinion that Lee gladly agreed to Grant's terms?

  (1) Lee accepted them.
  (2) These were the terms Lee had asked for.
  (3) Lee had sent a flag of truce.
  (4) Lee surrendered immediately.
  (5) There is no supporting fact.

2. Which of the following reveals the author's opinion about Grant?

  (1) Lee respected Grant.
  (2) Grant kept fighting until the end.
  (3) Grant agreed to meet with Lee.
  (4) Grant was generous in his terms.
  (5) Grant wanted Lee to surrender.

Read the following paragraph.

> Before the end of the Civil War, President Lincoln announced that all slaves held in the South and the North were to be regarded as free. This statement is known as the Emancipation Proclamation. Lincoln showed great political wisdom by making this announcement. The North benefitted in three ways. The proclamation encouraged Northerners who had opposed the war. It also guaranteed that England would not support the South; England had outlawed slavery in 1833 and would not help people who were fighting to maintain it. Also, almost 200,000 free blacks joined the Union army to fight for the freedom of the slaves in the South.

To check your answers, turn to page 95.

Questions 3 and 4 refer to the paragraph. Circle the best answer for each question.

3. Which of the following did <u>not</u> happen as a result of the proclamation?

   (1) It inspired the North to continue the war.

   (2) It weakened the Southern war effort.

   (3) It gained support for the North from foreign countries.

   (4) Slaveholders surrendered their slaves.

   (5) Equal rights were advanced.

4. Which of the following words is used to express an opinion in the paragraph?

   (1) statement

   (2) wisdom

   (3) support

   (4) outlawed

   (5) joined

Read the following paragraph.

During the Civil War, Lincoln's declared goal was not so much to end slavery but to keep the Union together. He, like other Northerners, believed that the Union was created by the people and was indivisible: no state had the right to secede. Lincoln's terms for planning Reconstruction were based on this belief. He wanted the nation to be reunited as quickly and painlessly as possible. The only requirements for acceptance back into the Union were to swear allegiance to the nation and to end slavery. The rebel states would then be pardoned and allowed to reestablish their state constitutions.

Questions 5 and 6 refer to the paragraph. Circle the best answer for each question.

5. According to the paragraph, Lincoln held the opinion that

   (1) the states had a right to secede

   (2) the Confederacy was legitimate

   (3) the South would win the war

   (4) slavery would be maintained

   (5) secession was not legal

6. Lincoln's position on secession of states is most similar to

   (1) Gorbachev's declaration that Latvia's claim of independence from the USSR is unjustified

   (2) the destruction of the Berlin Wall

   (3) the official Chinese reaction to the students' demand for democracy

   (4) the United States' acceptance of Texas into the Union

   (5) England's attitude toward the French

To check your answers, turn to page 95.

GED Mini-Test

Directions: Choose the best answer to each item.

Items 1 and 2 refer to the following information.

On November 19, 1863, President Lincoln dedicated a national cemetery at the Gettysburg battlefield. The speech he made there became famous as the Gettysburg Address. Lincoln saw the Union victory at that site as representing democratic ideals. He commented especially on the importance of a unified nation:

"Four score and seven years ago our fathers brought forth on this continent a new nation, conceived in liberty and dedicated to the proposition that all men are created equal. Now we are engaged in a great civil war, testing whether that nation or any nation so conceived and so dedicated can long endure. We are met on a great battlefield of that war. We have come to dedicate a portion of that field, as a final resting place for those who here gave their lives that that nation might live. It is altogether fitting and proper that we should do this. But, in a larger sense, we cannot dedicate—we cannot consecrate—we cannot hallow—this ground. The brave men, living and dead, who struggled here, have consecrated it, far above our poor power to add or detract. The world will little note, or long remember, what we say here, but it can never forget what they did here. It is for us the living, rather, to be dedicated here to the unfinished work which they who fought here have thus far so nobly advanced. It is rather for us to be here dedicated to the great task remaining before us—that from these honored dead we take increased devotion to that cause for which they gave the last full measure of devotion—that we here highly resolve that these dead shall not have died in vain—that this nation, under God, shall have a new birth of freedom—and that government of the people, by the people, for the people, shall not perish from the earth."

1. In this speech, Lincoln expressed the opinion that his words

    (1) would bless the cemetery
    (2) would soon be forgotten
    (3) would be long remembered
    (4) were of national importance
    (5) were fitting and proper

2. Which word does not reflect Lincoln's opinion of the men who fought at Gettysburg?

    (1) brave
    (2) consecrated
    (3) nobly
    (4) honored
    (5) dead

To check your answers, turn to page 95.

Following Reconstruction, President Hayes introduced a laissez-faire policy toward race relations in the South. The term is French for "to leave alone" and was meant to express the attitude of the government toward the people. He told black citizens that their rights and interests would be protected if the federal government did not interfere with Southern whites. And indeed, for a while Southern conservatives adopted a moderate policy toward black citizens. Blacks served as justices of the peace and in the legislature. There was little public discrimination.

However, in the 1890s difficult economic conditions changed the situation. Southern farmers, who were in the middle of a depression, blamed the former slaves whom they saw as taking away their livelihoods. People began to demand that blacks be segregated and denied voting rights.

The guaranteed rights of the black voters did not stop the angry white Southerners. The Southern states added restrictions that made voting more and more difficult for blacks. Strict residency requirements could not be met by migrant workers. Literacy tests and poll taxes, fees paid in order to vote, were effective because many blacks were unable to read or to pay the taxes. Also, laws were passed to set up social segregation on public transportation and in public buildings.

The new segregation codes were known as Jim Crow laws, named after a stage character who presented an unfavorable image of black people. In the Supreme Court case of *Plessy v. Ferguson*, the court ruled that the Jim Crow laws were legal as long as "separate but equal" facilities were provided for blacks. The problem was that the white population decided what "equal" meant.

3. According to the information, which was an opinion about Southern blacks?

    (1) Blacks held public office.
    (2) Blacks were taking jobs away from whites.
    (3) The right for blacks to vote was guaranteed.
    (4) Some Southern blacks could not read.
    (5) Some Southern blacks were poor.

4. Which conclusion is a fact that can be determined from the information?

    (1) Blacks should not vote.
    (2) Racial segregation is socially acceptable.
    (3) Jim Crow laws were upheld by the legal system.
    (4) Black people present an unfavorable image.
    (5) The laissez-faire attitude toward the South was effective.

To check your answers, turn to page 95.

Answers and Explanations

Practicing Analysis (page 87)

1. (Analysis) **(4) looking for shoes before the battle** This statement is something that can be proved. Options (1), (3), and (5) are the author's opinions. Option (2) is the opposite of what is stated.

2. (Analysis) **(3) Ten thousand men lost their lives or were injured.** It is horrifying that so many people were killed or hurt in such a short time. There is nothing particularly awful about options (1), (2), or (4). Option (5) is not a fact.

Exercises (page 89)

1. (Analysis) **(2) Lincoln would not represent their interests** The Southern states based this opinion on the antislavery position of the Republicans. There is not enough support for options (1) and (5). Option (3) had nothing to do with the secession. Option (4) is incorrect because the Southern states were part of the Union before they seceded.

2. (Analysis) **(4) The South probably resented the North even after the war.** The South had felt it was not being treated fairly before the war, then it was defeated and left in a shambles, so there was probably little warm feeling for the North. There is not enough evidence to support the opinions in options (1), (2), (3), or (5).

3. (Comprehension) **(2) needed to keep landowners wealthy** The support for this is in the second paragraph. Options (1) and (3) are the opposite of the facts. Option (4) is incorrect because other economic factors were involved. Option (5) is incorrect because the moral aspect of slavery is not discussed.

4. (Comprehension) **(1) they felt they had to support the Confederacy after the Fort Sumter incident** It would have been clear that war was about to start, so the slave states would feel obliged to stick together. There is no support for options (2), (3), and (5). Option (4) is the opposite of what they wanted.

5. (Comprehension) **(5) what led to the Civil War** Except for the last paragraph, the information explains the cause of the war. Nothing is said about option (1). Options (2) and (3) are discussed only in the last paragraph. There is no support for option (4).

6. (Application) **(3) the American Revolution** In both cases, many families had relatives fighting on the other side. This is not the case in options (1), (2), (4), and (5).

Reviewing Lesson 6 (pages 90–91)

1. (Analysis) **(5) There is no supporting fact.** There is no evidence other than the word <u>gladly</u> which reflects opinion, not fact. Lee probably would have surrendered and accepted the terms no matter how he felt, so options (1) and (4) are incorrect. Option (2) is not true. Option (3) happened before the terms were offered.

2. (Analysis) **(4) Grant was generous in his terms.** A comment on Grant's attitude would reveal the author's opinion. There is no evidence of how Lee felt about Grant, so option (1) is incorrect. Options (2), (3), and (5) are facts, not opinions.

3. (Comprehension) **(4) Slaveholders surrendered their slaves.** Actual freedom did not occur until the war was over. Options (1), (2), (3), and (5) are all results of the proclamation.

4. (Analysis) **(2) wisdom** This is a word that shows judgment, not fact. Option (1) is a noun that refers to a fact. Options (3), (4), and (5) refer to actual happenings.

5. (Analysis) **(5) secession was not legal** Lincoln believed that states had no right to leave the Union. This was his interpretation of the Constitution. Options (1) and (2) are the opposite of what Lincoln believed. There is no evidence that Lincoln expected the North to lose, so option (3) is incorrect. There is no support for option (4).

6. (Application) **(1) Gorbachev's declaration that Latvia's claim of independence from the USSR is unjustified** Both Lincoln and Gorbachev would agree that no section of the country has the right to separate from the nation, even though the two men's reasons might be different. Option (2) refers to breaking down a division, not preventing one. Option (3) refers to a request for change in government, not a separation. Option (4) is about a joining, not a separation. Option (5) has nothing to do with national unity.

GED Mini-Test (pages 92–93)

1. (Analysis) **(2) would soon be forgotten** Lincoln said that the world would not remember his speech, an opinion that was proven wrong. Therefore, option (3) is incorrect. There is no evidence for option (1). He did not believe option (4). Option (5) refers to the dedication of the cemetery, not to Lincoln's words.

2. (Analysis) **(5) dead** Many of the soldiers who had fought were dead; that is a fact. Options (1), (2), (3), and (4) are all words of praise that suggest Lincoln's high opinion of the soldiers.

3. (Analysis) **(2) Blacks were taking jobs away from whites.** This statement reflects the belief of farmers, not a fact that can be proven. Options (1), (3), (4), and (5) are all facts.

4. (Analysis) **(3) Jim Crow laws were upheld by the legal system.** The Supreme Court's ruling declared the laws to be legal. Option (1) was an opinion of some Southerners. There is no support for option (2). Option (4) is a misreading about the stage character that portrayed blacks in a negative way. Option (5) is the opposite of what is actually said.

LESSON 7 Analysis Skill: Identifying Cause and Effect

This skill will help you see how one thing can affect another.

A **cause** is what makes something happen. An **effect** is what happens as the result of a cause. When you understand the details, facts, and opinions presented in what you are reading, you will have other questions to ask yourself. You might ask why a certain event happened; that is, you want to know what caused it. Or, you might want to know what happened as a result of a situation: you want to know what the effect was.

Some cause-and-effect relationships are very simple. There is a basic pattern of Cause A produces Effect A. For example, "Because I didn't get the raise I needed, I started looking for another job."

In other situations, there may be more than one cause for an effect or more than one effect of a cause. In Lesson 6, you saw that two major issues—economic differences and opposing ideas about slavery—caused the Civil War. In Unit 1, you read about some of the effects of our heavy use of natural fuels. In the 1970s, there was an oil shortage. The price of gasoline went up, people had to wait in long lines to fill their tanks, and United States-based oil companies began to explore off-shore drilling.

A more complex type of cause-and-effect relationship involves a chain reaction. Cause A results in Effect A. Effect A then causes something else. So Effect A becomes Cause B and results in Effect B. For example, a severe thunderstorm causes the rivers to rise, the excess water causes flooding, and the flooding causes serious damage to people's homes.

Cause-and-effect relationships are often indicated by words such as because, therefore, and results in. The cause always happens before the effect, but a writer might not state the cause first. So you must read carefully. Also remember that just because one thing happens before another does not mean that the first actually causes the second. Check the facts and decide if the second event would have happened if the first one had not.

Practicing Analysis

Read the following paragraphs.

It is said that necessity is the mother of invention. It is also true that inventions give birth to many other situations. As industry developed in the United States because of technological inventions, the need for factory labor increased. As factories grew larger, the available labor force was getting smaller. The frontier of the West had attracted many homesteaders and young men in search of adventure, so there were fewer people to work in the factories. Skilled craftsmen were not interested in unskilled work, so factory owners had to look for other sources of labor. They found that women and children adapted well to the work and would accept low wages.

At first, workers in the Northeastern textile mills were treated and paid well because the companies needed to attract good workers. However, as the factory system spread, factory life worsened as workers faced long hours, hazardous conditions, and low pay. The arrival of large numbers of immigrants in the last half of the nineteenth century provided a cheap and plentiful source of labor, and wages dropped further. As a result of low wages, long hours, and unhealthy working conditions in the sweatshops of industries, workers began to organize together to correct the sources of their discontent.

Questions 1 and 2 refer to the paragraphs. Circle the best answer for each question.

1. According the the paragraphs, industry in the United States developed because

    (1) people were moving West
    (2) there were new technological inventions
    (3) more people wanted to work in factories
    (4) factory work was well-paid
    (5) there were no more skilled craftsmen

2. Which is a direct effect immigrants had on factory life?

    (1) Workers began to organize.
    (2) Wages dropped.
    (3) Women began to work in factories.
    (4) Working conditions improved.
    (5) Children were paid low wages.

To check your answers, turn to page 104.

Topic 7: Industrial America

The term **Industrial Revolution** is often used to describe the shift in the national economy from farming to manufacturing. Although the word <u>revolution</u> suggests a sudden change, the growth of industrial America was gradual and happened in two main segments.

The Industrial Revolution began in Great Britain in the 1700s and had moved to America by the early 1800s. Steam engines and machines began to replace hand labor. People began to use products made in factories instead of ones made at home. Two important ideas for speeding up the production process came from a young schoolteacher named Eli Whitney. He came up with the related ideas of mass production and interchangeable parts. Each special part of an item could be made by a machine instead of by hand. All parts made by that machine would be the same, so a worker could produce many identical items. The different parts could be fitted together easily by people on an assembly line thereby speeding up production. This process made America the world's leading manufacturer of goods.

Other American inventors had made important contributions to industry before the Civil War. Charles Goodyear had learned to treat rubber so that it hardened enough to hold its shape. Cyrus McCormick invented a reaper that could do the work of many people. Elias Howe invented a sewing machine that could handle heavy material such as sail cloth and leather. Walter Hunt gave us the paper collar, the tricycle, and the safety pin. All these inventions helped the growth of factories.

After the Civil War, manufacturing increased again, and the number of inventions soared. Even more machines were invented. A form of energy called electricity was discovered. The American way of life began to change. In the early 1800s, most Americans had lived on farms with no electricity, no running water, no furnaces, and only the transportation available from the horse and buggy. By 1900, many people had moved to the cities where they could get factory jobs. Many homes now had electric lighting, indoor plumbing, and good heating. Trains ran frequently and some people even had automobiles. The telegraph and telephone made communication easy over long distances.

Because most individuals did not have enough money to build factories on their own, they formed companies. Corporations formed by groups could raise large sums of money and reduce individual financial risk. To raise money, the corporations sold shares of stock to stockholders who would get dividends if the companies made a profit.

With the new machines and power sources, the developing companies could take advantage of the natural resources that could be found all over America. Coal, oil, natural gas, iron ore, and copper were plentiful. America was on its way to becoming a wealthy nation.

Exercises

Questions 1 to 4 refer to the previous information. Circle the best answer for each question.

1. What effect did machines have on manufacturing?

   (1) Production was speeded up.
   (2) Production was slowed down.
   (3) Goods were more easily transported.
   (4) Hand labor became more costly.
   (5) Products had to be made individually.

2. The inventions of the nineteenth century resulted in

   (1) the Civil War
   (2) a more comfortable way of life
   (3) a decrease in manufacturing
   (4) the safety pin
   (5) products of poor quality

3. The main reason the people formed corporations was to

   (1) protect their rights
   (2) make bigger profits
   (3) cheat shareholders
   (4) have enough capital
   (5) take greater risks

4. A heavy-duty sewing machine would make production of which of the following easier?

   (1) lace
   (2) paper goods
   (3) needles
   (4) shoes
   (5) blouses

To check your answers, turn to page 104.

Reviewing Lesson 7

Read the following paragraphs.

As people flocked to the factories, the working conditions became worse. The work was hard, the hours were long, and the pay was low. Individuals were forced to accept the conditions or lose their jobs. So workers started to band together against the owners. The workers realized that a group would have a stronger position to take demands to employers. Group efforts such as this came to be known as collective bargaining. The group could agree to strike and so shut down production until the workers' demands were met. Labor unions grew out of the need for organized collective bargaining with powerful companies. An early union, the Knights of Labor, was formed in the 1880s to achieve several specific goals. The Knights wanted to have an eight-hour work day, to eliminate child labor, and to organize consumer cooperatives. However, the Knights had little political support and the local leaders were not well-organized. These reasons, combined with a reputation for violence, led to the failure of the union by 1895.

Another group, the American Federation of Labor, was organized by Samuel Gompers in 1881. The A.F. of L. was successful for several reasons. Its membership of skilled workers could strike more effectively than unskilled workers who could be easily replaced. Also, the union was organized around the members' crafts, so the needs of each group were made more clear and could be taken care of quickly. Gompers also made a point of cooperating with employers who recognized the union. He realized that unions would otherwise be labeled as a threat to American business. Under his direction, skilled laborers got better pay and shorter hours.

Questions 1 and 2 refer to the paragraphs. Circle the best answer for each question.

1. Which of the following was one cause for the failure of the Knights of Labor?

    (1) The organization had too many goals.
    (2) The A.F. of L. was much more powerful.
    (3) The members were badly organized.
    (4) The Knights were not good at bargaining.
    (5) There was no real need for a union.

2. Unions were formed to confront employers because workers

    (1) realized there was strength in numbers
    (2) wanted to end unemployment
    (3) hoped to avoid strikes
    (4) wanted to increase production
    (5) wanted to invest in their companies

To check your answers, turn to page 104.

Look at the following table.

AVERAGE ANNUAL EARNINGS FOR SELECTED OCCUPATIONS—1890	
Farm laborers	$233
Public school teachers	256
Bituminous coal miners	406
Manufacturing employees	439
Street railway employees	557
Steam railroad employees	560
Gas & electricity workers	687
Ministers	794
Clerical workers in manufacturing & Steam RR	848
Postal employees	878

Question 3 is based on the table. Circle the best answer.

3. Based on the table, a probable reason for people to move from the country to the city in 1890 was that

(1) railroads did not go out into the country
(2) rural life was not interesting
(3) city jobs paid much better wages
(4) school teachers were needed in the city
(5) many government jobs were available

Read the following paragraphs.

Immigration has always played a major role in American history. It was also important in the development of American industry, especially after 1880. The technological advances in America had affected the rest of the world. Because the United States could produce more and cheaper grain than most European countries, the income of peasants in the Old World began to drop. Many came to the United States, the so-called land of opportunity.

Employers encouraged immigration because many of the new arrivals from Poland, Russia, Italy, and China would take any job. These immigrants could often speak little English and so did not complain about low wages or bad treatment. Large factories had found another source of cheap labor and would take advantage of it for many years.

Questions 4 and 5 refer to the paragraphs. Circle the best answer for each question.

4. According to the paragraphs, one effect of immigration to the United States was that

(1) conditions in industry improved
(2) factories could continue to pay low wages
(3) resident Americans were forced out of work
(4) the income of European peasants dropped
(5) American technology affected the world economy

5. Which word or phrase suggests the author's opinion that American industry was not upholding democratic ideals?

(1) technological advances
(2) opportunity
(3) so-called
(4) encouraged
(5) cheap labor

To check your answers, turn to pages 104 and 105.

GED Mini-Test

Directions: Choose the best answer to each item.

Items 1 and 2 refer to the following paragraph.

One person who helped influence the development of industry in the South had been born a slave around 1856. His name was Booker T. Washington. As a boy, he decided he wanted to learn to read. He taught himself the alphabet by studying the marked barrels at the salt mine where he worked. Washington managed to go to school part-time, learn two trades, and finally graduate. He is remembered for founding a school for black students. Tuskegee Institute was the first industrial college in the South. His students not only received academic education but also were trained in the skilled trades necessary in industry. The idea worked so well that white colleges began to imitate the practice.

1. According to the paragraph, Booker T. Washington's school

   (1) had an important effect on white colleges
   (2) was an ordinary college
   (3) prepared blacks to be teachers
   (4) has since been forgotten
   (5) was for slaves only

2. You can infer that at the time Tuskegee was founded

   (1) young blacks could go to any college they chose
   (2) blacks did not go to white colleges
   (3) all children were required to go to school
   (4) the South had become highly industrialized
   (5) skilled trades were commonly taught in colleges

Items 3 and 4 refer to the following paragraph.

As a result of rapid industrial growth, people flocked to large cities to find jobs or to be near urban society and culture. Cities served as markets for nearby farms and as centers of new industries. Improved transportation, trade, commerce, industry, and immigration all contributed to the growth of large urban areas, such as Chicago and New York. However, urban growth also caused problems such as overcrowded conditions in tenements that lacked basic necessities for health and cleanliness. As a result, diseases like typhoid destroyed entire neighborhoods.

To check your answers, turn to page 105.

3. Which of the following is <u>not</u> a reason for the growth of large cities?

(1) increased commerce
(2) job opportunities
(3) immigration
(4) spread of disease
(5) efficient transportation

4. An effect of the rapid growth of urban areas was

(1) overcrowded housing
(2) immigration laws
(3) better education
(4) improved health facilities
(5) job competition

Items 5 to 8 refer to the following information.

The rapid changes in urban areas led to serious problems in industry and daily life. A group of reformers and writers, known as "muckrakers," helped to arouse the American people to demand reforms. Listed below are four major works and themes that led to public awareness and congressional reform.

Literary Works	Themes
The History of the Standard Oil Company (by Ida Tarbell, 1904)	Exposed the ruthless tactics of oil monopolies
The Jungle (by Upton Sinclair, 1906)	Described the filthy conditions in the meat-packing industry
The Bitter Cry of Children (by John Spargo, 1906)	Documented the poverty that caused children to go to school hungry
The Shame of the Cities (by Lincoln Steffens, 1904)	Exposed corruption in city government

5. *The Jungle*, by Upton Sinclair, was written as a result of the exposure of

(1) unsanitary conditions in slaughter houses
(2) unfair labor practices
(3) poverty among industrial workers
(4) corruption in politics
(5) the manufacture of tainted food

6. A work that probably charged politicians with illegal voting practices was

(1) *The Bitter Cry of Children*
(2) *The Jungle*
(3) *The History of the Standard Oil Company*
(4) *The Shame of the Cities*
(5) *The Object of Ridicule*

7. One monopoly that was exposed was a result of

(1) *The Bitter Cry of Children*
(2) investigations into the Standard Oil Company
(3) charges against city politicians
(4) practices in the meat-packing industry
(5) *The Shame of the Cities*

8. The effect of the muckrakers' efforts was to

(1) provide solutions for society's problems
(2) inform the public of urgent problems
(3) reform society
(4) expand the sale of books and newspapers
(5) cause riots to protest high prices

To check your answers, turn to page 105.

Answers and Explanations

1. (Analysis) **(2) there were new technological inventions** Machines were invented that made factory work possible and efficient. Option (1) has nothing to do with industry. Options (3) and (4) are results of early industrialization, but they did not lead to development of industry. There is no evidence to support option (5).

2. (Analysis) **(2) Wages dropped.** This effect is indicated in the passage. The low wages accepted by the immigrants affected the wages of other workers. Immigrants had nothing to do with options (1), (3), and (5). Option (4) is the opposite of what happened.

1. (Analysis) **(1) Production was speeded up.** Machines could produce standard parts which could be quickly assembled. Options (2) and (5) are the opposite of the effect. Option (3) has nothing to do with the effect. There is no mention of option (4).

2. (Analysis) **(2) a more comfortable way of life** Inventions like electricity and indoor plumbing made life easier. Inventions did not cause the war, so option (1) is incorrect. Options (3) and (5) are the opposite of what is stated. Option (4) is one of the inventions, not a result of them.

3. (Analysis) **(4) have enough capital** Without a group of people, it was difficult to have enough money to build factories. Option (1) is not suggested. Option (2) is incorrect because profits do not depend on the formation of a corporation. No dishonesty is mentioned, so option (3) is incorrect. Option (5) is incorrect because a corporation reduced the financial risk.

4. (Application) **(4) shoes** Leather goods would need a heavy needle and strong pressure to make the holes for thread. Options (1) and (5) are lightweight products. Options (2) and (3) are not made by sewing.

1. (Analysis) **(3) The members were badly organized.** This is stated as a reason for the union's failure; a national group needs to be well-organized in order to work. Options (1) and (4) have no support. There is no evidence to support any rivalry between the two unions, so option (2) is incorrect. Option (5) is the opposite of what is suggested.

2. (Analysis) **(1) realized there was strength in numbers** Individual workers had no hope of having anyone listen to complaints about poor working conditions. There is no suggestion of option (2). Option (3) is incorrect because strikes are used by unions to get management to listen. There is nothing to suggest that options (4) and (5) were concerns of the early unions.

3. (Analysis) **(3) city jobs paid much better wages** Most of the jobs listed are city-based and pay more than farm labor. There is no support for options (1) and (2). Option (4) is incorrect because teachers are not necessarily trained in cities, and the salary in the table gives no reason for a move. There is no mention of how many postal positions (the only government job listed) were available, so option (5) is incorrect.

4. (Analysis) **(2) factories could continue to pay low wages** Employers had found a labor source that was grateful to work at all and had not yet learned to make demands. Option (1) is the opposite of what is stated. There is no reference to the effect on resident Americans, so option (3) is incorrect. Options (4) and (5) are causes, not effects, of immigration.

5. (Analysis) **(3) so-called** This phrase reflects a negative opinion, meaning there was not as much opportunity as there seemed to be. Options (1), (2), (4), and (5) refer to facts.

GED Mini-Test (pages 102–103)

1. (Analysis) **(1) had an important effect on white colleges** Other schools began to include the teaching of industrial-based trades with academic training. Options (2) and (4) are not true. There is no mention of option (3). Option (5) is incorrect because slavery was over by the time the school was founded.

2. (Comprehension) **(2) blacks did not go to white colleges** The most likely reason to build a black college is if there is no place for blacks to study. Options (1) and (5) are the opposite of what is implied. There is no support for options (3) or (4).

3. (Analysis) **(4) spread of disease** The growth of large cities was the reason, or cause, for serious overcrowding in tenements, which in turn caused the rapid spread of diseases like typhoid. As the paragraph states, options (1), (3), and (5) were all reasons for the growth of cities. Option (2) was a result of growth of trade and industry in cities.

4. (Analysis) **(1) overcrowded housing** The rapid growth of cities led to terrible problems in overcrowded housing. The influx of workers and immigrants outstripped available housing, and the result was the tenements of large inner cities. The paragraph does not indicate that options (2), (3), (4), or (5) were effects of rapid urban growth.

5. (Analysis) **(1) unsanitary conditions in slaughter houses** As indicated in the list, *The Jungle* exposed practices within the slaughter houses and meat-packing industry. Options (2), (3), (4), and (5) are not related to the reasons that *The Jungle* was written.

6. (Analysis) **(4) *The Shame of the Cities*** As indicated in the list, *The Shame of the Cities* exposed corruption in city government. One type of corruption you may infer concerned the illegal voting practices promoted by city politicians. Options (1), (2), and (3) refer to books dealing with other themes. Option (5) is not mentioned and is not a valid choice.

7. (Analysis) **(2) investigations into the Standard Oil Company** As indicated in the list, *The History of the Standard Oil Company* exposed the tactics of this monopoly. Options (1), (3), (4), and (5) do not refer to a monopoly.

8. (Analysis) **(2) inform the public of urgent problems** The efforts of the muckrakers served to inform the public about urgent problems in industry, politics, and inner-city poverty. They did not provide solutions to reform society, options (1) or (3). The muckrakers' books and articles were not written to effect large sales, option (4), or to cause riots in protest of high prices, option (5).

LESSON 8 Analysis Skill: Distinguishing Between Supporting Statements and Conclusions

This skill will help you separate a writer's conclusion from the ideas that were used to lead to that conclusion.

You have already learned to draw conclusions from what you read. Often writers will use information to lead up to their own conclusions. It is important to be able to identify the details and examples that are used to support those conclusions.

One way to decide which statement is the writer's conclusion is to try to draw a conclusion yourself. You should be able to take certain statements from a paragraph or longer reading, add the statements together, and arrive at about the same idea that the writer suggests. First, find the sentence or sentences that you think state the conclusion. Then imagine that the writer did not state the conclusion at all. Ask yourself what other statements can help you decide. If those statements support a conclusion similar to the one you picked, you have probably found the conclusion.

It is important to be able to tell a conclusion from its supporting details in order to judge if the conclusion is accurate. If you do not agree with a conclusion, you would want to examine the supporting details to find out how that decision was made. For example, in the 1960s, a patriotic American might have said, "I am a good American. I support the government's decisions. Anti-war protestors are anti-American." At first these sentences look like three separate statements. Actually, the third sentence is a conclusion based on the first two. What the patriot was actually saying was: "Good Americans support the government's decisions. Therefore, anti-war protestors are not good Americans." The problem with this conclusion is that it is based on an opinion: that person's definition of how a good American should act. Sometimes a conclusion will be separated from supporting statements with words such as <u>therefore</u> and <u>so</u> or <u>what we can learn from all this</u>. Use these words as guides.

Practicing Analysis

Read the following paragraph.

> After the end of World War I in 1918, Americans looked forward to better times. But first they had to deal with the economic problems left by the war. The 1920s began with deciding what to do with the millions of veterans who came home and had to find work. There were also thousands of domestic wartime employees who no longer were needed for government work. Factories that had enjoyed increased production of wartime items shut down to retool for peacetime products. Unemployment rose. The nation was involved in struggles between factory owners, workers, farmers, and consumers, all of whom demanded an end to inflation and recession.

Questions 1 and 2 refer to the paragraph. Circle the best answer for each question.

1. The information in the paragraph best supports the conclusion that

    (1) Americans were expecting better times
    (2) economic problems resulting from the war had to be solved
    (3) wars cause inflation and recession
    (4) thousands of Americans were out of work
    (5) the 1920s were depressing times

2. Even if it had not been stated in the paragraph, you would have been able to draw which of these conclusions?

    (1) Veterans had to look for work.
    (2) Wartime employees lost their jobs.
    (3) Factories shut down.
    (4) Unemployment rose.
    (5) People demanded an end to inflation.

To check your answers, turn to page 114.

Topic 8: The United States Involved With the World

By the end of the nineteenth century, the United States extended from the Atlantic to the Pacific coasts. The Alaskan and Hawaiian territories had come under U.S. jurisdiction, along with Cuba, Puerto Rico, Guam, and the Philippine Islands. The country had finally stopped growing physically and was getting ready to take an active role in world affairs.

The first involvement with world politics occurred when Cubans rebelled against Spain and requested help from the United States. The assistance turned into a 115-day war after an American ship, the *Maine*, was blown up in Havana harbor.

Despite this brief encounter with another nation, many Americans wanted to follow George Washington's advice to stay out of foreign countries' affairs. But when World War I began in 1914, the United States found that remaining neutral was not easy. At first, involvement was only on the level of trade. American goods were sold to the European Allies who did not have time for manufacturing. Eventually, Americans came to believe in the Allies' cause. England, France, Russia, and later, Italy claimed they were fighting for democracy. When three American ships were sunk in one day by the German and Austria-Hungary alliance, the United States finally joined the fight.

In 1939, the Axis Powers—Italy and Japan led by Hitler's Germany—attacked Poland. France, having promised to support Poland, declared war on Germany. World War II had begun. Again the United States wanted to stay out of European affairs. But many Americans objected to what the Axis dictators were trying to do. While Americans debated the question, Japan attacked Pearl Harbor, Hawaii. The next day—December 8, 1941—America declared war.

The peace that came in 1945 did not really settle world affairs. The Soviet Union went back on its promises to let neighboring countries be self-governing. China and many countries in Eastern Europe were dominated by communism, while Western Europe and the United States still vigorously supported democracy. The Communists and the Free World settled into a long cold war. Communists wanted other countries to join them, and the free world wanted to spread democratic principles.

The now-economically powerful United States found itself the leader of the Free World nations. Americans supported struggling countries with food, money, and people. The Cold War warmed up a bit when democratic forces in Korea and Vietnam fought against the Communist rulers. The United States supported the battle against the governments backed by the USSR and China.

As all great nations have discovered, maintaining world power is a difficult and costly process. In recent years, all of the major political powers have encountered internal upheavals. While the United States has been paying some much-needed attention to its own problems, it still plays an important role in world affairs.

Exercises

Questions 1 to 4 refer to the previous information. Circle the best answer for each question.

1. Which best supports the conclusion that staying out of World War I was not easy for the United States?

   (1) The encounter with Spain had been brief.
   (2) George Washington had encouraged remaining neutral.
   (3) Americans believed in fighting for democracy.
   (4) The Allies had trouble with manufacturing during the war.
   (5) Germany and Austria-Hungary were allies.

2. The details about the divisions between communism and democracy support the conclusion that

   (1) the Free World is right
   (2) the Cold War lasted a long time
   (3) Communists are right
   (4) peace came in 1945
   (5) world affairs were not settled by the war

3. A major reason the United States became involved in three wars is that

   (1) other countries requested assistance
   (2) American property had been attacked
   (3) America was eager to be involved
   (4) communism had to be stopped
   (5) the economy improved during war

4. Which of the following phrases suggests an opinion about America?

   (1) stopped growing physically
   (2) came to believe
   (3) debated the question
   (4) supported democracy
   (5) paid much-needed attention

To check your answers, turn to page 114.

Reviewing Lesson 8

Read the following paragraphs.

When Franklin D. Roosevelt took office in 1933, he promised "a new deal for the American people." The goal of his administration was to pull the nation out of the depths of the worst economic crisis in history. Like that of his progressive predecessors, his aim was to conserve natural resources, regulate business, break down monopolies, save the free enterprise system, and improve working conditions. Toward his goals, he formed a "brain trust" of college professors to advise and help him evaluate the government's courses of action. Important New Deal legislation included the Federal Emergency Relief Act to provide grants to states for relief of poor persons; the Agricultural Adjustment Act and the National Industrial Recovery Act to raise farm prices and set up codes of fair competition; the National Labor Relations Act to guarantee workers the right to collective bargaining; the Social Security Act to protect workers by providing insurance against unemployment and old age; and the Soil Conservation Act to raise farm prices by instituting soil conservation methods. Additional acts protected consumers, established minimum wages and maximum hours, and prohibited most child labor.

Roosevelt felt he was acting in the best interests of the people and the country as a whole. However, critics saw these reforms as leaning toward socialism. They believed that the New Deal was a dangerous break with the American tradition of self-reliance. To them, government's role was to leave free enterprise and competition alone.

Questions 1 and 2 refer to the paragraphs. Circle the best answer for each question.

1. Which of the following is a conclusion that the writer drew about President Roosevelt?

   (1) Roosevelt wanted to improve working conditions.
   (2) Roosevelt formed a "brain trust" to advise him.
   (3) Roosevelt promised a new deal for the people.
   (4) Roosevelt passed a number of reform acts.
   (5) Roosevelt was a socialist.

2. In which way does the writer support the critics' conclusion?

   (1) by discussing Roosevelt's political connections
   (2) by explaining the negative effects of the reform acts
   (3) by referring to the Declaration of Independence
   (4) by showing how the reforms did not work
   (5) no supporting facts are given

To check your answers, turn to page 114.

Read the following paragraphs.

As the 1980s were left behind, so were some of the accepted positions of the world's powerful nations. After years of cold war and a bitter nuclear arms race, many surprising political changes happened in a very short time. Chinese students demonstrated for democracy, and for a few hours, Americans were even able to watch the unrest on TV. Mikhail Gorbachev instituted liberal policies in the USSR and paid two visits to the United States. East and West Berlin residents joined in tearing down the Berlin Wall that had divided Germany since World War II.

Not all of these movements have been successful. But the world powers are talking, and for the first time in years, they are also listening. The United States, a major force for peace against the injustices of communism, now has to determine its new role in world relations.

Questions 3 and 4 refer to the paragraphs. Circle the best answer for each question.

3. Based on recent world events, the writer has concluded that

   (1) the civil rights movement has been successful
   (2) freedom is right around the corner
   (3) the United States will have to take a different role
   (4) freedom movements will not succeed
   (5) the Cold War is over

4. Which is the main effect of the recent political events?

   (1) Gorbachev came to the United States.
   (2) Americans have been able to see China on TV.
   (3) The Berlin Wall is down.
   (4) All of the movements have been successful.
   (5) The world powers are having real discussions.

Look at the following cartoon.

Question 5 refers to the cartoon.
Circle the best answer.

5. What has the cartoonist concluded?

   (1) Congress has a clear position about U.S. involvement with Panama.
   (2) Congress wants to back off from Panama.
   (3) Congress wants to get more involved with Panama.
   (4) President Bush has to make a difficult decision.
   (5) President Bush has already made up his mind about Panama.

To check your answers, turn to page 114.

GED Mini-Test

Directions: Choose the <u>best answer</u> to each item.

<u>Items 1 and 2</u> refer to the following information.

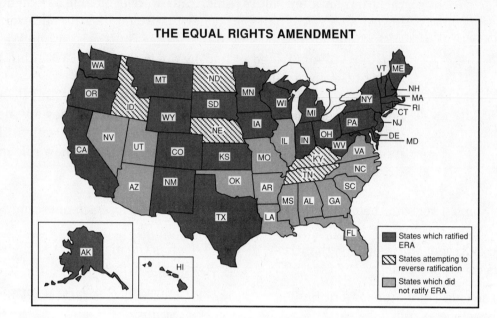

THE EQUAL RIGHTS AMENDMENT

The Equal Rights Amendment was intended to guarantee that a woman could not be legally or socially discriminated against on the basis of sex. To pass into law, an amendment needs ratification or approval by 38 states.

1. You can conclude from the map that

    (1) the ERA passed
    (2) the ERA had no support
    (3) the country was evenly divided about the ERA
    (4) the ERA was defeated by only a few states
    (5) the ERA would not have helped anyone

2. Which of the major areas of the United States would be the least likely to support another bill for women's rights?

    (1) New England
    (2) the Great Plains
    (3) the South
    (4) the Northwest
    (5) the Midwest

<u>Items 3 to 10</u> refer to the following information.

During the 1960s to 1980s in the United States, many new terms became part of our national vocabulary. Listed on the next page are definitions and descriptions of some of these terms. Each definition supplies support for concluding that there is a connection between a term and an important historical event or concept. Choose the term most likely related to the event or concept.

1. <u>Arms race</u>—Competition between the United States and the Soviet Union beginning in the 1950s to develop nuclear weapons
2. <u>New frontier</u>—President John F. Kennedy's 1960s challenge to fulfill national goals in economic development, civil rights, and space
3. <u>Civil disobedience</u>—A form of nonviolent protest against unjust laws or conditions in the 1950s and 1960s
4. <u>Watergate</u>—A political scandal caused by high-level cover-ups leading to the resignation of President Richard Nixon in 1974
5. <u>Reaganomics</u>—President Ronald Reagan's 1980s plan to curb federal spending in order to reduce huge budget deficits

3. The Civil Rights Act and NASA

  (1) Reaganomics
  (2) arms race
  (3) civil disobedience
  (4) Watergate
  (5) new frontier

4. Strategic Arms Limitation Talks (SALT)

  (1) arms race
  (2) Watergate
  (3) new frontier
  (4) Reaganomics
  (5) civil disobedience

5. Concern for discussion at summit meetings between world leaders

  (1) new frontier
  (2) Watergate
  (3) arms race
  (4) civil disobedience
  (5) Reaganomics

6. The involvement of high-level officials and accusations of obstruction of justice

  (1) civil disobedience
  (2) Watergate
  (3) new frontier
  (4) Reaganomics
  (5) arms race

7. Boycotts and marches to protest segregation

  (1) Reaganomics
  (2) arms race
  (3) new frontier
  (4) Watergate
  (5) civil disobedience

8. Legislation to reduce inflation, high interest rates, and federal deficits

  (1) arms race
  (2) Watergate
  (3) Reaganomics
  (4) new frontier
  (5) civil disobedience

9. NASA's goal to land astronauts on the moon within five years of the initial concept

  (1) Reaganomics
  (2) arms race
  (3) new frontier
  (4) Watergate
  (5) civil disobedience

10. Sit-ins at lunch counters and bus depots to protest against racial discrimination

  (1) arms race
  (2) Reaganomics
  (3) new frontier
  (4) Watergate
  (5) civil disobedience

To check your answers, turn to page 115.

Answers and Explanations

1. (Analysis) **(2) economic problems resulting from the war had to be solved** The supporting statements detail the financial difficulties that were caused by the shift from war to peace. Option (1) is not a conclusion that can be drawn from the supporting statements. Option (3) is a broad generalization that is not supported in the paragraph. Option (4) is a supporting detail. Option (5) is incorrect because it refers to the entire decade, not just to its start; it also is too general.

2. (Analysis) **(4) Unemployment rose.** The statements that come before this one support it as a conclusion. Options (1), (2), and (3) are support for the conclusion. Option (5) is an additional detail about the main idea.

Exercises (page 109)

1. (Analysis) **(3) Americans believed in fighting for democracy.** It is difficult to ignore a struggle over your basic beliefs. Options (1) and (2) have nothing to do with the difficulty of staying out of the war. Option (4) is related to the Allies difficulties with manufacturing, not to staying out of the war. The principles, not the countries themselves, were important factors; so option (5) is incorrect.

2. (Analysis) **(5) world affairs were not settled by the war** The information supports the idea that many agreements still had to be reached. Options (1) and (3) are not conclusions supported by the passage. Options (2) and (4) are supporting details, not conclusions.

3. (Analysis) **(2) American property had been attacked** In three cases, America did not declare war until its ships or land was attacked. Option (1) is a reason only for the Spanish-American War. Option (3) is incorrect because the United States wanted to remain neutral. Option (4) is true only for the Cold War. Option (5) is a result of being in a war, not a reason for waging it.

4. (Analysis) **(5) paid much-needed attention** This statement reflects a judgment about how much attention had been given to internal problems; it is not a fact. Options (1), (2), and (3) refer to things that actually happened. Option (4) is incorrect because it refers both to a fact and to more countries than just America.

Reviewing Lesson 8 (pages 110–111)

1. (Analysis) **(1) Roosevelt wanted to improve working conditions.** This statement is a decision based on what Roosevelt actually did. Options (2), (3), and (4) are supporting details. Option (5) is the opinion of Roosevelt's critics, not of the writer.

2. (Analysis) **(5) no supporting facts are given** A reference to the tradition of self-reliance is not support for the conclusion that the reforms were socialistic in nature. The writer does not provide any of the information in options (1), (2), (3), and (4).

3. (Analysis) **(3) the United States will have to take a different role** Because of the trend toward political openness, the focus of the U.S. will have to change to suit the situation. Option (1) is not a possible conclusion because there is no reference to the civil rights movement. Options (2), (4), and (5) are not adequately supported.

4. (Analysis) **(5) The world powers are having real discussions.** Rapid and radical changes have made the powers realize they cannot ignore the situation. Options (1), (2), and (3) are details related to the events, not the results. Option (4) is the opposite of what is stated.

5. (Analysis) **(4) President Bush has to make a difficult decision.** The cartoon indicates that Congressional opinion is split, and Bush does not want to choose between the two. Option (1) is the opposite of what the cartoon supports. Options (2) and (3) each refer only to one section of the cartoon. There is no support for option (5).

1. (Comprehension) **(4) the ERA was defeated by only a few states** Even without the states that tried to reverse ratification, thirty states were in favor of it. Option (1) is clearly incorrect; only 35 states had originally ratified the amendment. Option (2) is incorrect because over half the states were clearly in favor. Option (3) is incorrect for the same reason. There is no support for option (5).

2. (Application) **(3) the South** All the Southern states rejected the ERA. Options (1), (2), and (4) were primarily in favor of the bill and would probably vote for another one. Option (5) is incorrect because the states were divided, but were not entirely against the ERA.

3. (Analysis) **(5) new frontier** In 1960 President John F. Kennedy challenged the nation to fulfill the demands of a "new frontier" in areas of economic development, civil rights, and space explorations. Option (5) is most closely related to these issues. Options (1), (2), (3), and (4) are not supported.

4. (Analysis) **(1) arms race** Strategic Arms Limitations Talks have been ongoing since 1972 when U.S. President Nixon and USSR Premier Brezhnev first agreed to try to limit offensive weapons sysems. Options (2), (3), (4), and (5) are not supported.

5. (Analysis) **(3) arms race** During the 1950s, the United States and Russia began to accumulate nuclear weapons. This competition became known as the arms race. It has been the theme of many summit conferences between the U.S. and Soviet leaders. Options (1), (2), (4), and (5) are not supported by the information.

6. (Analysis) **(2) Watergate** The break-in at the Democratic National Committee at the Watergate Hotel in Washington was part of a covert effort to hinder the election of Democratic party rivals. Senate investigations eventually revealed cover-ups at the highest levels of politics. For his knowledge and involvement, President Nixon resigned rather than face impeachment procedures. Options (1), (3), (4), and (5) are not supported.

7. (Analysis) **(5) civil disobedience** The Reverend Martin Luther King, Jr., advocated these forms of nonviolent protest against unjust laws as the best way to protest segregation. Options (1), (2), (3), and (4) are not supported.

8. (Analysis) **(3) Reaganomics** President Reagan felt that the nation's ills were due to excessive government spending, high taxes, inflation, and high interest rates. His economic program, called Reaganomics, called for major cutbacks in federal spending and lower interest rates, in addition to other measures. Options (1), (2), (4), and (5) are not supported.

9. (Analysis) **(3) new frontier** Since the concept of having astronauts on the moon arose nearly twenty years before the Reagan presidency, option (1) is incorrect. Option (2) involves nuclear arms, which were not a part of the goal of landing astronauts on the moon. Option (4) deals with political scandals during the Nixon presidency, which did not affect the moon program. Option (5) does not apply to the issue.

10. (Analysis) **(5) civil disobedience** Civil disobedience was the chief means by which protesters in the 1950s and 1960s protested segregation and racial discrimination, and worked to integrate food counters and bus depots. There is no support for options (1), (2), (3), or (4).

Review: History

In this unit, you learned to make inferences, identify facts and opinions, understand causes and effects, tell the difference between conclusions and their supporting statements, and apply what you learn to other situations. In the following review, you will practice the skills from the unit and review details of American history.

Directions: Choose the best answer to each item.

Items 1 and 2 are based on the following paragraph.

America is famous all over the world for its Wild West, its cowboys riding the range to corral the great herds of cattle. Historians have suggested that this familiar image would not have existed if it had not been for Christopher Columbus and a few other explorers. Neither horses nor cows lived on the North American continent before the first ships arrived from Europe. Columbus left much of his extra livestock when he headed back home. It is probable that most of the beef cattle in the United States are descendants of cows that helped discover the New World.

1. According to the paragraph, an unusual effect of Columbus's landing in the West Indies is that

   (1) he introduced cattle to America
   (2) he made cowboy movies popular
   (3) the Wild West became popular
   (4) America became known all over the world
   (5) he was able to report a discovery to the Spanish queen

2. It is implied in the paragraph that Columbus also left

   (1) pigs
   (2) chickens
   (3) sheep
   (4) turkeys
   (5) horses

One of the many religious groups that helped to settle the New World was called the Friends, or Quakers. The Quakers were led by William Penn, the son of an admiral in the English Navy. Like other groups who disagreed with the teachings of the Church of England, the Quakers wanted to take advantage of the new territory. The Quakers had special luck. King Charles owed money to Penn's family. He paid the debt with a grant of American land claimed by England.

In 1682, William Penn and the Quakers colonized the rich lands of the New World which they named Pennsylvania. They met the Indians who lived there, paid them for the land, and made a peace treaty which was never broken. The gentle Quakers then built their main city, Philadelphia, whose name means "City of Brotherly Love."

Unlike some of their religious neighbors, the Quakers accepted people of other faiths and nationalities and encouraged them to settle on Quaker land. People as different as Catholics, Jews, and blacks answered the invitations and were offered inexpensive land and a say in the colony's government.

3. One opinion expressed about this group of colonists is that they were

(1) Quakers
(2) religious
(3) Friends
(4) gentle
(5) from England

4. According to the paragraphs, if an Asian family had come to Philadelphia, they most likely would have been

(1) sent back home
(2) asked to become Quakers
(3) forced to live outside the city
(4) welcomed
(5) referred to another colony

5. The conclusion that the Quakers were lucky is supported by the statement that

(1) the colony was rich
(2) the lands of Pennsylvania were rich
(3) they were able to make a treaty with the Indians
(4) Penn was able to get land in repayment of a royal debt
(5) they were able to go to America

6. It is implied in the paragraphs that other religious-based colonies

(1) were very tolerant of other faiths
(2) were not tolerant of other faiths
(3) had asked Quakers to join them
(4) agreed with the teachings of the Church of England
(5) were jealous of William Penn

To check your answers, turn to page 124.

Items 7 and 8 refer to the following paragraph.

The first president of the United States, George Washington, was not a very good general. He won only a few battles because his military strategy basically was to react to whatever the enemy did. However, Washington became known as the "Father of His Country" because he had a forceful personality that inspired his troops to fight against overwhelming odds and to go back to war after terrible defeats. His dignity and honesty held together the often-disorganized cause of the American rebels.

7. George Washington became known as the Father of His Country mainly because he

(1) was the president of the United States
(2) was a good general
(3) fought against the British
(4) understood the rebels' cause
(5) had an inspiring character

8. The main reason that Washington is fondly remembered in history is most similar to the reason for the reputation of

(1) Dwight D. Eisenhower, a good general but a weak president
(2) Richard M. Nixon, a fine politician but a poor judge of character
(3) Gerald R. Ford, a good-natured man who may have felt he was not suited for the presidency
(4) Dan Quayle, a little-known senator who became vice-president
(5) John F. Kennedy, a politically average president who charmed and impressed the world

Items 9 to 12 refer to the following maps.

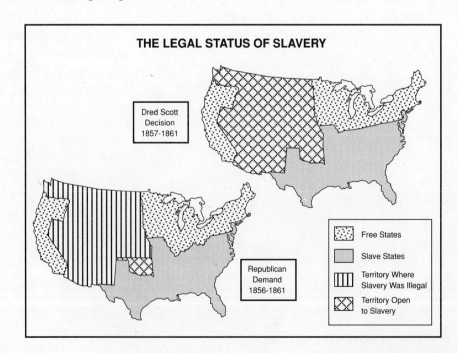

THE LEGAL STATUS OF SLAVERY

Dred Scott Decision 1857-1861

Republican Demand 1856-1861

Free States

Slave States

Territory Where Slavery Was Illegal

Territory Open to Slavery

9. The maps support the conclusion that Republicans

(1) were in favor of slavery
(2) were successful in getting what they wanted
(3) lived mainly in the South
(4) never owned slaves
(5) were opposed to legal slavery in the territories

10. According to the map of Republican demand, in which of the following states was slavery legal?

(1) Oregon
(2) California
(3) Minnesota
(4) Texas
(5) Wyoming

11. If the Civil War had not happened and the Dred Scott decision was upheld, which would probably be true?

(1) Any new state admitted to the Union could have slaves.
(2) No new states could have slaves.
(3) Only one new state could have slaves.
(4) The slaves would have rebelled.
(5) The Republicans would have changed their minds.

12. The positions taken by the two sides of the slavery issue are most like the positions taken by

(1) Quakers and Jews
(2) two parents arguing over money
(3) two children, each claiming all the toys
(4) England and France during World War I
(5) Germany and Japan during World War II

Items 13 and 14 on page 120 refer to the following paragraph.

The end of the Civil War did not bring an instant solution to the problems of the former slaves. The slaves were free, but they had no place to go and few ways to make a living. By 1866, the plan for Reconstruction had ground to a halt. President Andrew Johnson and the Congress could not agree on terms that would solve the economic and civil issues that faced the freed slaves. While the federal government argued about the situation, Southern state governments set up a system of employment called the black codes. Under these codes, blacks were treated as second-class citizens. In some states, blacks could work only as servants or farmhands. In others, blacks were legally barred from living in towns and cities. Some freedmen had to sign 12-month labor contracts just to get a job. Not until the Fortieth Congress in 1867 were the former slaves able to enjoy many of the civil liberties stated in the Bill of Rights.

To check your answers, turn to pages 124 and 125.

13. The effect of the black codes was to

   (1) help former slaves get jobs
   (2) deny blacks their legal rights
   (3) help the rural economy
   (4) make Reconstruction succeed
   (5) solve the problems of the slaves

14. The limiting of jobs available to blacks is similar to

   (1) employing children in factories
   (2) hiring women for wartime work
   (3) barring women from many professions
   (4) making it illegal for children to do most work
   (5) legalizing a minimum wage

Items 15 to 19 refer to the following information.

The writers of the U.S. Constitution realized that conditions would change, so they allowed for additions, or amendments, to the document. An amendment must be discussed and agreed on by Congress. The following amendments guarantee some of the rights that we now all take for granted.

1. First Amendment—Prohibits Congress from interfering with freedom of speech, press, and religion, and with the right to assemble peacefully.

2. Second Amendment—Guarantees the right of the state militia to keep weapons and the rights of citizens to bear arms.

3. Fourth Amendment—Prohibits unreasonable search and seizure of persons and property.

4. Fifth Amendment—Provides that a person accused of a crime shall be entitled to a fair trial by a jury of peers and that a person shall not be compelled to testify against himself or herself.

5. Fifteenth Amendment—Provides that no citizen shall be denied the right to vote on account of race, color, or previous condition of servitude.

6. Nineteenth Amendment—Provides that the right to vote shall not be denied or abridged on account of sex.

15. The amendment that has been the basis of controversies regarding federal aid to religious schools is the

   (1) first
   (2) third
   (3) fourth
   (4) fifth
   (5) fifteenth

16. A suspect is stopped, searched, and his property is taken from him. This action may violate which amendment?

   (1) the first
   (2) the fourth
   (3) the fifth
   (4) the fifteenth
   (5) the nineteenth

17. The amendment that provides that no person shall be compelled in any criminal case to testify against himself protects against

   (1) cruel and unusual punishment
   (2) self-accusation
   (3) unreasonable search
   (4) due process of law
   (5) clear and present danger

18. Which amendment extended the right to vote to a large part of the population after the Civil War?

   (1) the second
   (2) the fourth
   (3) the fifth
   (4) the fifteenth
   (5) the nineteenth

19. Which amendment gave women the right to vote?

   (1) the second
   (2) the fourth
   (3) the fifth
   (4) the fifteenth
   (5) the nineteenth

Items 20 and 21 refer to the following graph.

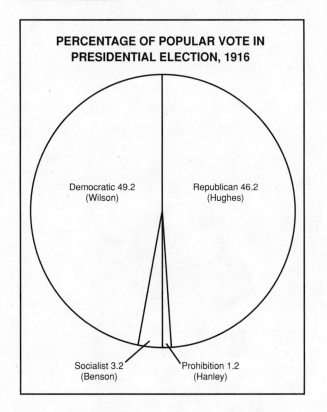

PERCENTAGE OF POPULAR VOTE IN PRESIDENTIAL ELECTION, 1916

Democratic 49.2 (Wilson)

Republican 46.2 (Hughes)

Socialist 3.2 (Benson)

Prohibition 1.2 (Hanley)

20. According to the graph, in 1916 the Democratic Party

   (1) was very unpopular
   (2) lost by a small margin
   (3) won by a small margin
   (4) won by a landslide
   (5) lost by a landslide

21. A fact about the Socialist and Prohibition parties that can be determined from the graph is that

   (1) the Socialist party was better organized
   (2) neither party had much support
   (3) neither party deserved to win
   (4) both parties should have received more support
   (5) both parties had admirable goals

To check your answers, turn to pages 125 and 126.

Items 22 and 23 refer to the following paragraph.

Martin Luther King, Jr.'s most memorable speech was delivered to an enormous crowd at the Lincoln Memorial in Washington, D.C. The theme "I Have a Dream" declared that blacks should not have had to wait one hundred years to enjoy their rights. King challenged Americans by appealing to their ideals. His speech contained Biblical quotations, references to Lincoln and to black history, and his own experiences that were similar to those of his audience. His appeal to America concluded with the moving words: "Black men and white men, Jews and Gentiles, Protestants and Catholics, will be able to join hands and sing in the words of the old Negro spiritual: "Free at last! Free at last! Thank God Almighty. We are free at last!"

22. The conclusion that King appealed to the audience's ideals is

   (1) not supported in the paragraph
   (2) supported by general examples and a quotation
   (3) supported by references to moral issues
   (4) based on the logic of his speech
   (5) based on 100 years of oppression

23. If King had spoken about the plight of Asian refugees, which would he have been most likely to use?

   (1) what hard workers they were
   (2) what awful conditions they came from
   (3) how well their children do in American schools
   (4) what their civilization has contributed to the world
   (5) how their cooking style can improve our diets

Items 24 and 25 refer to the following cartoon.

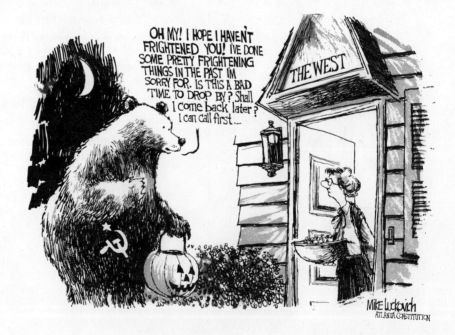

24. The cartoon is intended to support the conclusion that the Soviet Union

(1) celebrates Halloween
(2) is very frightening
(3) is trying to make peace with the United States
(4) is acting childishly
(5) is trying to play a trick on the United States

25. With which statement would the cartoonist be most likely to agree?

(1) You can take the bear out of the country, but you can't take the country out of the bear.
(2) Beware of a wolf in sheep's clothing.
(3) A leopard can't change its spots.
(4) You can catch more flies with honey than with vinegar.
(5) Don't change horses when crossing a stream.

Item 26 is based on the following graph.

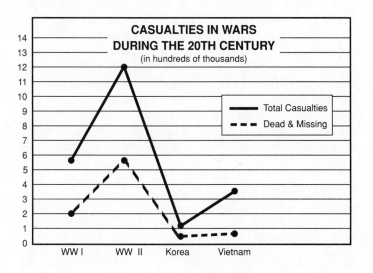

CASUALTIES IN WARS DURING THE 20TH CENTURY (in hundreds of thousands)

Total Casualties
Dead & Missing

WW I   WW II   Korea   Vietnam

26. The information in the graph best supports the conclusion that

(1) World War II had the highest total casualty rate of 20th-century wars
(2) no war is worth the cost in human lives
(3) few Americans lost their lives in World War I
(4) more people died in Korea than in Vietnam
(5) the Korean War and the Vietnam War happened recently

To check your answers, turn to page 126.

Answers and Explanations

1. (Analysis) **(1) he introduced cattle to America** We do not usually think about explorers leaving things. We think only of them finding things. Options (2), (3), and (4) are not direct effects of the landing. Option (5) is true but is not mentioned in the paragraph.

2. (Comprehension) **(5) horses** The opening example and the mention of horses suggest that horses were also left behind. Options (1), (2), and (3) are not suggested. Option (4) is not mentioned; it is native to the Americas.

3. (Analysis) **(4) gentle** This option is a judgment about the group, not a fact. Options (1), (2), (3), and (5) are all facts.

4. (Application) **(4) welcomed** The Quaker policy was to accept all people. Options (1) and (5) are incorrect because Quakers invited people of all nationalities. Option (2) is incorrect because all faiths were tolerated. Option (3) has no support; there is no evidence in the paragraphs that any group was asked to live apart.

5. (Analysis) **(4) Penn was able to get land in repayment of a royal debt** The colonists did not have to petition for or purchase land from the king. There is no evidence for option (1). Option (2) is true but does not support the conclusion. Option (3) has nothing to do with luck. Option (5) may be true but is not support for the stated conclusion.

6. (Comprehension) **(2) were not tolerant of other faiths** Intolerance can be inferred from the idea that Quakers were unlike the other colonists. Option (1) is the opposite of the idea suggested. There is no evidence for options (3) or (5). Option (4) is the opposite of what is stated about Quaker beliefs.

7. (Analysis) **(5) had an inspiring character** Good leaders must be able to make people follow them; Washington had that ability. Option (1) is what happened after he got his reputation. Option (2) is denied in the paragraph. Option (3) is incorrect because <u>all</u> the patriots fought against the British. There is no evidence in the paragraph for option (4).

8. (Application) **(5) John F. Kennedy, a politically average President who charmed and impressed the world.** In both cases, it was the personality of the man that caused people to remember him. The men in options (1) and (2) are remembered for other reasons, military and political. Options (3) and (4) are incorrect because Ford and Quayle are not thought of as having forceful personalities.

9. (Analysis) **(5) were opposed to legal slavery in the territories** The demand map supports the Republican position. Option (1) is the opposite of what is shown. Since the end date of both maps is the same, option (2) is incorrect. There is no evidence of where Republicans lived or if any of them owned slaves, so options (3) and (4) are incorrect.

10. (Comprehension) **(4) Texas** Texas is the only listed state marked as a slave state. Options (1), (2), and (3) are all free states. Option (5) is incorrect because Wyoming was not a state at the time.

11. (Application) **(1) Any new state admitted to the Union could have slaves.** Since all the territories were open to slavery under the Dred Scott decision, any section that wanted to be a state could come in as a slave state. Option (2) would not be true even under the Republican demand because the Oklahoma territory was open to slavery. Option (3) would have been true only under the Republican demand. There is no support in either map for options (4) and (5).

12. (Application) **(3) two children, each claiming all the toys** Each side wanted all the territories to follow its principles. Option (1) is incorrect because neither group demands that other people follow its ways. Option (2) is incorrect because slavery was a moral issue as well as a financial issue. Options (4) and (5) are incorrect because the countries in each option were on the same side.

13. (Analysis) **(2) deny blacks their legal rights** The black codes violated the Bill of Rights. Options (1) and (5) are the opposite of what happened. Option (3) is not clearly supported. Option (4) is incorrect because the black codes served only to make the problems worse.

14. (Application) **(3) barring women from many professions** Both practices deny human beings the opportunity to achieve better situations. Options (1) and (2) are examples of exploiting people, but not limiting them. Options (4) and (5) were helpful steps not hindrances.

15. (Analysis) **(1) first** The First Amendment provides for freedom of religion, but controversies such as state aid for transportation to parochial schools and prayer in public schools have raised this amendment for clarification in court decisions. There is no support for options (2), (3), (4), and (5).

16. (Analysis) **(2) the fourth** The Fourth Amendment, known as the "search and seizure" amendment, demands "probable cause" and specific warrants to search and seize people and places. Options (1), (3), (4), and (5) are not supported by the definitions.

17. (Analysis) **(2) self-accusation** The Fifth Amendment prohibits the government from forcing one accused of a crime to testify against oneself during trial. Testifying against oneself would be self-accusation. Options (1), (3), (4), and (5) are not supported by the definitions.

18. (Analysis) **(4) the fifteenth** The Fifteenth Amendment barred voting discrimination on the basis of race or "previous condition of servitude," referring to former slaves and to blacks who were free before the Civil War. Options (1), (2), (3), and (5) are not supported by the definitions.

19. (Analysis) **(5) the nineteenth** The Nineteenth Amendment gave women suffrage—the right to vote in all federal and state elections. Prior to this amendment in 1919, only some individual states had extended suffrage to women. The definitions do not support options (1), (2), (3), and (4).

20. (Comprehension) **(3) won by a small margin** There is only a three percent difference in the popular vote, running in the Democrat's favor. Since the Democrats won, options (1), (2), and (5) are incorrect. Option (4) is incorrect because they won only by a margin of the vote.

21. (Analysis) **(2) neither party had much support** The percentage of voters indicates this as a fact. Options (1), (3), (4), and (5) are not supported by the graph.

22. (Analysis) **(2) supported by general examples and a quotation** The examples of the content of the speech and the quotation are all emotional subjects. Option (1) is not true. Option (3) is incorrect because morality is not mentioned. Option (4) is the opposite of what was stated. Option (5) has nothing to do with an emotional appeal.

23. (Application) **(2) what awful conditions they came from** This subject would appeal to the listeners' compassion. Options (1), (3), (4) and (5) are not related to difficulties faced by Asian refugees.

24. (Analysis) **(3) is trying to make peace with the United States** The bear's apology and the innocent context of a child's action support this conclusion. Option (1) is incorrect because the cartoon is not supposed to represent a real situation. Option (2) is incorrect because the bear is trying not to be frightening. Options (4) and (5) rely on the image of Halloween but ignore the bear's speech.

25. (Application) **(4) You can catch more flies with honey than with vinegar.** Polite words lead more quickly to friendly relations than harsh words. Options (1) and (3) refer to a person not being able to change; the intention of the cartoon is to suggest that change is possible. Option (2) is incorrect because the bear in the cartoon is sincere not deceitful. Option (5) is incorrect because it warns about the dangers of change.

26. (Analysis) **(1) World War II had the highest total casualty rate of 20th-century wars** The figure 1,200,000 supports this conclusion. Option (2) is not supported. Option (3) is incorrect because although the figure is much less than that for World War II, 550,000 cannot be called only a few deaths. Option (4) is incorrect because the Vietnam figure is slightly higher. There is no mention of dates, so although accurate, option (5) is not supported by the graph.

Use the chart below to identify your strengths and weaknesses in each thinking skill area in the History unit.

Circle the number of each item that you answered correctly on the review.

Skill	Questions	Lesson(s) for Review
Comprehension	2, 6, 10, 20	1, 2, 3, 5
Analysis	1, 3, 5, 7, 9, 13, 15, 16, 17,18, 19, 21, 22, 24, 26	6, 7, 8
Application	4, 8, 11, 12, 14, 23, 25	4

If you answered 23 or more items correctly, congratulations! You are ready to go on to the next section. If you answered 22 or fewer items correctly, determine which areas are most difficult for you. Then go back and review the lessons for those areas.

Jobs are an important part of the economy.

- **goods**
  material items made and used by people

- **services**
  work that does not produce material items

- **production**
  the creation of goods and services

- **labor**
  the human work that goes into production of goods and services

- **land**
  the natural resources of the earth

Economics is the study of the use of **goods** and **services** in a community. Economists look at how goods and services are produced, how they are distributed, and how they are consumed, or used.

In economic terms, **production** has three basic parts. **Labor** is the human effort involved in making goods or providing services. It can be either physical or mental work. **Land**, or natural resources, is what is supplied by nature. This term includes land, water, and whatever is attached to the earth's surface. Anything from fish and animals to minerals and forests is called a natural resource. **Capital**, which most of us think of as money, is really the manmade products that help us make things. Tools and any other equipment needed to produce items or services are known to the economist as capital. Money is not called capital because it does not really produce anything. It is a means of exchange for goods or services.

- **capital**
  the manmade goods used in production

- **distribution**
  how income is divided in a society

- **consumption**
  how goods and services are used

Distribution is the way the total income of a society is divided. It covers income, interest, profit, and wages.

Consumption is the way goods and services are used by people. It also refers to the use of labor, land, and capital in producing goods and services.

Topic 9 will introduce you to general economic behavior. You will learn about the way national economies work. You will also read about the role of manufacturers and consumers in the economic marketplace. Because writers take many things for granted about their readers, you will learn to identify assumptions writers make.

Topic 10 explains the role of labor in the economy. You will read about workers and unions. You will also learn about problems of income and unemployment. As you read, you will also be reviewing cause-and-effect relationships.

Topic 11 discusses the way government works in the economy. You will see how governments get money, how they spend money, and how they protect the interests of consumers. You will also learn how to evaluate, or make judgments about, the information you read.

☞ *See also: GED Exercise Book Social Studies, pages 26-35*

LESSON 9 Analysis Skill: Recognizing Assumptions

This skill will help you watch for and understand what information a writer believes the reader already knows.

When you **assume** something, you take it for granted. You believe it to be true, and usually you think that other people also believe it. People assume things every day, and every day they make decisions based on the strength of those **assumptions**.

In daily life, you assume many things. When you are driving and come to a stoplight, you stop. You believe that the people in the cars behind you will see the red light and stop before they run into you. When you get home and flip the light switch, you expect the lights to come on. In each case, you are making assumptions about how systems work.

We usually assume that people know what we are talking about, but sometimes that is not the case. A baseball fan might strike up a casual conversation with a stranger and mention a game that was played the day before. Much to the fan's surprise, the other person has no idea what teams were playing or what the final score was. The fan incorrectly assumed that everyone knows what is happening in the world of baseball.

Most writers are like the baseball fan. They assume that people are interested in the subject being written about. They also assume that most people have certain basic knowledge about various subjects. A historian would believe that the reader knows what the Civil War was, if not when or why it happened. An economist would assume that the reader knows basic facts about money. When writers feel that the information is not common knowledge, they usually explain the idea or define a term.

Sometimes assumptions are made on the basis of what people believe to be right or wrong; these assumptions are not always based on facts. You, as a reader, have to decide if you agree with the assumption and if the assumption is based on reliable information. Remember that an assumption can be questioned, but a fact cannot.

Practicing Analysis

Read the following information.

> Businesses are organized in three basic ways. Each type of organization has certain advantages and disadvantages. The following definitions explain the main features of each type.
>
> 1. <u>Individual proprietorship</u>—a business that is owned and operated by one person. The single owner gets all the profits, but also has to pay all the debts. The single owner has total control of how the business is managed.
> 2. <u>Partnership</u>—a business that is owned by at least two people. The profits are shared among the owners, usually according to the percentage each person owns. The responsibility for paying the debts is also shared by the partners. In fact, each partner usually is held responsible for the debts of any of the other partners. The partnership has to share management decisions.
> 3. <u>Corporation</u>—a business that is owned by a group of people, but that is a legal unit in itself. The owners of a corporation buy shares of stock in the company. They each make a profit according to how much stock they own. The individual owners are not held responsible for the business's debts. The corporation itself is responsible. Shareholders usually do not manage the corporation. They hire other people as managers.

Questions 1 and 2 refer to the information. Circle the best answer for each question.

1. Dan and Ann decide to become partners in a print shop. They invest equal amounts of money. Dan's main job is to run the presses. Ann's main job is to handle the customers and finances. Which of the following do both Dan and Ann most likely assume?

   (1) Ann will make all the management decisions.
   (2) Dan will make more profit than Ann.
   (3) They will be able to agree on management decisions.
   (4) Ann will be able to handle all the debts.
   (5) Dan will eventually take over the business.

2. People who buy shares in a corporation most likely assume that they will

   (1) lose their money
   (2) help manage the company
   (3) make a profit
   (4) be in a partnership
   (5) become rich

To check your answers, turn to page 138.

Topic 9: General Economic Behavior

The study of economics is more complex than just looking at how people use money. Remembering a few basic principles makes economics much easier to understand.

The economy of every country is based on exchange. Both goods and services form the basis for exchange. Goods are physical objects such as food, cars, houses, and clothing. Services are the types of work that a person does for you, such as car repair, house painting, and health care.

Most countries have **monetary economies**. In a monetary economy, goods and services are paid for with money. The money represents a certain value that is placed on the product or service. Some countries still have **barter economies**. In a barter economy, goods are exchanged for other goods or for services.

A common way to measure a country's economic status is through its **Gross National Product**, or **GNP**. The GNP is the total monetary value, either at current prices or at a fixed price, of everything produced and sold over the year in that country. The GNP includes manufactured goods, farm products, public services such as education, and private services such as legal advice.

Prices in the overall economy are set by two main things. The first is the law of supply and demand. As the price of a product increases, the supplier will want to sell more in order to make money. As prices decrease, consumers will want to buy more. The second thing that influences prices is the cost of making the product. For example, a lipstick might cost a dollar to make. It could be sold at a normal profit for $2.00. However, the cost of advertising and packaging can bring the price up to $6.00.

In order to afford goods, people need to have an income. Most people get their money by working and being paid wages. The wage for any job is usually determined in two ways. One is the value of the work performed. A doctor is paid more than a doctor's receptionist because the doctor can do specialized work that is important to the community. The other way is how many people are qualified to do the work. A job that takes a lot of training will pay more than a job that takes less training. So a teacher would earn a higher wage than a teacher's assistant.

Exercises

Questions 1 to 6 refer to the previous information.

1. The writer assumes that any country's economy

   (1) operates according to certain principles
   (2) is well-balanced
   (3) cannot be understood
   (4) is based on money
   (5) is set at fixed prices

2. The use of a country's GNP as a measure of its economy assumes that

   (1) all economic exchanges have a monetary value
   (2) the same amount of products are made each year
   (3) everyone uses the barter system
   (4) the economy is improving
   (5) the economy is stable

3. In following the law of supply and demand, manufacturers most likely assume that consumers

   (1) will buy only inexpensive products
   (2) will demand high quality
   (3) can be persuaded to pay high prices
   (4) can save a lot of money
   (5) can be easily fooled

4. According to the information, advertising most affects

   (1) the consumer's income
   (2) the packaging of a product
   (3) the GNP
   (4) the price of a product
   (5) normal profits

5. According to the information, it can be inferred that the value of work is

   (1) always the same
   (2) always changing
   (3) determined by the community
   (4) not important to economics
   (5) up to the individual

6. Which of the following is the best example of the barter system?

   (1) exchanging a sweater for a larger one at a department store
   (2) giving a friend an IOU for a loan
   (3) buying a secondhand car from a neighbor
   (4) getting a meal at a restaurant
   (5) trading some of your garden vegetables for your neighbor's quilt

To check your answers, turn to page 138.

Reviewing Lesson 9

Read the following paragraphs.

When more goods are being made, we say that the economy is expanding. In an expanding economy, manufacturers must find more people to buy their goods. They use advertising to let people know something special about the product. They also provide coupons that lower the price and make buyers feel they are getting a bargain. Another way manufacturers attract customers is through rebates. A rebate is a refund of part of the purchase price. Buyers who take the time to send in rebates feel they are spending their money wisely.

When the manufacturer's normal market is already buying as much as it can, the manufacturer starts to look for new customers. One way to find a new market is to change the packaging of the product in order to appeal to other groups of people. For example, in the 1970s many single people had their own households. Before then, food companies had packaged their products mainly for couples and families. To attract this new market, manufacturers began to sell food in single-serving packages. Another way to find new markets is to sell goods to another country. This practice is called exporting and can double or triple a company's sales.

Questions 1 to 4 refer to the paragraphs. Circle the best answer for each question.

1. A manufacturing company will begin a new advertising campaign when it

   (1) has more customers than goods
   (2) has more goods than customers
   (3) wants to limit markets
   (4) manufactures food packages
   (5) wants to appeal to old customers

2. According to the paragraphs, a new cost for a manufacturer in an expanding economy could be the cost of

   (1) labor problems
   (2) packaging
   (3) producing the product
   (4) early retirement plans
   (5) finding new markets

3. Information in the paragraphs indicates that in an expanding economy

   (1) exports will increase
   (2) imports will increase
   (3) exports will decrease
   (4) imports will decrease
   (5) exports and imports will stay the same

4. The writer assumes that the use of advertising to expand markets is

   (1) an economic fact of marketing
   (2) a trick played on consumers
   (3) wasteful and ineffective
   (4) damaging to the economy
   (5) helpful to the economy

To check your answers, turn to pages 138 and 139.

Read the following paragraph.

The American economy is said to go through an eight- to ten-year business cycle. This cycle has four phases: expansion, peak, recession, and trough. During expansion, business activity increases until it reaches a peak. During recession, business activity decreases until it reaches a low point, or trough. Although minor upswings and downswings happen all the time, the overall pattern is a rise followed by a fall followed by a rise.

Questions 5 and 6 refer to the paragraph. Circle the best answer for each question.

5. The best description of the American business cycle would be

(1) positive
(2) negative
(3) unchanging
(4) always changing
(5) huge

6. The writer of the paragraph assumes that the American economic cycle is

(1) seriously affected by minor variations in the pattern
(2) not seriously affected by minor variations in the pattern
(3) currently on the rise
(4) falling
(5) at a peak

Look at the following graph.

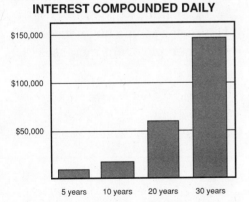

SAVINGS OF $100 A MONTH AT 8% INTEREST COMPOUNDED DAILY

Questions 7 and 8 refer to the graph. Circle the best answer for each question.

7. The maker of the graph assumes that

(1) people know exactly how interest rates work
(2) people are able to save as much as $100 a month
(3) interest rates will go up
(4) interest rates will go down
(5) people start saving when they are five years old

8. Which is best supported by the information in the graph?

(1) A bird in the hand is worth two in the bush.
(2) All that glitters is not gold.
(3) A penny saved is a penny earned.
(4) Money is the root of all evil.
(5) A good beginning makes a good ending.

To check your answers, turn to page 139.

GED Mini-Test

Directions: Choose the <u>best answer</u> to each item.

<u>Items 1 and 2</u> refer to the following paragraph.

One of the most important factors in the economy is the consumer. Every person in the country has some influence, one way or another, on the economic health of the nation. Ordinarily, people buy something almost every day. The sales of items from gumballs to houses are a good part of what keeps the money moving. When consumers feel that they have enough money to buy more than just what they need to live, the businesses in the nation profit. Interest rates go down, and people feel freer to borrow more money and spend it. But when consumers begin to feel a pinch in the pocketbook, they spend less. The decrease in spending hurts business. A decrease in business activity often results in more unemployment and people having even less money to spend. The question then that the economists face is how to keep the consumer happy.

1. Which of the following does the writer assume in the paragraph?

    (1) Economists try to keep the economy stable.

    (2) People would rather borrow money than earn it.

    (3) American consumers spend more than they can afford.

    (4) Housing is one of the most important economic factors.

    (5) Consumers are not aware of their role in the economic picture.

2. According to the paragraph, which is an effect of decreasing interest rates?

    (1) Business activity slows down.

    (2) People borrow more money.

    (3) People feel they have less money to spend.

    (4) Fewer people buy houses.

    (5) Unemployment increases.

<u>Items 3 and 4</u> refer to the following information.

There are two basic questions about economic production. What should be produced? How should it be produced? Neither of these questions is easy to answer.

If it is decided that farming in general is important, how should the farm industry be approached? Should labor and land be devoted to growing more food? Or should labor and money go first to develop better farm equipment? The second approach would mean a better use of the land in the long run.

Each question must be asked and answered by business executives. It is up to businesses and consumers to come up with answers that best serve the nation as a whole.

3. The writer assumes that businesses are concerned with

   (1) only making the highest short-term profit
   (2) only long-term benefits
   (3) coming up with easy answers
   (4) both the economic and the social effects of their decisions
   (5) supporting national defense

4. Which is the best summary of the information?

   (1) Economic theories do not really work.
   (2) Economic production involves two difficult issues.
   (3) Businesses do not care about the public good.
   (4) Consumers have no say in production.
   (5) Economic production has several simple solutions.

Items 5 and 6 refer to the following cartoon.

"The meek will inherit the earth, but NEVER the market."

5. The cartoonist assumes that the readers knows that "market"

   (1) refers to the grocery store
   (2) refers to the stock market
   (3) refers to a shopping mall
   (4) is a slang word for "power"
   (5) means what a rich man leaves in his will

6. The opinion of the speaker in the cartoon is that

   (1) religion is not important in money matters
   (2) only aggressive people can succeed in money matters
   (3) being quiet and gentle will bring success
   (4) the earth is better than the market
   (5) there is no risk in dealing with money

To check your answers, turn to page 139.

Answers and Explanations

1. (Analysis) **(3) They will be able to agree on management decisions.** Because partnerships are shared businesses, neither Ann nor Dan can make decisions alone; they must be able to agree or nothing will get done. Option (1) would be true only if both partners agreed on it. Option (2) is incorrect because each partner is entitled to half the profits. Option (4) is incorrect because both partners are financially responsible. There is no support for option (5).

2. (Analysis) **(3) make a profit** Most people who invest in a business do it to make money. Option (1) is the opposite of what is usually true. Option (2) is incorrect because shareholders do not manage corporations. Option (4) is incorrect because a corporation is not a partnership. Option (5) is incorrect because that would be a hope, not an assumption.

1. (Analysis) **(1) operates according to certain principles** The writer states that economics has basic principles. Options (2), (3), and (5) have no support. Option (4) is incorrect because some economies are based on barter.

2. (Analysis) **(1) all economic exchanges have a monetary value** The GNP can work as a measure only if a value in money is given to each exchange, even those that are not paid for in money. The quantity of products does not affect the accuracy of the GNP, so option (2) is incorrect. Option (3) is incorrect because the barter system would best be measured by something else. Options (4) and (5) are incorrect because the economy does not need to be improving or stable to be measured.

3. (Analysis) **(3) can be persuaded to pay high prices** Manufacturers would not try to sell even more high-priced goods if it were not believed that people would buy them. Option (1) suggests the opposite. There is no mention of quality, so option (2) is incorrect. Savings is not involved in the law of supply and demand, so option (4) is incorrect. Fooling the customer has nothing to do with the law of supply and demand, so option (5) is incorrect.

4. (Analysis) **(4) the price of a product** Advertising adds to the price of a product. Advertising has nothing to do with options (1), (2), or (3). Normal profits, option (5), probably would not increase much because the cost would go to the advertisers.

5. (Comprehension) **(3) determined by the community** If a person's work has no value to the community, it will not be in demand and will not provide that person with an income. There is no support for options (1) and (2). Option (4) is incorrect because the value of work helps to set income levels. Option (5) is incorrect because the community, not the individual, sets the value.

6. (Application) **(5) trading some of your garden vegetables for your neighbor's quilt** In this case, the value of the goods is not set by money but by how much each person wants the other's goods. Option (1) refers to exchanging one item for another of equal monetary value. Options (2), (3), and (4) are all based on monetary value.

Reviewing Lesson 9 (pages 134–135)

1. (Comprehension) **(2) has more goods than customers** Advertising is defined as a way of getting people to buy more. The company wants people to buy more when it has more goods than customers. Option (1) is the opposite of what is stated. If option (3) were correct, the company would not advertise. Option (4) is irrelevant. For option (5), a new advertising campaign is not necessary.

2. (Analysis) **(5) finding new markets** This can be understood from the main idea of the paragraphs; when more goods are produced, more people must be found to buy them. Options (1) and (4) would be costs when production was restricted. Options (2) and (3) will always be costs of manufacturing; therefore they are not new.

3. (Comprehension) **(1) exports will increase** This is correct from the information on developing overseas, or export, markets. Option (2) does not necessarily follow. Options (3) and (4) are more likely in a tightening economy. Option (5) is the opposite of what is stated.

4. (Analysis) **(1) an economic fact of marketing** The writer accepts marketing products as an economic fact. Option (2) is not mentioned. Although option (3) may be true for some marketing strategies, it is not mentioned. Options (4) and (5) are not related to these paragraphs on marketing.

5. (Comprehension) **(4) always changing** The pattern is one of change from activity to little activity and back to activity again. Options (1) and (2) are opinions about the cycle and are not supported in the paragraph. Option (3) is the opposite of what is stated. Option (5) has no support.

6. (Analysis) **(2) not seriously affected by minor variations in the pattern** The writer believes that the pattern remains constant. Option (1) is the opposite of what is stated. Options (3), (4), and (5) are not supported by the paragraph.

7. (Analysis) **(2) people are able to save as much as $100 a month** The choice of that figure as a reasonable basis of savings suggests this assumption. Option (1) is incorrect because the figuring has been done for the reader. Options (3) and (4) are incorrect because the rate is quoted at 8 percent. Option (5) is a misreading of the years of savings as years of age.

8. (Application) **(3) A penny saved is a penny earned.** In fact, after a while it becomes two pennies. Options (1) and (2) refer to value, but not to making the most of money. Option (4) is a judgment about greed, not careful money management. Option (5) may apply, but only in a general way.

GED Mini-Test
(pages 136–137)

1. (Analysis) **(1) Economists try to keep the economy stable.** The writer sees the economist as someone who is supposed to diagnose and solve the problems of the economy. There is no evidence that the writer assumes options (2), (3), (4), or (5) to be true.

2. (Analysis) **(2) People borrow more money.** When interest rates go down, the amount that has to be repaid on a loan is less, so that is the best time to borrow money. Options (1), (3), and (5) are not results of a decreased interest rate. Lower interest rates make buying a house easier, so option (4) is the opposite of what is implied in the paragraph.

3. (Analysis) **(4) both the economic and the social effects of their decisions** This assumption is suggested by the examples and the concluding sentence. Options (1), (2), and (3) are incorrect because the writer believes that businesses ask a number of questions before coming up with their decisions. There is no support for option (5).

4. (Comprehension) **(2) Economic production involves two difficult issues.** This is a restatement of the first paragraph. Option (1) is incorrect because there is no mention of evaluation of economic theories. Options (3) and (4) do not refer to the main idea of the passage. Option (5) is the opposite of what is stated.

5. (Analysis) **(2) refers to the stock market** The term "stock market" is often shortened to the "market." The two men are clearly businesspeople, so this choice would make sense. Neither option (1) nor (3) makes sense in the context of the cartoon. There is no support for option (4). Option (5) is based on looking at the word "inherit" rather than the cartoon as a whole.

6. (Analysis) **(2) only aggressive people can succeed in money matters** Meek people are not aggressive and rarely do well in the stock market, where buying and selling is a brutal business. Option (1) is incorrect because the biblical quotation is not intended to refer directly to religion. Options (3) and (5) are the opposite of what is suggested. Option (4) is incorrect because the contrast is not between the earth and the market but between types of people.

LESSON 10 Analysis Skill: Cause and Effect

This skill reviews the way one thing leads to another.

As you learned in Lesson 7, a cause is what makes something happen; the effect is the result. Remember that identifying a cause-and-effect relationship is a logical process. You need to use careful reasoning. Be sure that the effect is really the result of what you identify as the most likely cause.

Sometimes a cause is not stated; it is only implied. A writer may describe events in the order in which they happened and leave it up to the reader to decide which events caused other events. In this case, the reader must use information that is already known about the real world. The reader must also ask if the second or third events would have happened if the first event had not occurred. If the second or third events could have occurred without the first, the first event may not be the cause.

Another way that a cause is implied is by stating two or three related effects. You need to look at what those effects have in common to decide what the cause of all of them might be. If your lights go out, you might check to see if the refrigerator is working. If it is not, you can then reason that the cause is a power failure. From the two effects, you can also assume other related effects. For example, your electric alarm clock will have stopped, and your electric water heater will no longer heat water.

Looking at related effects can also help you to predict further effects. For example, the refrigerator will no longer keep things cold. If the temperature rises high enough, the frozen items will begin to thaw. Then you will have to use the items now that you were planning to save until another day.

Keep in mind that some causes are only partial causes that help to produce an effect but do not do so all by themselves. For example, a driver runs a red light. If another car is crossing the intersection or if a person is walking across the street, these things might combine to cause an accident.

Cause-and-effect relationships are often found in writings about economics, social behavior, and political science. Social scientists want to know how systems work, so they look for reasons why certain things happen. They also want to be able to predict what probably will result from future or possible events and situations.

Practicing Analysis

Read the following paragraph.

> Mergers between companies and the takeover of one company by another have become a fact of American business life. Some large department stores such as Bloomingdale's and Saks Fifth Avenue have run into financial trouble and have put themselves up for sale. Some retail managers and suppliers who have been employed by such companies are now worried about job security. New owners may want to hire an entirely different management staff or reorganize the existing team. The goods that a supplier had previously sold might not be what the new owners want to feature in their stores. Even stores that are not undergoing change can be affected by the companies that are. The financially troubled companies might get into price wars to cut prices and increase immediate sales. On the other hand, some people can benefit from the shifting business scene. The newly formed companies are often more independent and more financially secure than the old ones. Top executives can be fairly sure that their special knowledge is needed to keep the companies running smoothly. In addition, secure companies are taking advantage of the shake-ups by offering jobs to the skilled employees of the companies in transition.

Questions 1 and 2 refer to the paragraph. Circle the best answer for each question.

1. Which of the following is the most probable cause for a new owner to hire a new staff and/or new suppliers?

   (1) to correct the financial problems the old company had
   (2) as a goodwill gesture
   (3) to hire his or her relatives
   (4) to please the top executives
   (5) to save money

2. One unstated effect on the public would be that

   (1) the public would not know whom to trust
   (2) for a while companies would offer bargain prices
   (3) taxes would go up
   (4) fewer choices of products would be available
   (5) more jobs might be available

To check your answers, turn to page 148.

Topic 10: Labor and the Economy

Profit, the difference between how much production costs and how much the consumer pays, is the goal of businesses. Companies see wages paid to workers as a major part of the expense in production costs. To a business, it is important to keep the cost of labor down. However, the wage that is an expense to the company is an income to the worker. Workers want to keep their wages high so that they can buy what they need and want for themselves and their families. Employers and employees are constantly trying to improve their own positions.

A worker alone has only one small voice, but workers who are union members can be heard because they have a loud collective voice. The organization of workers can influence a company's decisions about wages, benefits, and working conditions. When a large group of laborers strike, or refuse to work, the company is forced to pay attention to the demands of the union.

When unions were first established, labor's power was limited by law and by the lack of financial support for striking workers. Now American law recognizes the workers' right to join a union, to organize others, and to strike. The National Labor Relations Act (NLRA) of 1935 requires employers to bargain with a union favored by a majority of the workers and defines certain labor practices as unfair. These unfair and illegal labor practices include firing because of union activity, discrimination against union members in favor of nonunion members, and interference with employees trying to organize unions or bargain collectively. Many concerned citizens felt that the NLRA was excessively pro-labor. The Labor Management Relations Act of 1947 (Taft-Hartley Act) was passed to balance the power of company management and the power of labor; it requires labor to bargain with employers, thus setting the stage for collective bargaining.

Collective bargaining is the discussion between management and union leaders who speak for all the employees. The two groups negotiate, or present and agree on, terms for employment contracts. Often each side has to compromise in order to arrive at an agreement. Since the 1930s, collective bargaining has increased wages and salaries, health and vacation benefits, and company liability for accident and health hazards. If a union comes to the bargaining table and management and the union cannot agree on a new contract, the union may choose to strike. Sometimes the threat of a strike causes management to agree to a wage increase. Sometimes the threat is put into action before management agrees to raise wages.

Exercises

Questions 1 to 6 refer to the previous information. Circle the best answer for each question.

1. Which is **not** an effect of the conflict between labor and management?

   (1) Laws had to be made to protect both sides.
   (2) Labor unions were established.
   (3) Labor has one voice and management has many.
   (4) Management and labor practice collective bargaining.
   (5) Workers have the right to strike.

2. What probably would happen first if a city did not want to increase teacher salaries?

   (1) The teachers would strike.
   (2) Teachers would take a cut in pay.
   (3) The teachers' union would picket the school board building.
   (4) The city would close the schools.
   (5) The teachers' union would bargain with the school board.

3. According to the information, labor unions

   (1) have no power
   (2) are too powerful
   (3) allow workers a voice in their jobs
   (4) have no financial support
   (5) are betraying workers' trust

4. Which is an important effect of collective bargaining?

   (1) Management and labor have social gatherings.
   (2) More tables are being manufactured.
   (3) Unions have gotten many benefits for laborers.
   (4) No labor contract can be broken.
   (5) Strikes have been made illegal.

5. It can be concluded from the information that labor and management will probably

   (1) join forces
   (2) never agree
   (3) usually have tension between them
   (4) try to make collective bargaining illegal
   (5) destroy the business world

6. Which supports the concern that the NLRA was too pro-labor?

   (1) The act specified only the rights of labor.
   (2) The act made some practices illegal.
   (3) The act prevented management from firing a person just because of a union affiliation.
   (4) The act recognized union rights.
   (5) The act prohibited labor unions.

To check your answers, turn to page 148.

Reviewing Lesson 10

Read the following paragraphs.

> Income in the United States is distributed unequally. Although the U.S. is considered a middle-class society, the poorest fifth of our country earns only 5 percent of the income while the richest fifth earns 40 percent of the income. In 1984, 11 percent of U.S. adults and 21 percent of U.S. children were at poverty levels. Many of these poor lack the education necessary to hold a job in our technological society.
>
> The difference in income between the wealthy and the poor has increased over the past decade. Prices for necessities like food and housing have increased more rapidly than the minimum wage. Consequently, the poor have become poorer in terms of their ability to pay for necessities.

Questions 1 to 4 refer to the paragraphs. Circle the best answer for each question.

1. According to the writer, what is a partial cause for unequal distribution of income?

   (1) The cost of food has become higher than the cost of housing.
   (2) There is a lack of appropriate schooling.
   (3) People pretend to be middle class.
   (4) Prices have increased more rapidly than wages.
   (5) Many people are at poverty level.

2. According to the writer, which is an effect of the more rapid increase in prices?

   (1) increased inequality of income
   (2) more equal income
   (3) less money for social welfare programs
   (4) more poor children
   (5) more people in the middle class

3. Twice as many children as adults were at poverty level in 1984. What reason for this can be inferred from the paragraphs?

   (1) The children of middle-class parents do not have as much money as their parents do.
   (2) A family usually has more than one child per parent.
   (3) Supporting a child costs money.
   (4) Many poor children are orphans.
   (5) Children of poor families are not paid enough.

4. It can be concluded from the paragraphs that

   (1) only 5 percent of Americans are at poverty level
   (2) at least 32 percent of Americans are at poverty level
   (3) three fifths of Americans are middle-class
   (4) 32 percent of Americans earn the minimum wage
   (5) 40 percent of Americans are wealthy

To check your answers, turn to page 148.

Look at the following cartoon.

"We plan to bargain all night until an agreement is reached."

Questions 5 to 8 refer to the cartoon. Circle the best answer for each question.

5. The main idea of the cartoon is

(1) collective bargaining is exhausting
(2) management always lies
(3) labor always lies
(4) the media has a right to know the facts
(5) labor and management agreed to maintain the image of round-the-clock negotiations

6. What is the probable result of the action depicted in the cartoon?

(1) Agreement will be reached.
(2) Negotiations will continue after both parties have rested.
(3) The press will spread more lies to the public.
(4) The negotiators will give up and the workers will go on strike.
(5) The corporation will win.

To check your answers, turn to pages 148 and 149.

7. The cartoonist assumes that the reader will recognize

(1) which company is negotiating with the union
(2) which union is negotiating with the company
(3) the man with the notebook as a reporter
(4) the identity of the speaker with the pillow
(5) the issue being negotiated

8. The message in the cartoon is intended to have an effect on the public that is most similar to the effect of

(1) crying "Fire" in a crowded theater
(2) publicly criticizing a popular politician
(3) saying "The check is in the mail"
(4) a suspected criminal saying "No comment"
(5) admitting no agreement is possible

GED Mini-Test

Directions: Choose the best answer to each item.

Items 1 to 4 refer to the following information.

Teenage unemployment is a serious problem in the United States. Many teenagers drop out of high school. Many others do not go on for further training or degrees.

The statistics are frightening. About a third of the teenagers who are not in school are unemployed. While many of the females are married or caring for young children, many others have simply given up the search for jobs. For either boys or girls, working at a fast-food restaurant or cleaning motel rooms is a short-term solution, but few teenagers look forward to a lifetime of frying hamburgers or cleaning toilets. In fact, McDonald's now is hiring retired persons to replace the number of teenagers who are no longer even applying for jobs. The looming question is how these teenagers will be able to support themselves and their families.

Education is a major factor in finding good, steady employment. The more education a person has, the better the chance of getting and keeping a job. Vocational training is available to help teenagers prepare for and find skilled jobs. Apprenticeship and work-study programs also train teenagers while paying them a wage. Unemployed teenagers need to look for such programs that are offered in their communities. Their futures and the futures of their children depend on taking positive action.

1. A probable effect of continued teenage unemployment is

   (1) a better-educated public
   (2) more children at poverty level
   (3) more satisfied citizens
   (4) fewer workers in fast-food industries
   (5) increased minimum wage

2. Which government program to increase teenage employment would the writer probably support most?

   (1) more government cafeteria jobs
   (2) home-based industries
   (3) more day care centers
   (4) literacy training
   (5) parenting classes

3. Exact figures to support the conclusion that the statistics are frightening

   (1) are not given
   (2) prove that many teenagers are out of work
   (3) are stated in the second paragraph
   (4) show that dropouts cannot get jobs
   (5) are compiled by the government

4. An assumption the writer makes is that vocational programs are

   (1) the best solution to teenage unemployment
   (2) not as effective as apprenticeship programs
   (3) available in most communities
   (4) not available in many places
   (5) a teenager's last resort

Items 5 and 6 refer to the following information.

In 1986, the International Ladies Garment Workers' Union (ILGWU) became concerned over what it called "sweatshop conditions" in rural Iowa. It accused Bordeaux, Inc., of Clarinda, Iowa, of violating the federal regulations that outlaw womenswear being commercially made at home.

The company began manufacturing decorated sweatsuits in 1980, and within six years had sales figures in the three-million-dollar range. It employed from 100 to 150 women who worked at home using their own sewing machines and the company's material. The company paid about $2.45 per piece, or $1.12 if the work did not pass inspection.

Some workers figured they earned from $4.00 to $9.00 an hour and, in this economically depressed farm area, were pleased to have the work. Other workers complained to the ILGWU that the hourly rate was more like $1.85 (which is illegal under the minimum wage law).

The Labor Department investigated the claims. At first, the Labor Department proposed a new system in which home employers would register with the department, providing it with lists of workers so that on-the-spot inspections could be made. They felt that fair employers should be allowed to operate. The ILGWU felt that piecework at home could not be monitored effectively and wanted the Labor Department to uphold the federal regulations that protected home workers. Later the Labor Department filed a suit against Bordeaux, Inc. During the time the suit was being heard in court, the company opened a factory, employed factory workers, and stopped using home workers. The court judged in favor of the Labor Department and ordered Bordeaux, Inc. to pay back wages to all the home workers it had employed before the suit.

5. The ILGWU favored strict government control of working conditions because

   (1) their union would gain power
   (2) poor people are often exploited
   (3) Bordeaux, Inc. would grow
   (4) the minimum wage would rise
   (5) the minimum wage would remain the same

6. The Labor Department saw the main cause of the dispute as

   (1) labor vs. management
   (2) unions vs. unorganized labor
   (3) responsible vs. irresponsible management
   (4) sweatshops vs. pieceworkers
   (5) ILGWU vs. Bordeaux, Inc.

To check your answers, turn to page 149.

Answers and Explanations

1. (Analysis) **(1) to correct the financial problems the old company had** The former managers or products were probably the reason for the old company's financial problems. Options (2) and (4) would not make sense. Options (3) and (5) have no support.

2. (Analysis) **(2) for a while companies would offer bargain prices** The price wars would offer a temporary drop in prices. No support is offered for options (1), (3), (4), and (5).

Exercises (page 143)

1. (Analysis) **(3) Labor has one voice and management has many.** This option is the only effect that has not come out of the conflict. Labor has unions or a collective voice, as does management. Options (1), (2), (4), and (5) are all results of the conflict.

2. (Application) **(5) The teachers' union would bargain with the school board.** This is the best option because the union would negotiate before it would strike, option (1), accept a pay cut, option (2), or picket, option (3). Cities try to avoid closing schools, option (4).

3. (Comprehension) **(3) allow workers a voice in their jobs** This is a restatement of the information in the second paragraph. Options (1) and (2) are not supported by the information. Option (4) refers to the early unions, not the modern ones. There is no evidence for option (5).

4. (Analysis) **(3) Unions have gotten many benefits for laborers.** The last paragraph details the benefits that have resulted. Options (1) and (2) are not related to collective bargaining. Options (4) and (5) are the opposite of what is stated.

5. (Comprehension) **(3) usually have tension between them** The two groups have different and opposing goals, and they will rarely see eye to eye. Option (1) is unlikely. Options (2) and (4) would not be to either side's advantage. There is no support for option (5).

6. (Analysis) **(1) The act specified only the rights of labor.** A balance of rights would have made the act seem less biased. Options (2), (3), and (4) are true, but they are details that do not summarize the apparent impact of the act. Option (5) is not true.

Reviewing Lesson 10 (pages 144–145)

1. (Analysis) **(2) There is a lack of appropriate schooling.** This is the best option, based on the last sentence in the first paragraph. Options (1) and (3) are not stated or implied. Options (4) and (5) relate to cost rather than distribution.

2. (Analysis) **(1) increased inequality of income** If the poor can afford even less than before, they are suffering from an even greater burden than before. Option (2) is the opposite of what is suggested. Options (3) and (4) are not related to the increase in prices. Option (5) is not a clear result of the increase in prices.

3. (Comprehension) **(2) A family usually has more than one child per parent.** If a family of five is poor, there will be three poor children to two poor adults. A single-parent family of three would have two poor children to one poor adult. Option (1) is incorrect because the children of a middle class family are assumed to be supported by the family, thus having the same income. Option (3) is true but does not account for the number of poor children. There is no support for option (4). Option (5) is incorrect because children are rarely the moneymakers in the family.

4. (Comprehension) **(2) at least 32 percent of Americans are at poverty level** The figure is the result of adding the stated figures for adults and children. Option (1) uses the figure for percent of income, not percent of Americans. Option (3) is incorrect because no income figures are given for the three fifths between the poorest and the wealthiest. Option (4) is incorrect because the actual wages are not mentioned. Option (5) uses the figure for percent of income, not percent of Americans.

5. (Comprehension) **(5) labor and management agreed to maintain the image of round-the-clock negotiations** When asked a main idea question, try to bring all the information together. In this cartoon, labor, management, and the press are all involved. Options (1) and (4) are concerned with details, not with the main idea. Options (2) and (3) are not suggested in the cartoon.

6. (Analysis) **(2) Negotiations will continue after both parties have rested.** Both parties have agreed on one thing and so will probably be willing to continue talking. Option (1) is a possible outcome but ignores the graphic information (negotiators sleeping). Option (3) is an opinion. Options (4) and (5) are not supported.

7. (Analysis) **(3) the man with the notebook as a reporter** The man with the pad has clearly asked a question, as reporters do, and is in front of a man with a microphone. The cartoon refers to general union-management negotiations, not to a specific situation, so options (1), (2), (4), and (5) are incorrect.

8. (Application) **(3) saying "The check is in the mail"** Both messages are intended to reassure the listener while buying a little time for the speaker. Option (1) would cause panic. Option (2) would start an argument. Option (4) would make the listener doubt the speaker's innocence. Option (5) is the opposite of the intended message.

GED Mini-Test (pages 146–147)

1. (Analysis) **(2) more children at poverty level** An unemployed teenage parent would mean that a child will probably not have enough financial support. Options (1) and (3) are the opposites of the likely effect. There is no support for options (4) and (5).

2. (Application) **(4) literacy training** If education is the key to employment, knowing how to read well is a basic requirement. Options (1), (2), and (5) would have little effect on the problem discussed. Option (3) is worthwhile but would affect only those with children, a small portion of the teenage job-seekers.

3. (Analysis) **(1) are not given** The only figure referred to is a generalized percent. Since no exact figures are given, options (2), (3), and (4) are incorrect. The source of any statistics is not mentioned, so option (5) is incorrect.

4. (Analysis) **(3) available in most communities** By referring teenagers to these programs, the writer indicates a belief that they are plentiful. Options (1), (2), and (5) are not supported. Option (4) is the opposite of what is implied.

5. (Analysis) **(2) poor people are often exploited** People who have little money or power need a strong voice to protect their rights. There is no basis in the information for options (1), (4), and (5). Option (3) is incorrect because the ILGWU is interested in protecting workers' rights, not the corporation's.

6. (Analysis) **(3) responsible vs. irresponsible management** The passage states that the Labor Department searched for a way to allow fair employers to operate, while penalizing exploitative employers. Options (1) and (2) do not reflect the Labor Department's view. Option (4) is incorrect; the passage states that a sweatshop and piecework are similar. Option (5) is a true dispute, but does not state the main cause of the dispute.

LESSON 11 Evaluation Skill: Interpreting Information

This skill helps you to decide if the facts you are given are enough to support conclusions drawn by you or by the writer.

When you draw a conclusion, you are basing your decision on the facts you know or have available. When you do this, it is important to be sure that you have enough information to reach your conclusion. A writer may give you a number of facts and draw a conclusion from them. While all the facts needed to add up to the conclusion may be available to the writer, you might not have been told all of them. Sometimes a writer will assume you know certain facts. At other times, what might appear to be a fact is actually an opinion that is based on facts.

To decide if the information is adequate, or enough, to support a specific conclusion, you need to identify and understand the main idea and to recognize all the supporting details. Ask yourself what conclusions you can draw from the stated facts. See if you can make any inferences based on the facts and on your general knowledge about the situation being discussed.

When you are sure that you understand all the facts, try to analyze the information. Look for opinions and assumptions. See if there are stated or unstated cause-and-effect relationships. Be sure that you can tell supporting details from any conclusion that the writer comes to. Now ask yourself, "Are these facts enough to support the conclusion?" Also, be sure to ask if there is anything else you would need to know in order to logically draw that conclusion. If the information is enough, the conclusion is accurate. However, you might find that there is not enough information or that the conclusion is not right.

This process is very much like following a recipe for making a cake. When you read a recipe, you look to see if all the ingredients are listed. Sometimes the recipe assumes that you know certain information, such as what a medium oven temperature is. If your recipe gives all the ingredients you expect to find, gives you step-by-step directions for mixing, and tells you the proper oven temperature and the needed baking time, you can be fairly sure that the result of following the recipe will be a well-baked cake.

As you read to decide if the information given is adequate, imagine that you have to explain the conclusion to someone else. Ask yourself if the facts you give as support will convince the other person that the conclusion is correct.

Practicing Evaluation

Read the following paragraphs.

Three major economic systems exist in the world today: capitalism, communism, and socialism. The main differences in the systems are the ways ownership and decision-making are treated.

Capitalism, the economic system favored by the industrialized Western world, has private or corporate ownership of goods and the means of production. Decisions and planning are in private hands. Under communism, the economic system of the Soviet Union and the People's Republic of China, the state owns the means of production and plans its economy. The goal of communism, in theory, is that everyone has everything he or she needs; individuals give their best to the community and in return receive what they need for daily living. Socialism is similar to communism; the state owns all the major means of production and plans the economy for the good of all, but competition among small businesses is encouraged. The state provides certain social services for its citizens, such as free or inexpensive medical care.

In the modern world, these economic systems have become confused with political systems. Because communism and socialism depend so much on central planning, they have become associated in people's minds with dictatorships. Capitalism, which depends on private ownership and free enterprise, is associated with democratic or representative governments.

Questions 1 and 2 refer to the paragraphs. Circle the best answer for each question.

1. Enough support for the conclusion that the differences among capitalism, communism, and socialism are economic is

   (1) not given
   (2) provided by the statement that three major economic systems exist
   (3) provided by the example of capitalism
   (4) provided by the contrast between communism and socialism
   (5) provided by examples of all three systems

2. In order to draw the conclusion that the theory of communism is not the same as the reality, you need to know

   (1) only what is stated in the paragraphs
   (2) what the theory of communism is
   (3) what the reality of communism is
   (4) more details of communist theory
   (5) how socialism is different from communism

To check your answers, turn to page 156.

Topic 11: Government and Economics

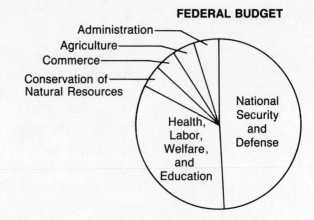

FEDERAL BUDGET

Administration
Agriculture
Commerce
Conservation of Natural Resources
Health, Labor, Welfare, and Education
National Security and Defense

The U.S. Government spends more money and has a larger payroll than any business in the world. Its budget runs into billions of dollars. Almost 50 percent of the federal budget is spent on national security and defense; a third is spent on health, labor, welfare, and education; and the rest is divided among conservation of natural resources, commerce, agriculture, and administration. The amount of government spending affects the economy.

Whenever there is spending, there must be income. Government spending is paid for by taxes paid by citizens and businesses. The federal income tax pays for federal spending. Traditionally, the federal income tax has been a graduated income tax. People with higher income taxes pay a higher percentage of their income to the government in taxes; people with lower incomes pay a lower percentage of their income in taxes.

For citizens to be taxed, they also must have income, or money, coming into the household. This income may be salaries or wages from employment, interest or dividends from investments, or rental income from properties. Income can also come from benefits like welfare, Medicaid, and unemployment compensation.

In this century, the government has steadily increased its control of the economy. It limits monopolies, regulates interstate commerce, restricts or expands the amount of money in the economy, uses the Federal Reserve System as a central bank, and sets up international trade agreements.

Through spending, taxation, and regulation, the government touches the economic life of every citizen.

Exercises

Questions 1 to 6 refer to the previous information. Circle the best answer for each question.

1. In order to draw a conclusion from the pie graph on page 152, a reader must first

   (1) know the total figure for the federal budget
   (2) read the first paragraph
   (3) understand how the government gets its money
   (4) read the entire passage
   (5) know the exact figures for each expense

2. Thomas Jefferson said that "government governs best which governs least." The information in this passage is enough to support the conclusion that modern Americans disagree with Jefferson because they have chosen a government that

   (1) spends a lot of money
   (2) taxes all its citizens
   (3) is heavily involved in the economy
   (4) taxes luxury items
   (5) has a welfare program

3. Budget legislation promised a balanced budget by cutting down on government spending. One effect of this legislation would be

   (1) more support for Star Wars defense plans
   (2) higher taxes for people in every tax bracket
   (3) more financial support for public education
   (4) less financial support for welfare programs
   (5) less income for the government

4. The type of business *most* influenced by the government budget is

   (1) secretarial
   (2) agricultural
   (3) child care
   (4) publishing
   (5) arms manufacturing

5. The national debt reached a peak in the early 1940s. This high debt was most likely caused by

   (1) unemployment
   (2) taxation
   (3) defense spending
   (4) budgeting
   (5) high income levels

6. Through 1986, the United States had a graduated income tax. In practice, the tax law offered many benefits, tax shelters, and loopholes to higher-income individuals. In 1987 a flat-rate income tax with few tax shelters was begun. Why did the Congress pass a flat-rate income tax law?

   (1) The government needed more money.
   (2) The government needed less money.
   (3) The graduated income tax was not practiced fairly.
   (4) The graduated income tax was too difficult to enforce.
   (5) The graduated income tax was hated by the citizens.

To check your answers, turn to page 156.

Reviewing Lesson 11

Read the following paragraph.

> Many state governments collect money through a state income tax or a sales tax or both. However, most states need more money than they can raise through taxes. Some get extra money by having lotteries, but Montana has come up with an idea that is based on something that many Americans have begun to take for granted—the credit card. Montana is going to issue its own credit card. By sponsoring the card, the state will receive part of the annual fee paid by the user. Between that and a percentage of the value of the purchases charged, Montana expects to take in as much as $12.2 million a year.

Questions 1 and 2 refer to the paragraph. Circle the best answer for each question.

1. The information in the paragraph supports the conclusion that

   (1) other states should issue credit cards

   (2) Montana's plan will increase state income

   (3) lotteries raise more money than credit cards do

   (4) consumers pay too much in annual fees for credit cards

   (5) Montana's money problems have been solved

2. The state of Montana assumes that

   (1) people will pay their annual fees

   (2) people in Montana use credit cards

   (3) Montana citizens will no longer play the lottery

   (4) Montana does not want to raise its taxes

   (5) more people will move to Montana

Look at the following cartoon.

© 1989 BARNETT—INDIANAPOLIS NEWS

Question 3 refers to the cartoon. Circle the best answer.

3. A conclusion about government spending can be drawn if the cartoonist is correct in assuming that the reader recognizes the

   (1) street sign as representing government money

   (2) unemployment crisis

   (3) problem of homeless people

   (4) beggars as representing government agencies

   (5) bums

To check your answers, turn to page 157.

Read the following paragraph.

One way government is involved in the economy is in its attempts to protect the consumer. In the past, shoppers had little protection. Every store should have been posted with large signs saying "Buyer, beware!" If a baker bought flour that was full of bugs, he would have to sift them out, cook with them, or toss out the flour and lose money. Now public awareness of consumer rights, increased federal controls, public relations on the part of manufacturers and store owners, and self-policing by various groups have combined to increase consumer protection. Most large supermarkets will replace food that has gone stale or sour, and, in fact, include the cost of returns in the amount of markup on the groceries.

Questions 4 to 7 refer to the paragraph. Circle the best answer for each question.

4. In order to decide how much influence government has on consumer protection, the reader needs to know

   (1) only what is in the paragraph
   (2) what problems face the consumer
   (3) what problems are controlled by law
   (4) what consumers want
   (5) how much businesses are fined for violations

5. The conclusion that consumer protection is a widespread concern is best supported by

   (1) reference to public awareness of consumer rights
   (2) reference to federal controls
   (3) reference to self-policing by retail groups
   (4) none of the above
   (5) options (1), (2), and (3)

6. Which is the best example of government control for consumer protection?

   (1) articles in *Consumer Reports*
   (2) rating of movies by the Motion Picture Association of America
   (3) state laws on seat belts
   (4) neighborhood stores removing pornographic magazines from public shelves
   (5) comparison testing in advertisements

7. The manufacturer's cost of recalling defective merchandise is probably paid for by the

   (1) government
   (2) manufacturer
   (3) automobile industry
   (4) consumer
   (5) labor union

To check your answers, turn to page 157.

Answers and Explanations

1. (Evaluation) **(5) provided by examples of all three systems** All three examples refer to economic differences. The evidence is given, so option (1) is incorrect. Option (2) is a generalization that does not support the conclusion. Options (3) and (4) are not enough by themselves to support the conclusion.

2. (Evaluation) **(3) what the reality of communism is** Information about the reality of communism is needed to draw a conclusion about how it differs from theory. This information is not given in the paragraphs, so option (1) is incorrect. Option (2) is not enough to make the contrast. Details of theory would not give any information about reality, so option (4) is incorrect. Option (5) would not lead to a conclusion about communist theory and practice.

1. (Evaluation) **(2) read the first paragraph** The graph alone does not give enough information for a reader to interpret it accurately; the first paragraph acts as a key to the graph. Exact figures are not necessary to draw conclusions about percentages, so options (1) and (5) are incorrect. Option (3) refers to income, not to the spending shown in the graph. Option (4) is incorrect because only the first paragraph is needed for supporting information.

2. (Evaluation) **(3) is heavily involved in the economy** Government involvement in the economy supports the idea that government is taking an active part, not that it is standing apart—or governing less. Jefferson believed in government that governed as little as possible. Options (1), (2), (4), and (5) are all supporting details for the conclusion.

3. (Analysis) **(4) less financial support for welfare programs** This is the best choice because it would cut government spending. Options (1), (2), and (3) would increase spending. Option (5) relates to government income, not spending.

4. (Application) **(5) arms manufacturing** The supporting detail in the text is "almost 50 percent of the federal budget is spent on national security and defense." Any increases or decreases in the federal budget are most likely to affect businesses dependent on the budget, that is, defense-related businesses. Options (1), (3), and (4) are not mentioned in the text or listed in the graph. Option (2) refers to an area that has less government funding.

5. (Analysis) **(3) defense spending** National debt is high when government spending is high without adequate income from taxation. U.S. participation in World War II began in the early 1940s. The government had to finance a larger army and produce many weapons for the U.S. and its allies. Option (1) might increase spending, but unemployment was low in the early 1940s because many were involved in the war effort. Option (2) increases income, not spending. Option (4) equalizes income and spending. Option (5) has nothing to do with the national debt.

6. (Analysis) **(3) The graduated income tax was not practiced fairly.** This is correct from information about tax benefits for high-income citizens. No information is given on options (1) and (2). Option (4) is a possible inference, but not well supported. Option (5) is an unsupported opinion.

1. (Evaluation) **(2) Montana's plan will increase state income** Even if the goal is not reached, the state's income will increase. There is not enough information to support options (1), (3), (4), or (5).

2. (Analysis) **(2) people in Montana use credit cards** The essential element of success is that Montana citizens use credit cards to make purchases. If that is true, then they will probably also do option (1), but not the other way around. There is no support for options (3) or (5). Option (4) has nothing to do with the success of the project.

3. (Evaluation) **(1) street sign as representing government money** The bailout sign is government money that agencies and companies ask for in order to get out of financial trouble. Options (2) and (3) are not suggested by the cartoon. Option (4) is incorrect because only two of the beggars are connected to the government. Option (5) is not related to an assumption by the cartoonist.

4. (Evaluation) **(3) what problems are controlled by law** The way government influences consumer protection is through making laws; this information is not given in the paragraphs. Therefore, option (1) is incorrect. Options (2), (4), and (5) will not supply the needed information.

5. (Evaluation) **(5) options (1), (2), and (3)** The three references indicate that consumer protection is the concern of many people. Therefore, option (4) is incorrect. Options (1), (2), or (3) alone are not enough to support the conclusion.

6. (Application) **(3) state laws on seat belts** This is the only example of specific government regulation. Option (1) is non-profit advice. Options (2), (4), and (5) are private-sector efforts at consumer protection.

7. (Comprehension) **(4) consumer** This answer is implied by the statement that supermarkets often pass the cost of returned merchandise on to the consumer in product markup. Options (1), (2), (3), and (5) are not supported or implied in the paragraphs.

Review: Economics

In this unit, you have seen the relationships among money, goods, and services. You have read about production, prices, and costs. You have also studied the relationships among labor, government, and the general economy. All of these things have patterns that economists use to understand how the economy works and to predict what will happen in the future. Pay attention to the cause-and-effect relationships that you see in readings about economics. Look for assumptions that people make about the economy and what people really know about how it works. Also pay close attention to the information that is used to support conclusions.

Directions: Choose the best answer to each item.

Items 1 and 2 are based on the following paragraph.

A common idea in economics is the wage-price spiral. When union bargaining results in increased wages for workers, prices of products also go up. Corporations want to keep their profits steady. If wages go up, the increase in the cost of production is passed on to the consumer as an increase in the cost of the item. Since the company continues to profit, labor demands even higher wages. Again production costs go up and so does the price. The result is inflation. However, unions oppose limiting wage increases and companies do not want to limit price increases.

1. An economist who wanted to stop the wage-price spiral would probably be in favor of

(1) unionization
(2) higher profits
(3) government control of prices
(4) socialism
(5) price increases

2. According to the paragraph, if the wage-price spiral continues, the result will be

(1) good for the consumer
(2) lower profits for companies
(3) rising prices
(4) lower prices
(5) labor-management deadlocks

Item 3 refers to the following graphs.

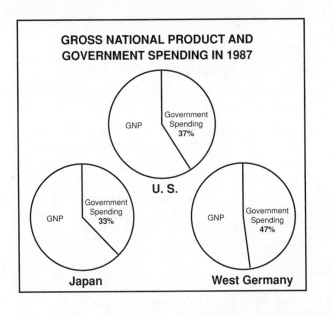

GROSS NATIONAL PRODUCT AND GOVERNMENT SPENDING IN 1987

GNP / Government Spending 37% — **U. S.**

GNP / Government Spending 33% — **Japan**

GNP / Government Spending 47% — **West Germany**

3. It can be concluded from the graphs that in 1987

(1) West Germany had a higher GNP than Japan
(2) the West German government spent less than the United States and Japan
(3) the United States had a higher GNP than Japan
(4) government spending was a main contributor to the GNP of these countries
(5) government spending does not affect the GNP of major countries

---

Items 4 and 5 refer to the following information.

Movement of the economy is classified by many different terms that explain the effects that wages, production, and cost-of-living expenses have on one another at a given time. Listed below are five of these terms and brief descriptions of the economic trends they indicate.

1. inflation—continuing rise in the prices of goods and services
2. demand-pull inflation—caused by a demand for goods that are in short supply
3. cost-push inflation—caused by a push for higher wages resulting in higher prices. Also called the wage-price spiral.
4. recession—production declines and people have less money
5. depression—severe reduction or slowing of business activity and cash flow

4. When an oil embargo was imposed in the 1970s, Americans had to wait in long lines on alternate days of the week to get fuel for their cars. The prices paid for this fuel demonstrate

(1) cost-push inflation
(2) demand-pull inflation
(3) inflation
(4) recession
(5) depression

5. In 1980 it cost more than $2.00 to purchase an item that had cost less than $1.00 in 1970. This is an example of

(1) demand-pull inflation
(2) cost-push inflation
(3) inflation
(4) depression
(5) recession

To check your answers, turn to page 164.

Items 6 and 7 refer to the following graph.

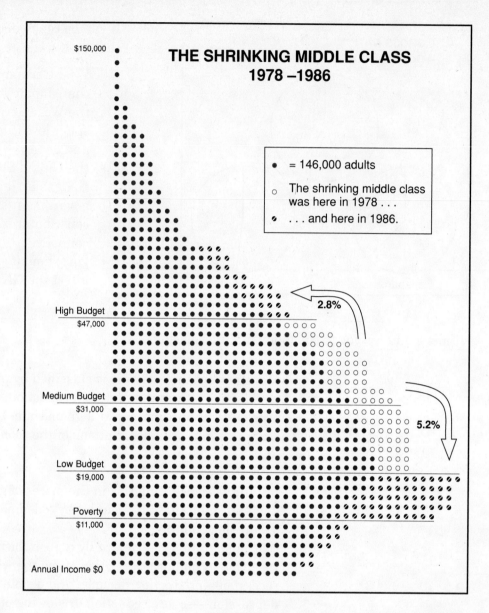

6. Which is a fact that can be determined from the graph?

   (1) People really want to get out of the middle class.
   (2) There is nothing wrong with living on a low budget.
   (3) Americans are going to have to get used to a lower standard of living.
   (4) Many people living below poverty level have to support families.
   (5) Fewer people were in the middle-class income range in 1986 than in 1978.

7. The information in the graph supports the conclusion that

   (1) the middle class is easily defined
   (2) the economy is seriously unstable
   (3) income is evenly distributed
   (4) the distribution of income is changing
   (5) the middle class is unsatisfied

Items 8 to 11 refer to the following paragraphs.

Congress has created several regulatory commissions that protect citizens from certain economic problems. Regulatory commissions make rules and come to decisions that affect banking, transportation, labor unions, communications, and other corporations. These commissions make rules about what businesses can and cannot do. They also help to settle disputes between opposing parties.

One of these commissions is the Federal Communications Commission, or FCC. The FCC licenses all radio and television stations. It decides how broadcasting wavelengths and channels are used based on whether "public convenience, interest, or necessity" is well served. If the FCC doesn't think that a station is operating for the public benefit, it can take away the station's license to broadcast.

When Congress establishes a commission, it makes sure that the commission is independent. The president is not allowed to fire commission members or chairpersons. In this way, Congress keeps the commissions from being pressured by political issues. Instead, the commission is free to act in the public interest.

8. A regulatory commission would probably rule in a dispute between

(1) a public-interest group and a toy manufacturer
(2) Congress and the president
(3) a TV station and an advertiser
(4) two political parties
(5) a supermarket and an employee

9. According to the paragraphs, Congress has assumed that a committee that is free of political pressure will

(1) listen more carefully to the president
(2) act only for the public good
(3) seek political support
(4) be reappointed
(5) not be independent

10. The information in the paragraphs supports the conclusion that

(1) most television stations follow the FCC's rules
(2) the FCC is the most powerful regulatory commission
(3) broadcast wavelengths have to be shared carefully so that stations do not overlap
(4) the FCC has the final say about what the public benefit is
(5) the FCC never makes an unfair ruling

11. What is the most likely reason that Congress formed regulatory commissions?

(1) Citizens had too much control over their economic lives.
(2) The economy was depressed.
(3) The president felt it was important.
(4) Certain businesses were sometimes operating against the public interest.
(5) Congress was overwhelmed by economic problems.

To check your answers, turn to pages 164 and 165.

Items 12 and 13 are based on the following table.

UNEMPLOYMENT AS A PERCENTAGE OF THE LABOR FORCE, 1929-1941	
Year	Unemployment
1929	3.2
1931	15.9
1933	24.9
1935	20.1
1937	14.3
1939	17.2
1941	9.9

Source: U.S. Department of Commerce

12. According to the table, unemployment was the worst during

(1) 1929
(2) 1933
(3) 1935
(4) 1939
(5) 1941

13. In order to draw an accurate conclusion about the effect World War II had on unemployment, you would need to

(1) use only the information given in the table
(2) know the dates for the Great Depression
(3) know when America joined the war
(4) understand the causes of the war
(5) have the total figure of the available labor force

Items 14 to 17 refer to the following paragraphs.

Massachusetts passed the first minimum-wage law in 1912 to guarantee decent pay for women and children in factories and retail stores. The action was taken because these two groups were paid such low wages that they could barely survive. The Fair Labor Standards Act was passed by Congress in 1938. This act called for a minimum wage of 25 cents per hour with an increase to 40 cents after seven years on the job. The federal minimum wage applies to most workers, with the exception of people who regularly receive tips. Workers such as waitresses, hairdressers, and taxi drivers can be legally paid less if their tips make up the difference.

Some states have their own minimum-wage laws, but those without their own use the federal figure. If a state's rate is lower than the federal rate, an employer in that state is required to pay the higher rate. In 1967, the minimum wage in most states was $1.00 and in some as high as $1.40. By 1981, the federal minimum wage had gone up to $3.35 an hour. During the early days of George Bush's presidency, Congress and the president argued over yet another increase. After much debate about what was reasonable, an agreement was reached, setting the new minimum at $3.80.

14. It can be inferred from the paragraphs that the minimum wage of $3.80 is

(1) unreasonable
(2) the final raise the minimum wage will have
(3) the federal rate
(4) the rate adopted by all states
(5) lower than the federal rate

15. The immediate effect of the first minimum-wage law was to

(1) force Congress to pass the Fair Labor Standards Act
(2) enable working women and children to survive
(3) set the rate for all other states
(4) draw women into the workplace
(5) eliminate children from the workplace

16. The exception to the minimum-wage law assumes that

(1) employers and employees will be able to agree on a fair wage
(2) Americans are good tippers
(3) waitresses and taxi drivers do not need as much money as other workers
(4) tips will not be considered income
(5) waitresses and taxi drivers are more honest than their employers

17. You could draw a conclusion about the reasons for increases in the minimum wage

(1) by looking at the figures shown in the paragraphs
(2) by looking at working conditions at the times of increase
(3) if you knew all the dates when the rate increased
(4) if you had figures about corresponding increases in the standard of living
(5) if you had figures about corresponding increases in the cost of living

---

Items 18 and 19 refer to the following cartoon.

"Made in Hong Kong! Made in Hong Kong! How can we compete with their cheap labor?"

To check your answers, turn to pages 165 and 166.

18. An appropriate government response to protect the U.S. economy in the situation pictured would be to

(1) increase sales taxes
(2) increase export quotas
(3) institute price controls
(4) increase import tariffs
(5) advertise "Buy American"

19. The most probable solution to the situation pictured in the cartoon is to

(1) buy more radios
(2) buy radios made in the U.S.
(3) buy radios made in Hong Kong
(4) avoid buying radios
(5) buy televisions instead of radios

Answers and Explanations

1. (Application) **(3) government control of prices** Outside control would have to be used to stop spiraling wages and prices. Option (1) is incorrect because unions would support increased wages. In order to have higher profits, option (2), manufacturers would have to charge higher prices. Option (4) is incorrect because socialism is an economic system that has nothing to do with the situation described in the paragraph. Price increases, option (5), would mean that workers would demand more money to pay for more expensive goods.

2. (Analysis) **(3) rising prices** As wages increase, prices rise. This situation means that the consumer has to pay more, so option (1) is incorrect. The increase in price is intended to prevent option (2). Option (4) is the opposite of the effect. There is no support for option (5).

3. (Comprehension) **(4) government spending was a main contributor to the GNP of these countries** For each country, government spending was close to or more than one third of the GNP. Options (1) and (3) are incorrect because no figures for the GNP are given. Options (2) and (5) are the opposites of the evidence.

4. (Application) **(2) demand-pull inflation** The scarcity of fuel caused prices to go up. There is no support for options (1), (3), (4), or (5).

5. (Application) **(3) inflation** Although the item remained the same, its cost more than doubled. The definitions for options (1), (2), (4), and (5) do not fit the example.

6. (Analysis) **(5) Fewer people were in the middle-class income range in 1986 than in 1978.** The broken circles indicate how the middle class has shrunk. Options (1), (2), and (3) are opinions. Option (4) is a fact but is not supported by the graph.

7. (Evaluation) **(4) the distribution of income is changing** The graph shows movement from the middle-class range to both higher and lower income levels. The range of income between low budget and high budget is so broad that option (1) is incorrect. There is not enough information to support options (2) or (5). Option (3) is the opposite of what the graph shows.

8. (Application) **(1) a public-interest group and a toy manufacturer** This answer follows from information in the paragraphs that regulatory commissions work for the general welfare of the consumer, represented by the public-interest group, when the consumer is being threatened by the manufacturer. Such a dispute might result from what parents believed to be a defective or hazardous toy. The disputes suggested in options (2), (3), (4), and (5) would be handled by other people, agencies, or a union.

9. (Analysis) **(2) act only for the public good** Political independence is believed to free the committee members to act in the public interest, not for private parties or political gain. There is no support for option (1). Options (3), (4), and (5) are all opposite to what is suggested.

10. (Evaluation) **(1) most television stations follow the FCC's rules** If stations do not follow the rules, they can lose their licenses. As stations are still in business, it can be concluded that they follow the rules. There is no evidence for option (2). Option (3) is true but is not supported in the paragraphs. There is not enough evidence to conclude either option (4) or (5).

11. (Analysis) **(4) Certain businesses were sometimes operating against the public interest.** This is an unstated cause that is implied by the nature of regulatory commissions. There is no support for options (1), (2), (3), or (5).

12. (Comprehension) **(2) 1933** The highest figure for unemployment was 24.9 in 1933. The figures for options (1), (3), (4), and (5) are all lower.

13. (Evaluation) **(3) know when America joined the war** Knowing that America joined the war in 1941 would allow a conclusion that the war lowered unemployment. Option (1) is not enough by itself. Options (2), (4), and (5) would not help in drawing a conclusion.

14. (Comprehension) **(3) the federal rate** The rate was set by Congress; therefore, this must be the federal minimum wage. There is no support for option (1). Option (2) is unlikely because the rate keeps going up as time passes. Option (4) is not suggested by the paragraphs. Option (5) is incorrect because $3.80 is the federal minimum wage.

15. (Analysis) **(2) enable working women and children to survive** The law was intended to provide at least survival wages for the groups that had been grossly underpaid. Option (1) is incorrect because the act came 26 years after the first minimum-wage law. There is no mention of other states' reaction, so option (3) is incorrect. There is no evidence of how the law affected the population of the workplace, so options (4) and (5) are incorrect.

16. (Analysis) **(1) employers and employees will be able to agree on a fair wage** Agreement on a fair wage would be necessary since tips can vary. There is no support for options (2), (3), or (5). Option (4) is incorrect because tips are regarded as income.

17. (Evaluation) **(5) if you had figures about corresponding increases in the cost of living** The cost of living is the only thing listed that could have a possible effect on increases in the minimum wage. Option (1) alone is not enough. Options (2), (3), and (4) would have no effect on the value of the minimum wage.

18. (Application) **(4) increase import tariffs** The government wants to protect American business, so the government will make it more difficult—that is, more expensive—to buy Hong Kong radios. Options (1), (2), and (3) would not affect the cost of goods coming into the United States. Option (5) is not an action that the government would take.

19. (Application) **(2) buy radios made in the U.S.** If more American radios were purchased, the problem faced by the businessmen pictured would not exist. Consumers would probably "buy American" if the prices were competitive with foreign merchandise. Option (1) is too general. Option (3) is the opposite of a reasonable solution. Options (4) and (5) are avoiding the problem rather than solving it.

Use the chart below to identify your strengths and weaknesses in each thinking skill area in the Economics unit.

Circle the number of each item that you answered correctly on the review.

Skill	Questions	Lesson(s) for Review
Comprehension	3, 12, 14	1, 2, 3, 5
Analysis	2, 6, 9, 11, 15, 16	6, 7, 8, 9, 10
Application	1, 4, 5, 8, 18, 19	4
Evaluation	7, 10, 13, 17	11

If you answered 16 or more items correctly, congratulations! You are ready to go on to the next section. If you answered 15 or fewer items correctly, determine which areas are most difficult for you. Then go back and review the lessons for those areas.

POLITICAL SCIENCE

Voting is a crucial part of a democratic political system.

- **government**
  the person or people who make the rules for a society

- **politics**
  the processes used in government

Human beings live in societies, which are groups of people with common interests. In any group of people, there are disagreements about how things should be done. To deal with the arguments between individuals and between parts of the group, most societies have organized ways to govern themselves. Usually there is a leader or group of leaders that make laws and have the authority to enforce those laws.

Political science is the branch of the social sciences that studies how a people governs itself. Included in this kind of study is how the **government** is organized, what the theories behind the government are, and how political ideas are actually practiced.

policies
plans that are used to manage people's affairs

politicians
the people who make political decisions

propaganda
one way people try to influence other people's decisions

Although we often use the word politics to refer to the competition between two or more groups of people, it has a more specific meaning. **Politics** is the part of government that deals with policy-making. **Policies** are the methods or plans that help people manage their affairs. **Politicians** are not just people who make long speeches; they are the ones who make the important decisions about how cities, states, and countries are run.

Topic 12 will introduce you to the general nature of political systems. You will learn about the basic role of government in a society and about the types of modern governments. You will also learn about the basis for the American political system and how it differs from other systems. In this lesson, the skill of recognizing fact and opinion will be reviewed because of its importance to the political process.

The political processes of the federal, state, and local governments in the United States is the subject of Topic 13. In this topic, you will learn details of the political system and how elections take place. An important part of the process is the voter and the rights of the voter. You will also read about how to recognize the faulty logic that is often used in propaganda. **Propaganda** is the way people try to influence other people to support or reject a cause or idea.

Topic 14 discusses the role of government in the general welfare of the nation. Government has a hand in how money is earned and spent, how business is run, and how the land is cared for. You will also review applying an idea that you read in one context to a different situation.

Topic 15 explains how the United States acts in today's world. The United States has a **foreign policy**, that is, a general method of dealing with other nations. You will also read about the United States' role in international organizations. Because social problems have become part of government's concern, you will learn how the United States treats some of its major social responsibilities. In this lesson, you will learn more about faulty logic and the problems it can cause.

☞ *See also: GED Exercise Book Social Studies, pages 36-46*

LESSON 12 Analysis Skill: Fact and Opinion

This skill reviews recognizing facts and opinions and being able to distinguish between them.

As you learned in Lesson 6, a fact is information about something that actually happened or actually exists. If you say to yourself as you are reading this book, "I am reading a book," you are stating a fact. You could add more information to the statement by saying, "I'm reading a lesson about political science in a book that teaches skills needed to pass the GED." You would still be stating a fact.

Opinions are individual interpretations of facts. You might tell a friend, "The political science unit is more interesting than the economics unit." This statement would be your opinion about the units. It is not a fact. Your friend might have a different opinion and say, "You just aren't reading closely enough. The economics unit is very interesting." Your friend would be expressing two opinions. The first is about your reading habits and the second is about the unit. Both opinions are based on the way your friend sees the facts. Opinions about facts are influenced by people's interests, by what people know about a subject, and by their experience with related facts.

Opinions help people to act on the facts they know. A news reporter might attend an important political demonstration. The reporter probably will take notes about what the demonstrators are doing, what their signs say about the issue, what the people are saying, and how the crowd reacts. The events that take place are all facts. But how the reporter presents the situation to the public will be influenced by how the reporter feels about the issue. If the reporter is in favor of what the demonstrators want, the news article will probably color the facts to make the demonstrators look good. If you watch that reporter's story on TV and you disagree with the demonstrators' side, you may decide not to believe what the reporter says. In these two cases, the news report is influenced by opinion and so is your reaction.

Political arguments are full of opinions. While the opinions are always about facts, they are not always based on sound reasoning. Remember that political opinions usually are presented as if they are facts. It is up to you to decide if the statements made can be proven or if they are only one person's judgment about events or ideas.

Practicing Analysis

Read the following paragraphs.

Governments help people organize their lives. Groups of people have goals and need to be able to agree on what actions to take in order to achieve those goals. It would take individuals much too long to achieve those goals alone. According to Abraham Lincoln, government should do the things that people cannot do for themselves.

Governments have four basic functions in a social system. First, a government takes the responsibility for making laws and enforcing them. The laws of a society reflect the general ways in which people expect everyone to behave. A law against theft means that stealing is not regarded as proper behavior. Second, a government can help to settle arguments between conflicting interests. It sets up a process to decide how a conflict will be resolved. The government acts somewhat as an umpire. Third, a government develops a system of plans and direction. It coordinates ideas into policies for the society. Fourth, a government deals with other governments. The political, economic, and military relationships and agreements between different countries are all handled through government agencies.

Questions 1 and 2 refer to the paragraphs. Circle the best answer for each question.

1. Abraham Lincoln's statement is

   (1) false
   (2) true
   (3) a fact
   (4) an opinion
   (5) out-of-date

2. The opinion that a government acts like an umpire is

   (1) not supported
   (2) supported by the fact that it settles disputes
   (3) supported by the fact that governments make laws
   (4) supported by the fact that governments make policies
   (5) supported by the fact that governments make economic agreements with other governments

To check your answers, turn to page 178.

Topic 12: Modern Government

Most of us take the idea of a nation for granted, but the complex organization of a nation-state is relatively new in the history of humanity. Most modern countries are not governed by family groups, religious groups, or business groups. Instead, most of today's governments are based on one or more basic political principles.

The first principle is that of **centralized government**. Political power used to be divided among military rulers, church authorities, and aristocrats. Over the years, the state took over the functions performed by all these groups. The central government also has the duty of making sure the young are educated and that the elderly are cared for. Trade, warfare, agriculture, scientific research, public transportation, and other social issues have also become the concern of government.

The second principle is that of **legal authority**. Under traditional rule, a leader was thought of as having power because his or her family had always been powerful. Under a legal system, a leader's power comes from the authority of the political office. It is based upon and permitted by law, not by family background. Citizens in a modern state expect the leader to govern according to the laws they have established.

The third principle is called **mass political participation**. Several hundred years ago, most political decisions were made by a small group of wealthy people. Today, people of all income levels can have a say in how the government is run. The leaders are chosen by the people and are expected to govern in the best interests of the citizens.

The three major types of government structures traditionally have been classified by the political principles they use to govern. **Authoritarian** governments are centralized, but they are not based on legal authority and are not supported by mass participation. The word of the leader, or small group of leaders, is the only law in an authoritarian government. Political opposition is not permitted. Idi Amin, the violent leader of Uganda, is a recent example of an authoritarian dictator.

Totalitarian governments are also centralized. However, their leaders usually do not have the same type of personal control as in authoritarian governments. In fascist totalitarianism, the dictator must have the support of the party leaders, and his power lasts only as long as he can maintain that support. Hitler and Mussolini are two examples of this type of power. Totalitarian governments such as the Soviet Union and mainland China do not have dictators. The single political party is the power that regulates all aspects of the citizens' lives.

Democracies are centralized, are run according to law, and their power lies in the hands of the people. The United States is an example of a democracy.

Exercises

Questions 1 to 4 refer to the information. Circle the best answer for each question.

1. An opinion is expressed in the passage about which of the following?

   (1) mainland China
   (2) the Soviet Union
   (3) democracy
   (4) Mussolini
   (5) Idi Amin

2. The descriptions about the three major government types are supported by

   (1) opinions about how well they work
   (2) opinions about the role of citizens in government
   (3) examples of political leaders in each type of system
   (4) facts about basic political principles
   (5) facts about the history of each type of government

3. Which conclusion has adequate support in the passage?

   (1) Government has changed over the years.
   (2) Principles of government have remained the same.
   (3) All governments have the same basic structures.
   (4) Military rulers no longer have any power.
   (5) Dictators are evil people.

4. If the single leader in an authoritarian government dies, what is the most probable effect?

   (1) The government continues as usual.
   (2) The government fails.
   (3) The people demand democracy.
   (4) The opposite political party comes to power.
   (5) The people elect a new leader.

To check your answers, turn to page 178.

Reviewing Lesson 12

Read the following paragraphs.

Power is the ability to control people's behavior. There are three basic ways to get power over people: through influence, through force, and through authority. Influence is a form of persuasion. People can be persuaded to do things by someone's personal appeal, by someone's social importance or wealth, by force of numbers, or by good organization. Force is based on making people do things against their will. Because physical force makes people afraid, they will do things they do not want to do. Authority is based on people's belief that those in power have the right to rule.

A stable government is based on what is called legitimate power. Legitimate power is considered proper and acceptable by the people who obey it. The power of a government comes from having a leader who has the authority to make decisions that the people will follow, even if they do not always agree with the decisions. Influence is not usually enough in itself to provide the power to govern. Force is called an illegitimate power. It does not have the consent or support of the governed people.

Questions 1 and 2 refer to the paragraphs. Circle the best answer for each question.

1. According to the paragraphs, the people's opinion is

    (1) not at all important
    (2) important to having legitimate power
    (3) easy to change
    (4) influenced by force
    (5) the basis for all types of power

2. In the 1970s, Nguyen Van Thieu ruled South Vietnam because of his military strength which was backed up by United States forces. When American troops were withdrawn in 1975, Thieu fell from power because the people did not support him. Thieu's regime can best be described as

    (1) influential
    (2) authoritarian
    (3) decisive
    (4) legitimate
    (5) illegitimate

To check your answers, turn to page 178.

Read the following information.

After the Constitution of the United States was written, it had to be approved by all the states. The dedicated men who were appointed to study the document read it carefully and discussed all of its points thoroughly. The following is one comment thought to have been made by Richard Henry Lee: "It is doubtful whether the Vice-President is to have any qualifications; none are mentioned; but he may serve as President, and, it may be inferred, he ought to be qualified therefore as the President; but the qualifications of the President are required only of the person to be elected President."

Questions 3 and 4 refer to the information. Circle the best answer for each question.

3. Which is an opinion held by Lee?

(1) The Constitution lists the qualifications for the presidency.
(2) The Constitution lists the qualifications for the vice-presidency.
(3) The Constitution does not list the qualifications for the vice-presidency.
(4) The Constitution should list the qualifications for the vice-presidency.
(5) The Constitution is wrong to say that the vice-president can serve as president.

4. Which of the following is a fact that can be determined from the information?

(1) The readers of the Constitution were dedicated.
(2) Not everyone was satisfied with the way the Constitution was written.
(3) The Constitution was perfectly written.
(4) It was a good idea to have all the states approve the Constitution.
(5) Richard Lee was being too critical of this historic document.

To check your answers, turn to page 179.

GED Mini-Test

Directions: Choose the best answer to each item.

Items 1 and 2 refer to the following paragraph.

Democracies, authoritarian governments, and totalitarian governments have different goals as well as different structures. The admirable goal of a democracy is to ensure freedom and dignity for individuals. The repressive goal of an authoritarian government is to maintain state control of the political thought and actions of individuals. The goal of a totalitarian government is for the state to control all parts of an individual's life, nonpolitical as well as political.

1. According to the paragraph, the writer thinks that

   (1) all governments are alike
   (2) authoritarian governments are best
   (3) totalitarian governments are best
   (4) democratic governments are best
   (5) the state should control the individual's life

2. If you lived under a totalitarian government, you probably could expect to

   (1) be able to choose the leader
   (2) be told where you could or could not travel
   (3) make your own choices about your career
   (4) educate your children in the manner of your choice
   (5) retire early

Items 3 to 6 refer to the following information.

The United States follows the Western concept of democracy. The emphasis is on the process of government, or how government works. In a democracy, the process of government is carried on by the people. There are four foundations for the process:
   a. following the rule of law;
   b. freedom of political activity;
   c. participation of the majority (the winners of an election) and the minority (the losers of an election) in the government; and
   d. belief in the democratic tradition, freedom of choice, and the acceptance of responsibility.
By following these guidelines, American citizens can pretty much rule themselves.

In fact, for Americans, democracy has become more than a political system. It has become a way of life. Liberty, human rights, and human dignity are now basic values. We expect to be able to choose our own way of doing things in day-to-day living. Because personal freedom is taken for granted by so many Americans, there is a danger of imposing our own values on someone else. One individual's choice might not be suitable for another person. Also, Americans must be aware that freedom of choice does not mean freedom to do anything that seems like a good idea. It must be remembered that living up to the democratic ideal requires that we all give up some degree of freedom in order to maintain the freedoms of our society as a whole.

3. The writer holds the opinion that freedom

   (1) has its responsibilities
   (2) is a natural right
   (3) is not really possible
   (4) is leading the country into danger
   (5) has no limits

4. Abraham Lincoln defined democracy as "of the people, by the people, and for the people." His summary of the process assumes that "the people" will

   (1) respect all reasonable laws
   (2) allow all people to have political freedom
   (3) encourage the people in power to respect the rights and needs of the people who are not in power
   (4) guarantee freedom of choice as long as it does not interfere with other people's freedom
   (5) do all of the above

5. John F. Kennedy's famous words, "And so, my fellow Americans, ask not what your country can do for you; ask what you can do for your country," are an appeal to citizens to

   (1) act as responsible citizens
   (2) pay their taxes on time
   (3) send a ten-dollar donation to the government
   (4) support his presidency
   (5) use social services

6. Public demonstrations like those against the war in Vietnam measure the force of public opinion because people must actively participate in a public action. However, such demonstrations do not indicate that

   (1) some people feel strongly about the issue
   (2) some people agree with government policy
   (3) there is dissatisfaction with government policy
   (4) Americans have the right to express their opinions
   (5) individuals will act publicly to express their opinions

To check your answers, turn to page 179.

Answers and Explanations

Practicing Analysis (page 171)

1. (Analysis) **(4) an opinion**
Even a belief held by an authority can be an opinion, not a fact. Therefore, option (3) is incorrect. Options (1) and (2) are incorrect because an opinion cannot be either true or false. It can only be supported or unsupported. Option (5) has no support.

2. (Analysis) **(2) supported by the fact that it settles disputes** Settling disputes is the role of an umpire, so this opinion is validly supported. Therefore, option (1) is incorrect. Options (3), (4), and (5) are not reasonable supports for the opinion.

Exercises (page 173)

1. (Analysis) **(5) Idi Amin** The Uganda dictator is called violent in the fifth paragraph. No opinions are expressed about options (1), (2), (3), or (4).

2. (Analysis) **(4) facts about basic political principles** Each description is based on how the principles fit into the government structure. There is no mention of opinions about how the systems work or about the citizens' role, so options (1) and (2) are incorrect. Option (3) is incorrect because examples are not given for all systems. No history of specific systems is mentioned, so option (5) is incorrect.

3. (Evaluation) **(1) Government has changed over the years.** The discussion of basic principles supports this conclusion. There is not enough support for options (2), (3), (4), or (5).

4. (Analysis) **(2) The government fails.** Because all the power was in that one person's hands, the government would be in chaos. Therefore, option (1) is incorrect. Option (3) might happen, but it is not a direct effect. Options (4) and (5) would not be direct effects in an authoritarian government because it has no political opposition or citizen participation.

Reviewing Lesson 12 (pages 174–175)

1. (Analysis) **(2) important to having legitimate power** Because people act on their opinions, they have the ability to support or overthrow a government; support is necessary for a legitimate government. Therefore, option (1) is incorrect. There is no support for options (3) or (5). Option (4) is incorrect because force does not depend on people's opinions.

2. (Application) **(5) illegitimate** Thieu's reign was based on the use of force, not on support of the people. Options (1), (2), and (3) do not fit the description. Option (4) is the opposite of what is described.

3. (Analysis) **(4) The Constitution should list the qualifications for the vice-presidency.** Lee apparently believed that the vice-presidency was such an important office that the qualifications should be mentioned specifically. Options (1) and (3) refer to facts about the Constitution. Option (2) is the opposite of what is mentioned in the information. The opinion in option (5) is not suggested by the quotation.

4. **(Analysis) (2) Not everyone was satisfied with the way the Constitution was written.** Lee's criticism supports this as a fact. Option (1) is an opinion stated in the information. Options (3), (4), and (5) are opinions that have no support in the information.

GED Mini-Test
(pages 176–177)

1. (Analysis) **(4) democratic governments are best** The preference is shown by the words "admirable goal." Therefore, option (1) is incorrect. There is no support for options (2), (3), or (5).

2. (Application) **(2) be told where you could or could not travel** Under a government that wants to control your life, freedom of movement would be limited. Options (1), (3), and (4) would be unlikely. There is no support for option (5).

3. (Analysis) **(1) has its responsibilities** This opinion is shown in the last sentence; therefore, option (5) is incorrect. There is no support for options (2), (3), or (4).

4. (Analysis) **(5) do all of the above** Lincoln's definition rests on the foundations listed in the passage. Option (1), (2), (3), or (4) alone is not the best assumption.

5. (Application) **(1) act as responsible citizens** This concept refers to the basic principles of a democratic society. "Fellow Americans" and "what you can do for your country" are clues. Options (2), (3), (4), and (5) are incorrect because no reference is made to them in Kennedy's quoted words.

6. (Application) **(2) some people agree with government policy** People who agree with government policy would not take part in a demonstration against it. A demonstration is based on the democratic principle of having freedom of political activity and taking responsibility for the expression of opinion. Therefore, options (1), (3), (4), and (5) are not good endings to the item's sentence.

LESSON 13 Evaluation Skill: Recognizing Faulty Logic

This skill helps you to recognize flaws, or errors, in reasoning.

When an argument is being presented, a person can often slip from a logical progression of ideas into statements that make no sense. Because these statements are often only one sentence, it is easy to overlook them. But it is very important to be aware of the existence of faulty logic. Statements of faulty logic will often look reasonable at first glance, but they are actually making an appeal to people's hearts instead of to their heads. It is up to the careful reader to find where reasoning has gone wrong.

One of the most common types of faulty logic is called a **hasty generalization**. A hasty generalization happens when someone makes a broad statement based on inadequate evidence. A friend might say that her children are better than any of her children's friends. She backs this statement up with these two examples: her children are polite and they always say thank you. There is not enough evidence for her generalization. The two qualities are good, but we do not know anything else about her children. She also has not said anything about her children's friends. Words such as all, none, never, and always signal hasty generalizations.

A more serious type of hasty generalization is the **stereotype**. You can recognize a stereotype if someone makes a generalization about a religious, ethnic, racial, political, or social group. A person who has seen a movie in which motorcycle riders are shown as irresponsible people might say, "Bikers are untrustworthy wanderers." That person is placing a stereotype on the whole group without taking into account all the motorcycle enthusiasts who have good jobs and solid family lives. These ideas are prejudices, not facts based on adequate evidence.

A related type of faulty logic is called **oversimplification**, which happens when two events are incorrectly linked as cause and effect. A common statement is that poverty causes crime. If that were true, then all poor people should be criminals. However, many poor people always obey the law. Also, if that statement were true, we would have to wonder why people who are not poor commit crimes.

Practicing Evaluation

Read the following paragraphs.

American government divides its governing power among three branches: legislative, executive, and judicial. Each branch is separate and independent of the others.

Legislative power to make laws is held by Congress which is made up of two parts. The Senate has two delegates from each state, and the House of Representatives has a number of delegates based on the population of each state. The Constitution gave Congress many important powers, including the power to tax, borrow money, regulate foreign and interstate trade, coin money and punish counterfeiters, establish a post office, and declare war. Congress as a whole has the right to make laws for the United States, but only the House of Representatives may initiate bills for raising money.

Executive power to enforce the laws is held by the president. He is also commander-in-chief of the armed forces. He can make Supreme Court appointments with Senate approval.

The Supreme Court and lower courts have judicial power to settle disputes or cases in courts of law. The Supreme Court has original jurisdiction, or first hearing, of cases involving conflicts between states or foreign diplomats. All other cases are first heard in lower courts, but may go to the Supreme Court on appeal.

Questions 1 and 2 refer to the paragraphs. Circle the best answer for each question.

1. Based on the information in the paragraphs, which statement about Congress is not logically sound?

   (1) Congress is given the power to make laws.
   (2) Congress has been given too many powers.
   (3) The Senate cannot initiate fund-raising bills.
   (4) All states have the same number of senators.
   (5) The number of representatives is probably different from the number of senators.

2. Based on the paragraphs, which is not true about President George Bush?

   (1) He holds executive power because he is the president.
   (2) Because he is the commander-in-chief, he can make decisions about the military.
   (3) He can enforce laws because he is the commander-in-chief.
   (4) Because he is president, he can select a judge for the Supreme Court.
   (5) He acts as the leader of his party because he is the president.

To check your answers, turn to page 188.

Topic 13: The American Political Process

A basic part of the political process in a democracy is the party system. While some democracies, such as France and Italy, have many political parties, the American system tends to be limited to two major parties with a small third or fourth party. Each party represents certain beliefs about important government issues. The policies that a party wants to support are called its **platform**.

The parties that we are familiar with have grown out of several others. The debate about the ratification of the Constitution led to the first two political parties in the United States. The **Federalists** supported the Constitution, but the **Anti-Federalists** wanted to make many changes before adopting it. George Washington was elected president in 1792 on the Federalist ticket. In 1796, Thomas Jefferson headed the **Democratic-Republican** party in opposition to the Federalists. This new party supported a loose interpretation of the Constitution and a strong central government. The election of 1828 saw Andrew Jackson from Tennessee winning as a **Democrat** and defeating the **National Republican** John Quincy Adams. The **Republican** party ran in 1856 and became a strong political force with the election of Abraham Lincoln in 1860.

Many minor parties have come and gone over the years. Often their names reflect the platform they promoted. You can easily guess what Free Soil, Greenback-Labor, Prohibition, Union Labor, Socialist, and States' Rights candidates stood for. The most recent enduring third party is the Independent party. Interestingly enough, third parties have never attained national power even though they influence the support of the two major parties.

Exercises

Questions 1 to 5 refer to the previous information. Circle the best answer for each question.

1. Which can be said about third parties in America?

    (1) Third parties fail because they have strange names.
    (2) Minority parties have no support.
    (3) Third-party members are really Socialists.
    (4) Third parties have no place in a two-party system.
    (5) Third parties tend to represent special interests.

2. Over the years, Americans have elected candidates from different parties because

    (1) Democrats are better than Republicans
    (2) Republicans are better than Democrats
    (3) it is the fair thing to do
    (4) the needs of the nation change
    (5) people can't make up their minds

3. The best explanation for the disappearance of the Anti-Federalist party is that

    (1) George Washington was a Federalist
    (2) Thomas Jefferson formed a better party
    (3) ratification of the Constitution was no longer an issue
    (4) the supporters became Federalists
    (5) it wanted to ruin the Constitution

4. According to the information, the real differences between each of the major political parties are in

    (1) their platforms
    (2) their names
    (3) their financial support
    (4) the success of their candidates
    (5) their interpretation of the Constitution

5. The Independent party has recently gained more supporters. Which is the most likely reason for people to vote the Independent ticket?

    (1) fear of taking a political stand
    (2) laziness
    (3) failing to register to vote
    (4) feeling the major parties do not offer solutions to important problems
    (5) indifference to politics

To check your answers, turn to page 188.

Reviewing Lesson 13

Read the following paragraph.

> In order to make sure that no one branch of government has too much power, the Constitution of the United States set up a successful solution. Under a rule called checks and balances, any one government branch can put a stop to certain actions of another. Even though only the Congress can make laws, the president has the power to veto, or say no to, these laws. And the Supreme Court can declare a law to be unconstitutional, therefore, not legally binding. The president is in charge of foreign affairs and the military, but Congress has to approve any money to be spent and the Senate can refuse to approve treaties with other countries. Even though the judges on the Supreme Court are independent and can hold the office for life, they must be initially appointed by the president and approved by Congress. Any judge who acts improperly can be impeached and removed from office.

Questions 1 to 4 refer to the paragraph. Circle the best answer for each question.

1. Which of the following is a hasty generalization about legal matters?

(1) The law is always right.
(2) The Supreme Court makes important decisions.
(3) Laws can always be questioned.
(4) United States laws should follow the Constitution.
(5) Proposed laws do not always get passed.

2. According to the paragraph, the system of checks and balances causes

(1) Congress to spend money
(2) The president to veto laws
(3) judges to be dismissed from office
(4) careful action by all three branches
(5) arguments between the president and Congress

3. Which is the best example of how the system of checks and balances works?

(1) The president refuses to approve a tax bill written by Congress.
(2) The Supreme Court makes a legal ruling.
(3) The president meets with Queen Elizabeth of England.
(4) The Senate approves a law the House does not like.
(5) A member of the Supreme Court dies.

4. Which word suggests an opinion about the system of checks and balances?

(1) unconstitutional
(2) independent
(3) successful
(4) certain
(5) legally

Read the following paragraph.

One way in which citizens can influence government decisions is by forming an interest group. The purpose of an interest group is to promote the concerns of its members. One of the methods interest groups use to achieve their goals is an old political tradition called lobbying, which means trying to persuade government leaders to favor certain causes. Lobbyists are at work at all levels of government, all across the country. One criticism of lobbyists is that they often represent an uneven section of the population.

Questions 5 and 6 refer to the paragraph. Circle the best answer for each question.

5. Which statement is a result of faulty logic?

   (1) Because lobbying is an old political tradition, it is the best way to get something done.

   (2) Because lobbyists represent many different groups, they may be in conflict with each other.

   (3) Lobbyists got their name from having to wait in lobbies.

   (4) A problem with special interest groups is that they do not represent the good of all the people.

   (5) Lobbyists want to influence politicians.

6. A lobbyist is a(n)

   (1) product of twentieth-century politics

   (2) politician

   (3) activist for a group's cause

   (4) lawmaker

   (5) government employee

Read the following paragraphs.

Local government provides many different services. Nearly one-third of all state and local revenue is spent on schools. Local government also offers police protection, road building and repair, sanitation, and public welfare services.

Local government is usually paid for by a property tax. The property tax is a percentage tax on real estate owned in the city or county. It yields a lot of money, is easy to collect, and can be raised to provide more revenue, if necessary.

Question 7 refers to the paragraphs. Circle the best answer for the question.

7. Homeowners bear much of the burden of supporting local government because

   (1) their children go to school

   (2) they can afford to pay high taxes

   (3) they get the most benefits

   (4) they own property that can be easily identified

   (5) they don't have to pay high rents

To check your answers, turn to pages 188 and 189.

GED Mini-Test

Directions: Choose the <u>best answer</u> for each item.

<u>Items 1 to 4</u> refer to the following paragraph.

According to the Constitution, the states are responsible for determining who can vote for president and vice-president of the United States. However, the Fifteenth Amendment (ratified in 1870) extended the right to vote to all men, regardless of race. The Nineteenth Amendment (1920) allowed women to vote. The Twenty-Third Amendment (1961) permitted District of Columbia residents to vote for the president. The Twenty-Fourth Amendment (1964) abolished the poll tax, while the 1965 Voting Rights Act abolished literacy tests for voter registration. The Twenty-Sixth Amendment (1971) lowered the voting age, nationwide, to eighteen. Many states still refuse to allow criminals and insane people to vote.

1. What would be the best logical argument for allowing criminals to vote?

   (1) Criminals have learned their lesson.
   (2) Criminals are still United States' citizens.
   (3) If they cannot vote, criminals will never learn to be responsible.
   (4) Criminals have learned a lot about the law.
   (5) Being able to vote will make criminals feel better.

2. Who would <u>not</u> have been allowed to vote in a presidential election?

   (1) a Yankee farmer in 1800
   (2) a Southern black sharecropper in 1860
   (3) a Southern woman in 1964
   (4) a District of Columbia resident in 1968
   (5) a traffic violator in 1984

3. What is the most likely effect of national legislation and Constitutional amendments on the right to vote?

   (1) Fewer people are allowed to vote.
   (2) There are increased restrictions on the right to vote.
   (3) Conservative people may now vote.
   (4) There are fewer restrictions on the right to vote.
   (5) More unqualified people are now allowed to vote.

4. What conclusion about the relative power of the federal and state governments can be drawn?

   (1) The federal government controls the state governments.
   (2) The state governments control the federal government.
   (3) The federal government has become more powerful.
   (4) The state governments have become more powerful.
   (5) There has been no change in the relative power.

General political attitudes can be described by a number of terms. A person who wants immediate and basic changes in the government is often called a radical. A person who believes that government programs can help to solve economic and social problems is called a liberal. Someone who feels that the federal government is too large and has too much control over the individual is often called a conservative. A reactionary is a person who wants things to return to the way they used to be. None of these terms imply a judgment about a person's beliefs. However, because these beliefs are in opposition to each other, people sometimes use the terms in a negative way as insults. There is nothing wrong with having any one of these attitudes.

5. Which of the following would <u>not</u> be an example of using a stereotype to criticize people with different beliefs?

(1) Liberals are ruining the country.
(2) Conservatives are ruining the country.
(3) Radicals have no sense of reality.
(4) Democrats often have liberal beliefs.
(5) Republicans are worse than reactionaries.

6. According to the paragraph, these political terms are

(1) positive facts
(2) descriptive of attitudes
(3) negative facts
(4) inaccurate
(5) insults

To check your answers, turn to page 189.

Answers and Explanations

1. (Evaluation) **(2) Congress has been given too many powers.** There is no way to judge if the powers listed are too many. The statement is a hasty generalization. Options (1), (3), and (4) are true according to the passage. Option (5) is a reasonable conclusion because state populations vary.

2. (Evaluation) **(3) He can enforce laws because he is the commander-in-chief.** This statement is an oversimplification of the president's duties, not a true cause and effect relationship. Options (1), (2), (4), and (5) all state real cause and effect relationships.

Exercises (page 183)

1. (Evaluation) **(5) Third parties tend to represent special interests.** This statement is supported by the names of the parties. Option (1) is an oversimplification with no support; the parties' names have nothing to do with success or failure. Option (2) is a generalization that ignores the fact that a party must have some support to exist. Option (3) is a broad stereotype that lumps all third parties together under a familiar name. Option (4) is incorrect because it ignores the role that third parties do play.

2. (Evaluation) **(4) the needs of the nation change** Americans select the party they believe will best serve whatever issues are important at the time. Options (1) and (2) are oversimplifications based on opinion. Options (3) and (5) are oversimplifications that link a political decision with ideas that have nothing to do with politics.

3. (Evaluation) **(3) ratification of the Constitution was no longer an issue** The reason for the party's existence vanished when the Constitution was adopted. Option (1) is incorrect because it did not matter which party Washington himself belonged to; what mattered was that the Federalist party received the strongest support. There is no support for the generalizations in options (2) or (4). Option (5) is a hasty generalization based on an unfounded opinion.

4. (Comprehension) **(1) their platforms** The primary differences between each party lie in their policies. Option (2) has nothing to do with their main differences. There is no evidence of options (3) or (4). Option (5) refers only to the first two parties.

5. (Analysis) **(4) feeling the major parties do not offer solutions to important problems** The only way to express dissatisfaction with the policies of both parties is to vote against them. Options (1), (2), and (5) would more likely result in not voting at all. Option (3) has nothing to do with choosing a party.

1. (Evaluation) **(1) The law is always right.** The legal basis for a law can be questioned: just because it is a law does not mean it is right. Options (2), (3), (4), and (5) are not hasty generalizations.

2. (Evaluation) **(4) careful action by all three branches** Members of each branch will act more carefully knowing that their actions can be criticized or reversed. Options (1), (2), (3), and (5) are all oversimplifications of what can happen because of the system.

3. (Application) **(1) The president refuses to approve a tax bill written by Congress.** The veto is an example of the ability of the president to check, or halt, the action of the legislature. Options (2), (3), and (4) refer to normal functions of each branch. Option (5) has nothing to do with the system.

4. (Analysis) **(3) successful** This word indicates an opinion about the system. Options (1), (2), (4), and (5) do not refer to judgments about the system but rather to supporting facts.

5. (Evaluation) **(1) Because lobbying is an old political tradition, it is the best way to get something done.** This is a hasty generalization that ignores the fact that tradition does not make something right. It also does not allow for other effective ways of achieving certain results. Option (2) is a reasonable inference. Options (3) and (5) are restatements of information in the passage. Option (4) is a conclusion that can be logically drawn from the passage.

6. (Comprehension) **(3) activist for a group's cause** This option rephrases the definition in the paragraph. Options (1), (2), (4) and (5) have no support.

7. (Evaluation) **(4) they own property that can be easily identified** Local governments need a source of revenue that is stable and easily discovered. Ownership is a matter of public record. Options (1), (2), and (3) are hasty generalizations based on insufficient evidence or unfounded opinions. Option (5) is an over-simplification that links two unrelated ideas.

GED Mini-test (pages 186–187)

1. (Evaluation) **(2) Criminals are still United States' citizens.** Voting has come to be regarded as the right of all adult citizens. Options (1) and (4) have nothing to do with the right to vote. The cause and effect implied in option (3) is faulty. The cause and effect in option (5) has nothing to do with the criminals' qualifications as responsible voters.

2. (Application) **(2) a Southern black sharecropper in 1860** The dates show that black men were not allowed to vote until 1870. Options (1), (3), (4), and (5) all refer to eligible voters.

3. (Analysis) **(4) There are fewer restrictions on the right to vote.** This is a restatement of the main idea that as the years have gone by, more and more people have been allowed to vote for president. Options (1), (2), (3), and (5) do not apply.

4. (Comprehension) **(3) The federal government has become more powerful.** The paragraph tells you that the states were originally responsible for determining who could vote for president and vice president. General knowledge tells you that amendments and acts are enforced by the federal government, so you can conclude that the federal government has become more powerful. Options (1), (2), (4), and (5) are not supported.

5. (Evaluation) **(4) Democrats often have liberal beliefs.** This statement does not imply a criticism. It also is based on the observation that Democrats tend to support federal programs. Options (1), (2), (3), and (5) are all hasty generalizations that have no factual basis; the only purpose they serve is to show disapproval with no examination of evidence.

6. (Analysis) **(2) descriptive of attitudes** The terms describe four general opinions about political policy. Options (1) and (3) are incorrect because there is nothing positive or negative about the terms. Option (4) is incorrect because a term is inaccurate only if it is applied to the wrong person. Option (5) is incorrect because a term can be an insult only if it is misunderstood by the speaker and the listener.

LESSON 14 Application Skill: Using Ideas in a New Context

This skill reviews using what you already know in a new situation.

In Lesson 4, you were introduced to the skill of application. Remember that to apply an idea means to make a connection between the situation where you first learned it and another similar situation.

Sometimes the idea is first presented in a general way. If you understand the general idea, you can apply it to a specific example. You have read about the system of checks and balances and know that a bill can be vetoed by the president. On the news, you hear that Congress has approved a bill to raise the salaries of senators and representatives. You also hear that the president does not approve of the proposed law. Based on what you already know, you can predict that the bill might not become law because the president will veto it.

Sometimes you will learn about an idea through a specific example. You then read about another situation. You decide that the two situations are similar and that the idea in the first can be used in the second. You might read about one law that was declared by the Supreme Court to be unenforceable because it was unconstitutional. Then you hear about another law that cannot be enforced. You can apply your knowledge about the cause of the first decision and determine that the problem with the second law is that it probably is not supported by the Constitution. You have applied the analysis skill of cause and effect to decide about an event in another context.

When applying ideas, you are also using all your other reading skills. You need to be able to identify and understand main ideas, draw conclusions, and make inferences. You will also need to use the processes of analysis and evaluation.

Practicing Application

Read the following paragraphs.

Sometimes a law made under one set of circumstances is repealed or altered when those circumstances change. This type of Congressional decision often takes place when the law affects the economy of the nation or the nation's major businesses.

A clear example of such a change is the law that set standards for automobile fuel efficiency. Because of a 400 percent increase in the price of oil in 1973, the United States made a move to decrease the amount of energy used. In 1975, auto manufacturers were required by law to improve the fuel use of their new cars to 27.5 miles per gallon by 1985. However, in 1986, after the oil crisis was over and fuel was much cheaper, the National Highway Traffic Safety Administration agreed to reset the standards at 26 miles per gallon for 1987 and 1988 cars.

The change came about because General Motors and Ford claimed that reaching the higher standard would mean lowered production of their large cars. The decrease would mean that tens of thousands of workers would be laid off. The two companies were not going to be able to meet the requirements for 1986, 1987, or 1988 cars. This failure would result in over $600 million in fines.

Questions 1 and 2 refer to the paragraphs. Circle the best answer for each question.

1. In 1988, many failing savings and loan institutions were given government funds to bail them out. The reason for this probably was to

   (1) protect both the savers and the businesses
   (2) balance the economy
   (3) counteract the fall in the price of oil
   (4) protect government investments
   (5) obey the current laws

2. If the government agency had not lowered the standard for 1987, which probably would have happened?

   (1) 1988 cars would have used less fuel per gallon.
   (2) The manufacturers would have hired more workers.
   (3) There would have been more large cars on the market.
   (4) The manufacturers would have been in financial trouble.
   (5) Fuel prices would have gone up.

To check your answers, turn to page 198.

Topic 14: Government Money and the General Welfare

In a capitalist system, there will always be people who find themselves in financial trouble. A single parent may be unable to manage a full-time job because there is no one to take care of the children. The head of a household may suddenly become unemployed because employers are laying off workers or requiring workers to have more skills or training. The savings from a lifetime of working might not be enough to support a person during retirement. Parents might not be able to afford to send their children to college. Whole towns can be shattered by a natural disaster such as a tornado. The government has stepped in to help in situations like these by setting up social welfare programs under the supervision of various federal agencies.

Some programs affect all Americans, and some programs are designed for special groups. The following agencies and programs are used by many Americans at one time or another.

1. **Social Security**—a federal insurance plan that pays benefits to retired persons or their spouses, based on their income while working

2. **Veterans Administration**—provides people who have served in the armed forces with money for education, job training, and hospital care, as well as special rates for housing loans and life insurance

3. **Department of Housing and Urban Development**—provides funding for rental housing for low-income families, the handicapped, and the elderly; it also provides funds for rehabilitating urban areas

4. **Food Stamp Program**—issues food stamps to individuals and families having temporary or serious long-term financial difficulties

5. **Medicare**—pays for some or all medical costs for a U.S. citizen of 65 or over who has worked long enough to qualify for Social Security benefits

6. **Unemployment Insurance**—pays weekly cash benefits to unemployed workers who have lost their jobs involuntarily. Benefits usually last for up to 26 weeks and may be continued for another 13 weeks in cases of severe economic need.

Exercises

Questions 1 to 4 refer to the previous information. Circle the best answer for each question.

1. William Foster, a 40-year-old who fought in Vietnam, has quit his job in a small town and moved with his family to a large city. His wife has found a good job, but William has discovered that he needs more skills to be hired at a local factory. William's best course of action would be to apply to the

    (1) Department of Housing and Urban Development
    (2) Food Stamp Program
    (3) Social Security Program
    (4) Unemployment Insurance Program
    (5) Veterans Administration

2. David Honda, a construction worker for 45 years, died recently. His wife, Wanda, had worked only a few years, spending most of her time taking care of the children. David's son, Harley, has advised his mother to apply for government benefits. Harley probably told her to contact the

    (1) Department of Housing and Urban Development
    (2) Food Stamp Program
    (3) Social Security Program
    (4) Unemployment Insurance Program
    (5) Veterans Administration

3. Mark Mostwise has operated his own business since he was 30. Even though he just turned 68, he is still active in the company. Mark has been receiving treatment for severe headaches, but his insurance will not cover all the costs. Mark should see if he can get help from the

    (1) Food Stamp Program
    (2) Medicare Program
    (3) Social Security Program
    (4) Unemployment Insurance Program
    (5) Veterans Administration

4. The automobile parts company that Pete Hoyt worked for laid him off. Another company will probably hire Pete in a few weeks. In the meantime, Pete should apply for benefits from the

    (1) Food Stamp Program
    (2) Medicare Program
    (3) Social Security Program
    (4) Unemployment Insurance Program
    (5) Veterans Administration

To check your answers, turn to page 198.

Reviewing Lesson 14

Read the following paragraph.

> The government gets the money to pay for its programs in two ways: taxes and borrowing. The main source for the national treasury is the federal income tax. All Americans who make over a minimum income pay a part of it to the government. The Department of the Treasury borrows money from citizens by selling bonds or treasury notes. In return for the use of the money spent on a bond, the Treasury pays the citizen a set interest.

Questions 1 and 2 refer to the paragraph. Circle the best answer for each question.

1. Which is most likely to happen if the government spends more money on all of its programs?

    (1) Income taxes will go down.
    (2) Taxes will increase.
    (3) Americans will have to earn more money.
    (4) People will buy more bonds.
    (5) The Treasury will stop paying interest on bonds.

2. According to the paragraph, government programs are

    (1) free
    (2) paid for by the citizens
    (3) not dependent on the citizens
    (4) paid for with the interest from bonds
    (5) supported mainly by borrowed money

Question 3 refers to the information. Circle the best answer for the question.

> The Jenkins-Archer Bill proposed cutting the tax rate for capital gains from 28 to 19.6 percent. A capital gains tax is a national tax on the money made from the sale of personal property. The House Leadership Bill proposes raising the tax rate for the wealthy and reintroducing tax breaks for Individual Retirement Accounts.

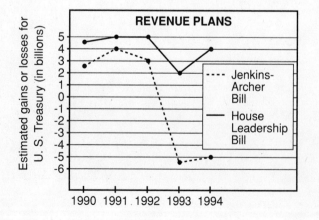

3. The Jenkins-Archer plan would most likely be supported by

    (1) high-income people
    (2) middle-income people
    (3) lower-income people
    (4) farmers
    (5) businesspeople

To check your answers, turn to page 198.

Look at the following graph.

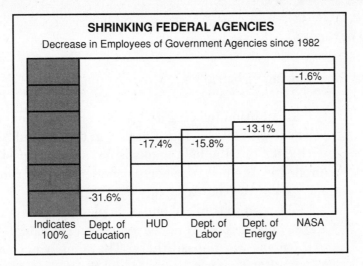

SHRINKING FEDERAL AGENCIES
Decrease in Employees of Government Agencies since 1982

	-1.6%
	-13.1%
-17.4%	-15.8%
-31.6%	

| Indicates 100% | Dept. of Education | HUD | Dept. of Labor | Dept. of Energy | NASA |

Questions 4 and 5 refer to the following bar graph. Circle the best answer for each question.

4. Based on the graph, you could most likely expect

(1) fewer teachers working for the government
(2) a decrease in interest in space travel
(3) no government interest in natural resources
(4) more public housing
(5) few scientists hired by the government

5. Which <u>cannot</u> be concluded from the graph?

(1) Government is cutting back on spending in federal agencies.
(2) The Department of Education has lost more employees than several other agencies.
(3) NASA has lost a few employees.
(4) Education is doing so well that it doesn't need help.
(5) The attitude toward some federal agencies has changed in the past few years.

Read the following paragraph.

The government announced that it will not release funds for highway construction to New York City unless air pollution standards are met by a specified date. New York City insists it must have the highway.

Item 6 refers to the paragraph. Circle the best answer.

6. What trend can you foresee for the city?

(1) easier automobile inspections
(2) more limits on car exhaust emissions
(3) less emphasis on public transportation
(4) more campaigning for industrial parks
(5) expanding the Lincoln Tunnel

To check your answers, turn to pages 198 and 199.

GED Mini-Test

Directions: Choose the best answer to each item.

Items 1 to 4 refer to the following paragraphs.

In addition to being able to coin money, Congress has some power to protect the use of money in the United States. The power to charter, or establish, banks is not specifically stated, but it is implied by the power to borrow money and to transfer funds from one part of the country to another.

We tend to think of banks as places where we have checking and savings accounts and where we can get loans. But what happens to the money we deposit there? That money does not simply sit in a vault. Banking is a business and the money needs to be used if a bank is to stay operative. Therefore, banks lend money to other people and businesses in exchange for interest.

In order to protect the use of money that people deposit in commercial banks, Congress wisely set up the Federal Reserve System (FRS) in 1913. The Federal Reserve System supervises commercial banks, checking their books and controlling their interest rates. Banks are supposed to be members of the FRS and keep a minimum amount of funds deposited in one of the twelve Federal Reserve banks.

1. If you are looking for a place to put your money, you should be sure that the institution you go to

   (1) is a member of the Federal Reserve System
   (2) keeps its money in the vault
   (3) doesn't lend out money
   (4) gives premiums for new accounts
   (5) makes good commercials

2. One national problem that you can probably expect the Federal Reserve System to be concerned about is

   (1) acid rain
   (2) inflation
   (3) drug abuse
   (4) child care
   (5) poverty

3. Which is an opinion expressed in the paragraphs?

   (1) Banks are supposed to join the Federal Reserve System.
   (2) There are twelve Federal Reserve banks.
   (3) Banks charge interest on loans.
   (4) Congress acted wisely.
   (5) Congress coins money.

4. Which conclusion can be drawn from the information in the paragraphs?

   (1) Bankers are trustworthy.
   (2) A role of government is to protect the people.
   (3) Interest rates are too high.
   (4) Members of Congress are interested only in money.
   (5) Moneylenders are greedy.

Items 5 and 6 refer to the following table.

'Rather Astronomical'

Loose lending policies at the Farmers Home Administration have led to huge losses that taxpayers will have to cover.

	Loan Losses*	Repossession Expenses	Total Losses
ALL FIGURES IN BILLIONS OF DOLLARS			
1990	$4.5	$1.9	$6.4
1991	$6.3	$1.8	$8.1
1992	$6.0	$1.7	$7.7

Total $22.2

* PRINCIPAL AND INTEREST.
ADMINISTRATION AND NEWSWEEK ESTIMATES.

SOURCES: FARMERS HOME

---

5. In order to solve the problem of loan losses, the Farmers Home Administration (FHA) should probably

   (1) lend even more money
   (2) lend more carefully
   (3) charge higher interest
   (4) repossess farms more often
   (5) stop lending altogether

6. Which proverb should the Farmers Home Administration have kept in mind?

   (1) Neither a borrower nor a lender be.
   (2) Money is the root of all evil.
   (3) Waste not, want not.
   (4) A penny saved is a penny earned.
   (5) Home is where the heart is.

To check your answers, turn to page 199.

Answers and Explanations

Practicing Application (page 191)

1. (Application) **(1) protect both the savers and the businesses** The passage suggests that the government changed a standard in order to protect the jobs of citizens and to keep businesses from paying crippling fines. This same idea underlies financial support of other private businesses such as the savings and loans. There is no support for options (2), (3), (4), or (5).

2. (Application) **(4) The manufacturers would have been in financial trouble.** The loss of the market for large cars, the firing of employees, and the payment of fines would have meant money problems for the companies. Options (1), (2), and (3) are the opposite of what would have happened. Option (5) has nothing to do with the agency's decision.

Exercises (page 193)

1. (Application) **(5) Veterans Administration** William needs further job training, offered by the VA. Option (1) provides housing and would not solve the problem. William would not qualify for options (2) or (4) because his wife has a good job and he left his job voluntarily. William is too young for option (3).

2. (Application) **(3) Social Security Program** Wanda is eligible to receive benefits from her husband's Social Security contributions. Because there is no evidence that Wanda needs housing or help with food money, options (1) and (2) are incorrect. Wanda is not eligible for help from options (4) or (5).

3. (Application) **(2) Medicare Program** Because Mark is over 65, he might be eligible for some medical benefits. Option (1) does not apply. Mark is not retired or unemployed, so options (3) and (4) are incorrect. There is no evidence that Mark was a veteran, so option (5) is incorrect.

4. (Application) **(4) Unemployment Insurance Program** Because Pete did not quit, he is eligible for unemployment insurance. There is no information about Pete's financial need, so option (1) is incorrect. Pete is probably not over 65, so options (2) and (3) are incorrect. There is no evidence that Pete was in the service, so option (5) is incorrect.

Reviewing Lesson 14 (pages 194–195)

1. (Application) **(2) Taxes will increase.** The main source of government income would be the most likely to increase. Option (1) is the opposite of what would happen. Option (3) has no support. The government's need for money would not necessarily encourage people to buy bonds, so option (4) is incorrect. Option (5) is incorrect because that would discourage people from buying bonds and so decrease the government's income.

2. (Comprehension) **(2) paid for by the citizens** Both sources of government income come from the citizens. The paragraph does not support options (1), (3), (4), or (5).

3. (Application) **(1) high-income people** High-income people would be the most likely to sell expensive property; they also would pay higher taxes under the other bill. The Jenkins-Archer bill would not be as beneficial for options (2), (3), (4), and (5).

4. (Application) **(1) fewer teachers working for the government** Teachers, who would logically be hired in the Department of Education, would find fewer positions available. Options (2), (3), and (5) are incorrect because the number of NASA and Department of Energy employees has not gone down much. If option (4) were correct, there would be more employees working for HUD.

5. (Evaluation) **(4) Education is doing so well that it doesn't need help.** This is a hasty generalization that is not supported by evidence in the graph. Options (1), (2), (3), and (5) are all supported by the evidence in the graph.

6. (Application) **(2) more limits on car exhaust emissions** From the information given, New York City has two choices: provide its own money or comply with the air pollution standards. Stricter controls on car exhaust emissions would help to meet the air pollution standards. Option (1) would probably increase air pollution by allowing cars that pollute the air to continue to operate. Option (3) would probably increase air pollution by causing more people to use private transportation like cars, which pollute. Option (4) would increase pollution because industry, even when regulated, always sends some pollution into the air. Option (5) would probably increase pollution by bringing more cars into the city.

GED Mini-Test (pages 196–197)

1. (Application) **(1) is a member of the Federal Reserve System** Membership in the FRS means that your deposit is insured. Options (2) and (3) are not very good bank policies. Options (4) and (5) have nothing to do with the safety of your money.

2. (Application) **(2) inflation** The concern of the FRS is money. Options (1), (3), and (4) refer to problems that are not financial. Although option (5) refers to lack of money, it is a social problem that would not concern the monetary system itself.

3. (Analysis) **(4) Congress acted wisely.** This is a judgment about the action taken by Congress, not a fact. Options (1), (2), (3), and (5) are all facts.

4. (Evaluation) **(2) A role of government is to protect the people.** The entire passage is about a government agency that protects the people's monetary interests. Options (1), (4), and (5) are unfounded stereotypes. Option (3) is an opinion with no support.

5. (Application) **(2) lend more carefully** If loose policies were the cause, then lending should be looked at more carefully. Options (1), (3), (4), and (5) would only make things worse.

6. (Application) **(3) Waste not, want not.** This answer is based on understanding the initial mistake made by the agency. The agency wound up wasting money on poor credit risks and so found itself with losses. The logical connection is between waste and want. Option (1) is incorrect, because the FHA is supposed to help the farmer. Options (2) and (5) have nothing to do with the problem. Option (4) is incorrect because the problem is not with saving but with poor judgment.

LESSON 15 Evaluation Skill: Identifying Faulty Logic

This skill helps you recognize errors in the way in which facts or ideas are presented.

When a person or group is trying to persuade you to buy a certain product or to support a certain idea, the facts are presented in such a way that it makes the product or idea look good. This use of selected facts is called **propaganda**. Some of the techniques used in propaganda are based on faulty logic, or errors in thinking.

In Lesson 13, you read about two errors that can occur in logical reasoning. There are several other ways facts can be misrepresented or even avoided. Two of these are the circular argument and the self-contradiction. A **circular argument** simply restates an idea in different words; that is, the argument winds up back where it started. A person might say, "Not wearing a motorcycle helmet is dangerous because it is unsafe." Unsafe means the same thing as dangerous. The argument does not explain what is unsafe about not wearing a helmet. It does not provide any new information. A **self-contradiction** occurs when two ideas that cannot happen at the same time are used together anyway. You might hear someone say the following: "Lee won't learn how to manage his money until he has spent every cent he has." The statement is self-contradictory because Lee cannot learn to manage his money if he has already spent all of his money.

A third type of faulty logic used in propaganda is called a **red herring**. A red herring transfers the reader's attention from a political issue to an unrelated issue that appeals to the emotions. Political campaigns are littered with red herrings. One candidate might distract attention from the opponent's stand on an economic issue by bringing up a question about the person's family life. The two issues have nothing to do with each other. When John F. Kennedy was running for President, some people argued that he should not be president because he was Catholic. Being Catholic, Protestant, or Jewish has nothing to do with a person's qualifications as a political leader.

Yet another misleading statement is called the **either-or error**. An either-or error sets up only two choices when others actually exist. There was a time when young women were told, "Either get married and raise children or be a failure as a woman." Such a statement implies that marriage is the only way that a woman can be successful.

Practicing Evaluation

Read the following paragraphs.

In June of 1990, the United States showed its support of international civil rights by honoring a visit from Nelson Mandela, a black South African. Mandela was imprisoned for years by the government of South Africa for speaking out against apartheid, the rigid separation of blacks and whites. Mandela now speaks worldwide against the South African white population's domination of black Africans. During his tour, there was discussion of whether the United States' sanctions against the South African government should be lifted.

A sanction is a political measure intended to deny trade with another country in order to protest a policy of that country. American sanctions against South Africa have cost that government over 10 billion dollars of income since 1985. The suggestion for doing away with the sanctions came about because the South African President has repealed a few of the restrictions applying to black citizens. Many Americans objected because they felt that lifting sanctions could slow the momentum of reforms in South Africa.

Questions 1 and 2 refer to the paragraphs. Circle the best answer for each question.

1. Which would be the best argument for continuing the sanction against importing South African wine?

    (1) There are too many drunken drivers on the road.
    (2) California wine is better.
    (3) Wine contains more alcohol than beer does.
    (4) South Africans are insensitive people.
    (5) Any import would suggest support of apartheid.

2. According to the passage, apartheid is wrong because it

    (1) is a bad policy
    (2) denies people their civil rights
    (3) costs the government too much money
    (4) is a serious mistake
    (5) offends many Americans

To check your answers, turn to page 206.

Topic 15: The United States and Foreign Policy

Every nation is affected by what happens in the rest of the world. A nation's behavior toward other nations is called its **foreign policy**. American foreign policy has developed over the years, based on changes in the world and in the nation itself. Because of the geographic position of the United States and its economic, political, and military strength, the United States now plays a major role in international affairs.

At first, the citizens of the United States believed that they were far enough from Europe and Asia that they could simply grow as a country without being concerned with the troubles of other nations. Washington and Jefferson even warned Americans to be wary of "permanent and entangling alliances." The concept of freedom from a superior power formed the basis for the country's initial foreign policy. For over one hundred years, **isolationism**, or separation from other countries, was the policy supported by Americans. Nonetheless, as the United States grew and established trade with other nations, it gradually became involved in world affairs.

Even within the framework of an isolationist policy, the United States developed policy for dealing with other countries. The Monroe Doctrine of 1823 warned European countries that interference in American affairs was not welcome. Because of industrialization, the end of the nineteenth century saw the beginning of the Open Door Policy. Communication and trade was encouraged between the United States and China and any other interested nations.

World War I ended America's policy of isolation. Citizens realized the importance of a political commitment to the rest of the world. In 1933, President Franklin D. Roosevelt established the Good Neighbor Policy which supported the right of Latin American countries to develop their own governmental systems without foreign interference. In 1947, President Harry Truman introduced the Marshall Plan and the Truman Doctrine. The Marshall Plan helped war-torn Europe to rebuild economies after the destruction of World War II. The Truman Doctrine stated that the United States would help any government that requested support against Communist influence.

Exercises

Questions 1 to 6 refer to the information. Circle the best answer for each question.

1. The statement that United States foreign policy has always been one of complete isolation or complete involvement is best disproved by the

   (1) Monroe Doctrine
   (2) Open Door Policy
   (3) Good Neighbor Policy
   (4) Marshall Plan
   (5) Truman Doctrine

2. The recent changes in the attitudes of major Communist nations and their friendliness toward the West show that

   (1) Communists will never change
   (2) Communists are good liars
   (3) communism no longer works
   (4) communism may no longer be a major threat
   (5) Communists are very friendly

3. America finally became seriously involved in world affairs because

   (1) it had been too isolated before
   (2) ignoring the world had been easy
   (3) it had to honor its political commitments
   (4) it had to be involved or be destroyed
   (5) Americans try to be the best that they can be

4. For years, China had been seen as a Communist opponent of the United States. In 1972, however, President Nixon visited that country and reopened diplomatic relations. This action was most closely related to the

   (1) Monroe Doctrine
   (2) Open Door Policy
   (3) Good Neighbor Policy
   (4) Marshall Plan
   (5) Truman Doctrine

5. The government of South Vietnam had asked for help against a Communist guerilla movement based in North Vietnam. The policy that led to the United States' involvement in the Vietnam war was the

   (1) Monroe Doctrine
   (2) Open Door Policy
   (3) Good Neighbor Policy
   (4) Marshall Plan
   (5) Truman Doctrine

6. Even though Germany's economy was ruined during World War II, it became very strong in the 1970s and 1980s. One reason for this recovery was probably the

   (1) Monroe Doctrine
   (2) Open Door Policy
   (3) Good Neighbor Policy
   (4) Marshall Plan
   (5) Truman Doctrine

To check your answers, turn to page 206.

Reviewing Lesson 15

Read the following paragraph.

The student commandos struck at dawn. They diverted police by tossing homemade bombs, then rapidly scaled the eight-foot wall surrounding the residence of Donald Gregg, the newly arrived U.S. ambassador to South Korea. Awakened by what sounded like fire-crackers, Gregg and his wife listened behind a locked bedroom door as the students smashed furniture, lamps and pottery with iron bars, doing about $30,000 worth of damage. "We oppose U.S. trade pressure!" they shouted. "Punish Gregg!" To keep police at bay, the students doused the floor with lighter fluid and threatened to set it alight. Finally, after evacuating the Greggs through a back door, police broke down the main entrance, firing tear gas as they charged. Six students were hauled away, including one who was draped in a South Korean flag. "I am interested in having dialogue with anyone who wants to talk," said the ambassador later in the day. "But I didn't see any opportunity for dialogue this morning."

Questions 1 and 2 refer to the paragraph. Circle the best answer for each question.

1. The students' cry of "Punish Gregg!" is not justified because they were confusing

   (1) Gregg with somebody else
   (2) the ambassador with the policies they resented
   (3) the South Korean police
   (4) America with South Korea
   (5) violence with protest

2. According to the paragraph, the role of a United States' ambassador is to

   (1) confront student protesters
   (2) call the police when violence erupts
   (3) talk to people in other countries
   (4) incite riots
   (5) keep the peace

Read the following paragraph.

Foreign aid is money, goods, and services given to another country. Sometimes foreign aid is offered with no strings attached, as when a country suffers a natural catastrophe like an earthquake. Sometimes foreign aid is offered in exchange for something. For example, a country might be offered a missile system and defense training in exchange for U.S. rights to establish and operate a naval base in that country.

Question 3 refers to the paragraph. Circle the best answer.

3. Which proverb would a critic choose to justify her criticism of using foreign aid as part of U.S. foreign policy?

   (1) Do not look a gift horse in the mouth.
   (2) Money cannot buy friends.
   (3) Birds of a feather flock together.
   (4) A bird in hand is worth two in the bush.
   (5) A stitch in time saves nine.

Look at the following cartoon.

"WHADDAYA MEAN 'IT'S EXTINCT!'?!"

Questions 4 and 5 refer to the cartoon. Circle the best answer for each question.

4. To which opinion is the cartoonist referring?

   (1) The army lives in the dark ages.
   (2) The military should not see Communists as the enemy.
   (3) Dinosaurs are not really extinct.
   (4) President George Bush is wrong.
   (5) The military uses outdated weapons.

5. If the speaker in this cartoon wanted to defend his position, which would be the most illogical thing he could say?

   (1) "It can't be extinct because it exists."
   (2) "Where's the proof?"
   (3) "How should we act now?"
   (4) "Was it our military strength that defeated it?"
   (5) "We'll wait to see if that's true."

Read the following paragraph.

   The United States is a charter member of the United Nations (UN), an organization that works for international cooperation. Since its founding in 1945, the membership of the United Nations has more than doubled. Most new members are small, developing third-world nations.

Question 6 refers to the paragraph. Circle the best answer.

6. The increase in membership has probably led to

   (1) strengthening of the international power of the U.S.
   (2) greater public awareness
   (3) more disagreement between the U.S. and other UN members
   (4) withdrawal of the U.S. from the UN
   (5) U.S. refusal to continue to host UN headquarters in New York City

To check your answers, turn to page 207.

Answers and Explanations

Practicing Evaluation (page 201)

1. (Evaluation) **(5) Any import would suggest support of apartheid.** This is the only politically sound argument. Options (1), (2), (3), and (4) are all red herrings.

2. (Evaluation) **(2) denies people their civil rights** This is the only real criticism listed. Options (1), (4), and (5) are examples of circular arguments that do not explain anything. Option (3) is a red herring that refers to an issue that is not related to the morality of the problem.

Exercises (page 203)

1. (Evaluation) **(3) Good Neighbor Policy** This policy neither supports staying away nor being involved. It advocates a country's right to establish its own government. Options (1), (2), (4), and (5) indicate more involvement.

2. (Evaluation) **(4) communism may no longer be a major threat** Friendly relations reduce the possibility of threat. Option (1) is a self-contradiction. Options (2) and (3) are red herrings because they transfer the reader's attention to an unrelated emotional issue. Option (5) is a circular argument.

3. (Evaluation) **(3) it had to honor its political commitments** This is stated in the second sentence of the last paragraph. Options (1) and (2) are circular arguments. Option (4) is an either-or error that ignores other possibilities. Option (5) is a red herring that appeals to a patriotic nature but is without a factual basis.

4. (Application) **(2) Open Door Policy** A renewed relationship suggests a willingness to deal with the other country rather than regard it only as an enemy. Options (1), (3), (4), and (5) do not apply.

5. (Application) **(5) Truman Doctrine** This policy supported aid to any nation fighting against a Communist influence. Options (1), (2), (3), and (4) do not apply.

6. (Application) **(4) Marshall Plan** This plan helped European countries to restore their economies. Options (1), (2), (3), and (5) do not apply.

1. (Evaluation) **(2) the ambassador with the policies they resented** The students were following the faulty logic of the red herring. The ambassador does not make policies. Options (1), (4), and (5) do not refer to the confusion of the students. Option (3) does not apply.

2. (Comprehension) **(3) talk to people in other countries** This conclusion can be drawn from Gregg's comment. Options (1), (2), (4), and (5) have no support.

3. (Application) **(2) Money cannot buy friends.** The paragraph implies that foreign aid is used to encourage allies. A critic of the use of foreign aid would assume that money could *not* buy allies. Options (1), (3), (4), and (5) would not support that critic's view.

4. (Analysis) **(2) The military should not see Communists as the enemy.** This opinion is suggested by the idea that communism as a target no longer exists. Even though the images are of cavemen, they do not support options (1) or (5) because it's really the idea of Communists as the enemy that is outdated. Option (3) is incorrect because the reference is not really to dinosaurs. There is not enough evidence for option (4).

5. (Evaluation) **(1) "It can't be extinct because it exists."** This statement is a circular argument that opposes the cartoonist's main idea that communism is no longer the enemy. Options (2), (3), (4), and (5) would be reasonable things to say.

6. (Analysis) **(3) more disagreement between the U.S. and other UN members** This is correct because the policy of the U.S. as a major superpower is likely to be different from the foreign policies of many small developing nations. Option (1) is inaccurate because the increase in the number of members dilutes the power of the U.S. Option (2) is irrelevant. Options (4) and (5) are incorrect based on general knowledge.

Review: Political Science

In this unit, you have reviewed two important reading skills that you need in order to understand the political world. In addition, you have gone further in understanding how to evaluate what you have read and how to make judgments about the logical basis of the information.

Directions: Choose the best answer to each item.

Items 1 to 4 refer to the following paragraph.

A special type of political leader can emerge in any of the basic political structures. These leaders have an extraordinary quality called "charisma." The force of such individuals' personalities is enough to inspire entire countries to follow them. Revolutions are often led by charismatic figures who appear to represent the principles of the revolt. Some famous charismatic leaders were the visionary Joan of Arc, France's Napoleon, the Nazi leader Hitler, India's gentle Ghandi, Mao of China, England's Churchill, and Cuba's Castro.

1. An opinion expressed by the writer of the paragraph is that

    (1) Joan of Arc said she had visions
    (2) Napoleon was from France
    (3) Hitler was a Nazi
    (4) Ghandi was gentle
    (5) Churchill was English

2. The best example of a stereotype is that charismatic leaders

    (1) have a special quality
    (2) are all revolutionaries
    (3) often represent revolutionary principles
    (4) can occur in any political system
    (5) are inspirational

3. The writer makes the assumption that

    (1) revolutions are necessary movements
    (2) the political figures listed will be familiar
    (3) having charisma is good
    (4) all revolutions have inspiring principles
    (5) the readers already know what charisma is

4. According to the paragraph, the power of certain leaders comes from their

    (1) willingness to sacrifice themselves
    (2) brilliant speeches
    (3) military leadership
    (4) government
    (5) characters

Items 5 and 6 are based on the following 1905 cartoon.

A GROWING MENACE

5. The main idea of the cartoon is that the American voting system was

    (1) working only on the national level

    (2) being abused at all levels

    (3) working only on the municipal, or city, level

    (4) supported by the will of the people

    (5) working only on the state level

6. Which is the most logical statement that might be used in an argument about the cartoon?

    (1) If people aren't paid, they won't vote.

    (2) We should not worry about the corruption of the voting system because the United States was founded as a democracy.

    (3) A purchased vote probably does not represent the opinion of the voter.

    (4) Buying votes is wrong because you have to pay for them.

    (5) Political corruption won't end until we put a stop to it.

To check your answers, turn to page 214.

7. Terrorism is the use of terror as a political weapon. Violent acts are used to force governments to conform to terrorist demands. Often terrorists operate in countries other than their own. Which of the following acts of violence could <u>not</u> be described as an act of terrorism?

(1) A Lebanese guerilla drives a truck armed with explosives into the American embassy in Beirut.
(2) An Irish girl, at the request of her Syrian boyfriend, carries a package of explosives onto a Pan Am airplane.
(3) The American ambassador to Afghanistan is abducted and shot in a hotel.
(4) A peaceful protester is critically injured in a demonstration against nuclear power plants in North Dakota.
(5) A Greek cruise ship is hijacked in the Mediterranean and an American is shot.

8. In 1965 President Lyndon Johnson created Medicare, a program that offers health insurance for the elderly. Currently the financial benefits for this program are no longer enough to insure adequate care for the eligible citizens. It can be concluded that

(1) the government no longer cares about the elderly
(2) there has been a rapid decline in the number of elderly citizens
(3) there has been a dramatic increase in the number of elderly citizens
(4) citizens should have a medical checkup yearly
(5) no one can rely on government programs

Items 9 and 10 refer to the following table.

THE TOP DOZEN STATES IN PROJECTED LOTTERY
Sales this year and how much revenue the states are expected to receive (in millions of dollars)

State	Gross Sales	Revenues
California	2,150	731
New York	1,688	756
Pennsylvania	1,511	N/A
Massachusetts	1,500	430
Ohio	1,455	530
Illinois	1,360	540
New Jersey	1,194	510
Michigan	1,050	420
Florida	890	312
Maryland	889	391
Connecticut	510	225
Arizona	250	82

Source: Handbook of Lottery Operations & Statistics, Public Gaming Research Institute, Inc.

9. Which statement has adequate support in the table?

(1) Lotteries provide enough revenue for the states that use them.
(2) Lotteries may supply millions of dollars in revenue for some states.
(3) Only twelve states operate legal lotteries.
(4) California has the best lottery system.
(5) States now have to rely on lotteries for their revenue.

10. It can be concluded from the table that gross sales of lottery tickets are usually

(1) at least twice the amount the states get as revenue
(2) the same in all states
(3) lowest in the Midwest
(4) higher than those of the previous year
(5) higher in Ohio than in Massachusetts

11. One clause in the Constitution of the United States reads, "The Congress shall have power to . . . provide for the common defense . . . of the United States." This clause has been used to justify

(1) ratification of treaties
(2) increases in bureaucracy
(3) growth of the economy
(4) government welfare programs
(5) building the Stealth Bomber

12. Poor people are more in favor of social welfare than rich people. Laborers are more in favor of Medicare and Medicaid than business owners. Executives are more in favor of tax shelters than clerical workers. These statements show that political opinions reflect

(1) self-interest
(2) union viewpoint
(3) educational training
(4) sex
(5) job status

Items 13 and 14 refer to the following map.

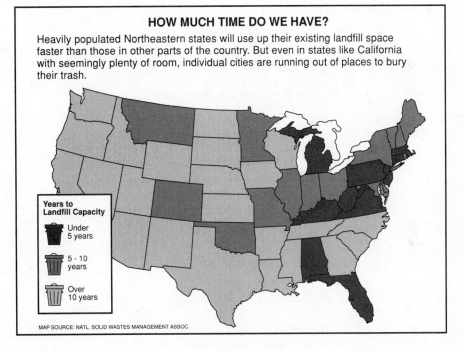

HOW MUCH TIME DO WE HAVE?

Heavily populated Northeastern states will use up their existing landfill space faster than those in other parts of the country. But even in states like California with seemingly plenty of room, individual cities are running out of places to bury their trash.

Years to Landfill Capacity

Under 5 years
5 - 10 years
Over 10 years

MAP SOURCE: NATL. SOLID WASTES MANAGEMENT ASSOC.

---

13. Which inference is supported by the information in the map?

(1) The United States government is responsible for this unfortunate situation.
(2) State and city governments should start looking for solutions immediately.
(3) Eastern states have been very irresponsible about their trash.
(4) Westerners do not produce much trash.
(5) Trash should be outlawed.

14. The predictions suggested by the map assume that

(1) Americans will continue to produce a certain level of trash each year
(2) everyone uses the same size trash can
(3) landfills are very effective for trash disposal
(4) people will recycle more
(5) there is no government control of the problem

To check your answers, turn to pages 214 and 215.

Items 15 and 16 refer to the following cartoon.

15. FICA are the initials used for Social Security deductions. The cartoon is implying that FICA deductions are

(1) a very small part of the average paycheck
(2) a large part of the average pay-check
(3) the same as income tax
(4) going to be raised
(5) going to be cut

16. Capital gains tax is a government tax on the sale of personal property. What process of faulty reasoning is the speaker on the TV using?

(1) Don't worry about the taxes you already pay. We are proposing a tax cut that probably won't affect you.
(2) Tax payers should pay more taxes so the government can cut them again.
(3) This tax cut will help some homeowners.
(4) All taxpayers are confused by the IRS.
(5) A tax break will really raise your taxes.

17. The Agency for International Development is responsible for foreign aid programs. Much of the food the agency sent to Africa and Asia to feed political refugees and people in famine areas rotted on the docks or in warehouses before it reached people who were starving. The most effective response of the Agency for International Development would be to

(1) send more food
(2) spray all foods with preservatives
(3) offer technical assistance in food distribution
(4) send money instead of food
(5) refuse to send foreign aid to countries suffering from famine

18. At the time of the 1980 Moscow Olympic games, the USSR had sent invasion troops to Afghanistan. President Jimmy Carter decided that a withdrawal of United States teams from the international games would be powerful evidence of United States

(1) disapproval of the Soviet action
(2) military strength
(3) athletic superiority
(4) acceptance of the Soviet action
(5) inability to compete

Items 19 to 22 refer to the following information.

Below are five major international political organizations.

1. United Nations (UN)—It is made up of a General Assembly, where most nations of the world send delegates; and a Security Council, where delegates of the five major powers (the U.S., France, Great Britain, the USSR, and the People's Republic of China) meet.
2. North Atlantic Treaty Organization (NATO)—North American and Western European nations joined to protect themselves and each other from an armed attack against any member nation.
3. Eastern European Mutual Assistance Treaty (EEMAT)—The USSR joined the Eastern European bloc nations in the Soviet bloc's equivalent of NATO. It is also called the Warsaw Pact.
4. Organization of American States (OAS)—Twenty-eight North and South American countries joined to defend each other.
5. European Community (EC, or the Common Market)—Western European nations joined to abolish trade barriers for a free movement of goods, services, and capital within the EC.

19. The Cuban Missile Crisis of 1962 involved the construction of Soviet-backed missile bases on the island of Cuba. Initially, the United States filed a complaint with an organization that represented the U.S. and Cuba. It ordered that the bases be disbanded. Cuba refused to cooperate and was expelled from which of the following?

(1) The UN Security Council
(2) NATO
(3) the EEMAT
(4) the OAS
(5) the EC

20. If Spain were militarily threatened by the USSR, it would most probably ask for aid from

(1) The UN Security Council
(2) NATO
(3) the EEMAT
(4) the OAS
(5) the EC

21. France and the Netherlands want to make a new agreement about taxes on imports and exports. They will probably negotiate through

(1) The UN Security Council
(2) NATO
(3) the EEMAT
(4) the OAS
(5) the EC

22. If the USSR felt threatened by a Western European nation, it would probably turn for military aid to

(1) The UN Security Council
(2) NATO
(3) the EEMAT
(4) the OAS
(5) the EC

To check your answers, turn to pages 215 and 216.

Answers and Explanations

1. (Analysis) **(4) Ghandi was gentle** This is a judgment that cannot be proven as a fact. Options (1), (2), (3), and (5) are all facts that can be proven.

2. (Evaluation) **(2) are all revolutionaries** That some of the most famous charismatic leaders were indeed leaders of revolutions does not mean that all were. Options (1), (3), (4), and (5) are all reasonable statements based on the information given.

3. (Analysis) **(2) the political figures listed will be familiar** In using these people as examples of charismatic leaders, the writer assumes that they will be recognized. There is no evidence that the writer assumes options (1), (3), or (4). Option (5) is incorrect because charisma is explained in the paragraph.

4. (Comprehension) **(5) characters** This generalization is a restatement of given information. Options (1), (2), and (3) may be true but are not specified in the paragraph. There is no mention of the role of government in the paragraph, so option (4) is incorrect.

5. (Comprehension) **(2) being abused at all levels** The ballot box for all three levels is stuffed with purchased votes. Therefore, options (1), (3), and (5) are incorrect. Option (4) is incorrect because Uncle Sam is shown as dropping the labeled paper.

6. (Evaluation) **(3) A purchased vote probably does not represent the opinion of the voter.** A purchased vote represents only the desire of the politician who bought it. Option (1) is an either-or error that suggests that there is only one reason for voting. Option (2) is a red herring that leads away from the issue to an unrelated idea. Options (4) and (5) are circular arguments.

7. (Application) **(4) A peaceful protester is critically injured in a demonstration against nuclear power plants in North Dakota.** This is correct because the protester is not acting in a violent manner. Instead, the paragraph states that the action is peaceful, although politically directed. Options (1), (2), (3), and (5) are all examples of violent political action.

8. (Comprehension) **(3) there has been a dramatic increase in the number of elderly citizens** This is the only logical conclusion. In the last few decades, medical advances plus a better standard of living have led to an increase in the number of elderly citizens. There is no support for options (1) or (5). Option (2) is the opposite of what is true. Option (4) is an opinion with no support in the paragraph.

9. (Evaluation) **(2) Lotteries may supply millions of dollars in revenue for some states.** The figures support this conclusion. Options (1), (3), (4), and (5) are not supported by enough information.

10. (Comprehension) **(1) at least twice the amount the states get as revenue** This is true for all twelve states, according to the figures given. The figures are different for all states, so option (2) is incorrect. Options (3) and (5) are not supported by the figures. Option (4) is incorrect because the only figures given are for projected sales.

11. (Application) **(5) building the Stealth Bomber** The bomber would be justified as a military expense necessary for defense of the country. Options (1), (2), (3), and (4) are not related to defense.

12. (Analysis) **(1) self-interest** Each group is influenced by its own needs. Options (2) and (5) refer to only one of the examples. Options (3) and (4) have nothing to do with the question.

13. (Evaluation) **(2) State and city governments should start looking for solutions immediately.** Landfill use is regulated by state and city governments, so they need to think about what to do when the space runs out. Options (1) and (3) are incorrect because the information in the map does not indicate who is responsible for the problem. Option (4) is incorrect because the amount of trash produced is not indicated; however, it is suggested that the West has more space to use. Option (5) is a red herring that ignores the problem.

14. (Analysis) **(1) Americans will continue to produce a certain level of trash each year** The figures are based on the idea that the problem will remain constant. Option (2) has nothing to do with the predictions. Option (3) is incorrect because soon landfill space will no longer be available. There is no support for options (4) or (5).

15. (Comprehension) **(2) a large part of the average paycheck** The size of the FICA deduction suggests this idea. Therefore, option (1) is incorrect. Option (3) is not suggested—the two are clearly different. There is no mention of what is going to happen to FICA deductions, so options (4) and (5) are incorrect.

16. (Evaluation) **(1) Don't worry about the taxes you already pay. We are proposing a tax cut that probably won't affect you.** The speaker is using a red herring technique to distract the taxpayer from what he actually has to deal with. The speaker is not suggesting option (2). Option (3) is probably true, but it is not the problem with the speaker's statement. Option (4) is a common stereotype but is not suggested by the speaker. Option (5) is self-contradictory but is not suggested by the speaker.

17. (Application) **(3) offer technical assistance in food distribution** This would be the best way to get food to the people who need it. Option (1) would add to the problem. Option (2) would be of only minor help. Option (4) would not guarantee that the money went for food. Option (5) would defeat the purpose of the organization.

18. (Analysis) **(1) disapproval of the Soviet action** Refusal to participate in a friendly competition would be a sign of disapproval. Therefore, option (4) is incorrect. Options (2), (3), and (5) would not be the causes of such an act.

19. (Application) **(4) the OAS** This is correct because the OAS is the organization that deals with interests in North and South America. Although Cuba is a member of the UN General Assembly, it does not qualify for membership in the Security Council; therefore, option (1) is incorrect. Cuba has never qualified for membership in options (2), (3), or (5).

20. (Application) **(2) NATO** Spain would be within its rights to ask for protection against a nonmember. Option (1) would not be immediately available to Spain. Spain would not be a member of options (3) or (4). Option (5) is an economic organization.

21. (Application) **(5) the EC** This is the only economic organization available to these countries. Options (1), (2), (3), and (4) would not handle this type of discussion.

22. (Application) **(3) the EEMAT** As the Eastern equivalent of NATO, the EEMAT would support its member. Option (1) would be correct only if the countries wanted to negotiate; the UN Security Council would not provide military aid. Options (2) and (4) would not be available to the USSR. Option (5) is an economic organization.

Use the chart below to identify your strengths and weaknesses in each skill area in the Political Science unit.

Circle the number of each item that you answered correctly on the review.

Skill	Questions	Lesson(s) for Review
Comprehension	4, 5, 8, 10, 15	1, 2, 3, 5
Analysis	1, 3, 12, 14, 18	9, 10, 12
Application	7, 11, 17, 19, 20, 21, 22	14
Evaluation	2, 6, 9, 13, 16	13, 15

If you answered 17 or more items correctly, congratulations! You are ready to go on to the next section. If you answered 16 or fewer items correctly, determine which areas are most difficult for you. Then go back and review the lessons for those areas.

Pueblo Indians participate in a ritual summer Corn Dance.

♦ **anthropology**
the study of the development of human culture

Scholars in the behavioral sciences study people in several ways. One way is to look at how people act as members of cultures. Another way is to observe how people act in smaller groups such as family, work, religious, and social groups. A third way is to look at how people behave as individuals. Each of these views is studied by specialists trained in human behavior. The areas studied cover **anthropology**, **folklore**, **psychology**, and **sociology**.

Anthropologists study both the physical and social development of human beings over the centuries. Some anthropologists concentrate on **ethnology**, a branch of anthropology that studies the processes that lead to the unique social life of a particular society at a particular time.

- **folklore**
  the study of people's beliefs and traditions

- **psychology**
  the study of how individuals think and feel

- **sociology**
  the study of how people behave in groups

Folklorists are more concerned with people's beliefs and traditions. Folklore studies cover many things from fairy tales to traditional building techniques to recipes that have been handed down through the generations.

Psychologists are interested in the way people's minds work. They look at and analyze the differences between normal and abnormal behavior.

Sociologists look at the relationship between individuals and society. Unlike psychologists, who study people's inner lives, sociologists are concerned more with group behavior.

In Topic 16, you will see how cultures in general work and why some cultures of human beings seem so different from others. As you read about various cultures, you will be asked to look at their values, or what is important to them.

Topic 17 will concentrate on the behavior of smaller groups and individuals. In this topic you will practice recognizing the importance of people's beliefs.

☞ *See also: GED Exercise Book Social Studies, pages 47-54*

LESSON 16 Evaluation Skill: Recognizing Values

This skill helps you to recognize the things that social groups feel are important to them.

Societies are held together by sharing things called values. **Values** are the goals and ideals that make life meaningful. Values include what people think is important, good, beautiful, worthwhile, and holy. Understanding values helps us understand why people act as they do. Human beings often make decisions about what to do in certain situations based on their values. They also use their values to make judgments about experiences they have and people they meet.

All societies and cultures have values, but the specific values vary from group to group. These differences sometimes make one group seem very strange to another group. For example, as you read in Unit 2, Americans value freedom, especially freedom of the individual. We also value success, especially when success is the result of hard work. We admire the "self-made" man or woman. On the other hand, Americans tend to feel a bit uneasy about inherited wealth. We even sometimes look down on individuals who did not earn their money. However, in Europe, many people still admire the nobility, the old families who passed power and money down from generation to generation. In this case, personal success is valued less than the history of the family.

You can often determine a group's values by looking at the way people act or the laws they set up about behavior. For example, a small Illinois farm town had a law that pigs were not allowed to wander loose in the streets. The citizens had nothing against pigs; in fact, most families had them. But the town placed a high value on cleanliness, and the law helped keep the streets clean. In fact, Americans as a whole value cleanliness. We are taught to bathe frequently and insist that children wash behind their ears. Even TV advertisements reflect that value by promoting toothpaste, soap, and household cleaning products.

As you try to discover other people's values, be sure that you do not judge them on the basis of your own. Values are not really right or wrong.

Practicing Evaluation

Read the following paragraph.

Cultural values sometimes make life a little awkward. Two sets of values can come into conflict with each other. For example, a mainland artist was hired to go to Alaska to paint murals and teach art classes in several isolated towns. Mr. Lee spent several months in each town, living in what rooms the townspeople could supply. Because they could not afford to pay Lee much, he was offered free meals, eating with a different family each night. The families all thought that having the artist as a guest was an honor. To express that feeling, they served their very best meal. In most of these towns, pot roast was regarded as an expensive treat, hard to get because beef usually had to be flown in by small planes. So night after night, each family served Mr. Lee the very best meal, pot roast. In town after town, Mr. Lee ate pot roast. When one family offered him a dinner of whale blubber, he was delighted. When Mr. Lee finally returned home and visited his mother, she served him pot roast. Mr. Lee, claiming that the airplane flight had made him feel ill, skipped dinner that night.

Questions 1 and 2 refer to the paragraph. Circle the best answer for each question.

1. The families who fed Mr. Lee probably spent more money than usual on his meal. The Alaskan townspeople clearly place high value on

   (1) self-sacrifice
   (2) being better than their neighbors
   (3) showing guests that they are welcome
   (4) serving nutritious meals
   (5) getting to know a guest's tastes

2. During all the months of eating pot roast, Mr. Lee did not complain. By continuing to eat the families' meals, he was demonstrating

   (1) that he really loved pot roast
   (2) that he had an iron stomach
   (3) respect for his elders
   (4) respect for his hosts
   (5) disrespect for his own values

To check your answers, turn to page 228.

Topic 16: People as Members of Cultures

All people of the world grow up in a culture. A **culture** is the sum of the knowledge, beliefs, arts, morals, laws, and customs of members of a society. Because each society's culture is determined by its physical environment and the makeup of its people, no one culture is exactly like any other. Each culture develops its own values. Societies that are near each other and exchange goods and residents will have many similarities, but they will each have special characteristics.

For many years, cultural behavior was thought to be biologically determined; that is, the way people acted was thought to be inherited like hair color or bone structure. In the early twentieth century, anthropologists Margaret Mead and Ruth Benedict did studies that supported the idea that culture was instead a learned way of behaving. They also said that each culture's behavior as a whole reflected a general personality for that group.

Within a particular culture, children learn what is expected of them. Children find out that there are acceptable and unacceptable ways of behaving. They learn that there are rules of conduct that govern how a person should think and act. Most of these rules are so old that we do not even think about them. We simply know that certain actions are right, at least, right in the eyes of the people we live with.

Some customs of one culture may look very strange to the members of another culture. However, customs that might seem to have no reason actually have functional bases. According to one anthropologist, all customs come from a way of fulfilling an emotional or biological need of the society. A general example of this idea is that a belief in magic is a way to explain things that cannot be explained by looking at facts. More specific ways of behaving are also influenced by culture. In most Christian societies, women wear hats or veils to church. The cultural background for such action lies in the Biblical statement that a woman's hair is her crown of glory and should be covered when worshipping in church. Another example can be seen in Asian children, trained from infancy to have an unquestioning respect for their parents and their ancestors and to uphold the reputations of their families.

Exercises

Questions 1 to 6 refer to the information. Circle the best answer for each question.

1. Women wearing hats in church are expressing a cultural value that can best be stated as

   (1) a person should be humble when worshipping
   (2) fashion is very important
   (3) women should not be jealous of each other's hairstyles
   (4) all women are vain
   (5) women are not as good as men

2. In the past few years, many of the winners of academic contests have been the American children of Asian parents. These children have studied very hard because they have been taught the value of

   (1) showing respect for their families' reputations
   (2) education as a means to success
   (3) winning contests
   (4) obeying rules
   (5) being right

3. According to the information, cultural values are

   (1) inherited
   (2) learned
   (3) the same in all societies
   (4) similar
   (5) unimportant

4. According to the information, customs are developed because

   (1) everyone believes in magic
   (2) emotional and biological needs have to be fulfilled
   (3) the Bible has set out cultural rules
   (4) life would be strange without them
   (5) children have to be taught something

5. Which of the following is most likely to be a custom among traditional Japanese?

   (1) Even after marriage, one son lives with his parents until they die.
   (2) Children leave home at age eighteen.
   (3) Old people are sent to live in the mountains.
   (4) Young children are sent to live with relatives until grown.
   (5) Children are not allowed to visit their grandparents.

6. The most likely reason that Alaskan Eskimos developed a culture which might seem strange to other people is that

   (1) Eskimos are strange people
   (2) they never came in contact with other people
   (3) they had to wear heavy furs all the time
   (4) their harsh environment made certain behavior necessary
   (5) they were the only Indian groups to remain in the North

To check your answers, turn to page 228.

Reviewing Lesson 16

Read the following paragraphs.

A recent study by a Harvard-educated sociologist born in India sought to explain why poor people in India tend to have large families. As one illiterate laborer said, despite the fact that he has no land and very little money, he considered his eight children to be his greatest wealth. He says, "It's good to have a big family. They don't cost much and when they get old enough to work, they bring in money. And when I am old, they will take care of me."

Because this is a view that millions of Indians share, it represents a major obstacle in the effort to curb the rapid growth of India's population. The report states, "People are not poor because they have large families. Quite the contrary, they have large families because they are poor."

Some of the reasons that poor people are reluctant to reduce the size of their families relate to social customs that the Indian government is trying to abolish. The dowry system, for example, often forces a couple to try to produce sons to offset the economic liability they face in providing money to marry off their daughters. Many Indians think they must have at least eight children to allow for those who may die during youth. Most Indians also want to ensure they will still have at least two adult sons to provide for them in their old age.

Questions 1 to 4 refer to the paragraphs. Circle the best answer for each question.

1. The main reason for this study was to

    (1) understand the reason for the size of Indian families
    (2) describe birth-control methods
    (3) describe the dowry system
    (4) explain why poor people live in India
    (5) caution people about overpopulation

2. According to the paragraphs, many poor Indians do not like the idea of limiting family size because of

    (1) antigovernment sentiment
    (2) the country's low birthrate
    (3) the desire to marry off their daughters
    (4) social and economic customs
    (5) religious beliefs

3. Which is a cultural value of India?

    (1) The old take care of the young.
    (2) A large family costs too much.
    (3) The dowry system produces only sons.
    (4) Indians all have eight children.
    (5) Having children is a great wealth.

4. Why is it important that the sociologist was born in India?

    (1) The sociologist was one of many children.
    (2) It supports the sociologist as an expert.
    (3) Indians can go to Harvard.
    (4) Illiterate people can become sociologists.
    (5) Not all sons die in childhood.

To check your answers, turn to page 228.

Read the following paragraph.

An individual's personality is made up of the special way that person thinks, feels, and behaves. Although each person is born with unique inherited characteristics, the culture in which that person lives has a powerful influence on personality development. Behavioral scientists say that certain general personality traits are the result of what is called <u>cultural conditioning</u>. In other words, each culture tends to produce a certain range of characteristics. For example, in traditional Arab societies, most women behave in a shy and withdrawn manner, but women in some Polynesian groups tend to be very outgoing. Such aspects of personality are learned from life experiences in the family. So, much of a child's personality is shaped by the culturally "correct" way the parents behave.

Questions 5 to 8 refer to the paragraph. Circle the best answer for each question.

5. What is highly valued in traditional Arab societies as described in the paragraph?

(1) family life
(2) girl children
(3) boy children
(4) quiet women
(5) aggression

6. The Marquesan tribe of the South Pacific believes that prolonged nursing of infants makes a child difficult to raise. The Chencho people of India do not wean their children until they are five or six years old. What explains this difference?

(1) Marquesan women do not know how to nurse.
(2) The Chencho culture encourages prolonged nursing behavior in their children.
(3) Marquesan women are more civilized and liberated.
(4) Chencho women are born to be better mothers.
(5) Climate differences affect how families raise their children.

7. According to the paragraph, what is the relationship of a person's personality to his or her culture?

(1) Personality is one of the causes of culture.
(2) The relationship between culture and personality depends upon the individual.
(3) Culture is the result of personality.
(4) Personality is influenced by culture.
(5) Culture has no influence on personality.

8. Which statement is best supported by evidence presented in the paragraph?

(1) Early influences on personality cannot be measured.
(2) Persons raised in the same culture eventually look alike.
(3) Polynesian women are bashful and quiet.
(4) Persons raised in the same culture tend to have similar characteristics.
(5) Many Arab women wear veils.

To check your answers, turn to page 229.

GED Mini-Test

Directions: Choose the <u>best answer</u> to each item.

<u>Items 1 to 4</u> refer to the following paragraphs.

The first great civilizations of the world developed along the banks of great rivers. From the beginning, conditions in the Nile Valley in Egypt, and in areas like the Nile Valley in what is now the Middle East, were favorable for agriculture. It was in river valleys that early people first worked out rules for living together in communities. The earliest rules dealt with irrigation. Cooperation was needed to build systems of dams and canals, leaders were needed to supervise the building, and laws were needed to ensure fair use of materials and water.

The well-watered, fertile soil produced abundant harvests, which in turn made possible a large increase in population. As a consequence, cities and villages arose. So fertile was the soil of the Nile Valley that farmers could produce more than enough food for themselves and their families. As a result, surplus goods could be sold. This resulted in the development of trade and commerce, and with these came the exchange of ideas and inventions between people of different regions.

Since there was ample food available, not everyone had to be engaged in farming. Some people left farming to develop arts and crafts. Potters learned to shape clay to make decorative vases; weavers learned to make fabrics and patterns of intricate designs; carpenters learned to build different types of furniture; and architects learned to construct elaborate buildings for government and worship. Thus, civilization and culture grew and prospered in the river valleys of the Middle East.

1. Which of the following tells why civilization first developed in the Nile River Valley and in the Middle East?

   (1) It was a major center for trade.
   (2) The soil was fertile and produced abundant harvests.
   (3) The area had a large population.
   (4) People were deeply religious.
   (5) It was customary to live beside rivers.

2. According to the paragraphs, what was most likely highly valued by the early Egyptians who left farming?

   (1) beauty
   (2) agricultural knowledge
   (3) water rights
   (4) law and order
   (5) individual freedom

3. Early laws were established as a result of the need to

    (1) build enough housing
    (2) limit surplus goods
    (3) create a just system of water distribution
    (4) govern commerce and trade
    (5) educate craftspeople

4. The early Egyptians as a group apparently placed a high value on

    (1) competition
    (2) cooperation
    (3) selfishness
    (4) education
    (5) independence

<u>Item 5</u> refers to the following paragraph.

    The Samali are Moslem camel herders. Often family groups feud with other groups and steal their camels on raids. If a man or woman is hurt during one of these encounters, the offending family group has to pay fines. For injuries to the eye, ear, arm, or leg, the payment is 25 to 50 camels. For an injury that causes death, the fine can be up to 100 camels.

5. The Samali apparently place a high value on

    (1) family life
    (2) religion
    (3) human life
    (4) money
    (5) peace

<u>Item 6</u> refers to the following information.

    In the 15th century, the area we now know as Central America was occupied by a large population that had true cities. The state governments directed building and labor, maintained armies, and collected taxes. Although they did not use the wheel or have domesticated animals, they had an intensive system of agriculture and specialized trades. In addition, they had systems of writing and mathematics and used a working calendar.

6. Apparently this culture placed a high value on

    (1) war
    (2) self-expression
    (3) simple living
    (4) politeness
    (5) organization

To check your answers, turn to page 229.

Answers and Explanations

1. (Evaluation) **(3) showing guests that they are welcome** By serving what is regarded as a special meal, the family is saying that having the guest is a pleasure. Option (1) refers to what the family will do in order to uphold their values, not to the value itself. Option (2) is incorrect because there is no suggestion that the families were competing with each other. There is no support for option (4). Option (5) is incorrect because they clearly assumed he would like pot roast.

2. (Evaluation) **(4) respect for his hosts** Mr. Lee clearly valued politeness and did not want to offend his hosts. Option (1) is incorrect because he obviously got tired of eating pot roast. There is no evidence for option (2) even though it may have been true. Option (3) is incorrect because we do not know the ages of Mr. Lee or of his hosts. Option (5) is incorrect because he was following his own value system by not complaining.

Exercises (page 223)

1. (Evaluation) **(1) a person should be humble when worshipping** By covering their heads, women are covering their beauty, according to the Bible. Options (2) and (3) are not suggested cultural values. Options (4) and (5) are unfounded stereotypes.

2. (Evaluation) **(1) showing respect for their families' reputations** By doing well academically, the children are maintaining the families' good names. Options (2), (3), (4), and (5) are possible but are not as specific as option (1).

3. (Evaluation) **(2) learned** This information can be concluded from the passage. Therefore, option (1) is incorrect. Option (3) is the opposite of what is stated. There is no support for options (4) or (5).

4. (Analysis) **(2) emotional and biological needs have to be fulfilled** This cause is stated in the paragraphs. There is no support for options (1) and (3). Options (4) and (5) may be generally true but are not the cause.

5. (Application) **(1) Even after marriage, one son lives with his parents until they die.** Parents are highly respected, so constant care would be an appropriate custom. Because of the importance of family in Asian cultures, options (2), (3), (4), and (5) are unlikely.

6. (Evaluation) **(4) their harsh environment made certain behavior necessary** Environment has a role in shaping culture. Harsh living conditions would require extreme adaptations. Option (1) is a circular argument that says nothing. Option (2) is an oversimplification of their relative isolation. Option (3) is a circular argument that simply describes one aspect of the culture. Option (5) is a red herring that leads away from the idea of cultural development.

Reviewing Lesson 16 (pages 224–225)

1. (Analysis) **(1) understand the reason for the size of Indian families** As stated in the first sentence (the topic sentence), the study sought to explain why poor people in India have large families. Although the text mentions options (2), (3), (4), and (5), they are not the major reasons for the study.

2. (Evaluation) **(4) social and economic customs** As stated in the third paragraph, social and economic customs such as the dowry system and having at least two adult sons to support parents make limiting family size unpopular in India. The paragraphs do not mention antigovernment sentiment, nor do they discuss religious beliefs in India. You can infer that India has a very high birthrate, so option (2) is incorrect. Options (1), (3), and (5) have no support.

3. (Evaluation) **(5) Having children is a great wealth.** Look for facts that support the notion that having a large family is a great wealth. See the first and last paragraphs that discuss the notion that children, not land or money, are a great wealth. Options (1), (2), (3), and (4) are not substantiated by facts in the paragraphs.

4. (Analysis) **(2) It supports the sociologist as an expert.** A person who is born in the country being studied probably has a better understanding of the culture than an outsider. Options (1), (3), (4), and (5) have no support.

5. (Evaluation) **(4) quiet women** The women's personalities would be shaped by a cultural value that placed emphasis on silence. Therefore, option (5) is the opposite of what is described. There is no information to support options (1), (2), or (3).

6. (Evaluation) **(2) The Chencho culture encourages prolonged nursing behavior in their children.** The differences between what these two groups of people consider the best approach to nursing imply that one culture values and encourages prolonged nursing, while the other culture does not. According to the information, child-rearing practices are culturally influenced. The example given provides an explanation for these differences. Options (1), (3), and (4) are opinions and are not based on any material presented. Option (5) is not a valid inference.

7. (Analysis) **(4) Personality is influenced by culture.** According to the paragraphs, each culture produces certain typical personality traits. Therefore, it may be said that personality is one of the effects, or results, of cultural influence. Options (1) and (3) are false cause and effect relationships. Option (2) might be true, but the question asks for a relationship discussed in the paragraphs. Option (5) is incorrect, based on the information given.

8. (Analysis) **(4) Persons raised in the same culture tend to have similar characteristics.** This statement is supported by both the explanation and the examples. Option (1) is incorrect because it contradicts the main idea of the paragraph. Option (2) is incorrect, since the paragraph states that persons raised in the same culture eventually <u>act</u> alike, not <u>look</u> alike. Option (3) is the exact opposite of what is stated. Option (5) may be known to be true from your general knowledge, but there is no evidence to support it here.

GED Mini-Test (pages 226–227)

1. (Comprehension) **(2) The soil was fertile and produced abundant harvests.** The Nile River Valley provided fertile soil for abundant harvests, which favored population growth. This was a major reason for the development of early civilization in this region. Options (1) and (3) are results (effects) of, not reasons (causes) for, the development of civilization in the Nile Valley. Options (4) and (5) are not reasons for development of a civilization.

2. (Evaluation) **(1) beauty** Many of the people who left farming went into arts and crafts, so beauty is the most likely thing to have been valued. Options (2) and (3) would have been valued by farmers, not artists. Option (4) would apply to all early Egyptians, not just those who left farming. There is no evidence for option (5).

3. (Analysis) **(3) create a just system of water distribution** The last two sentences of the first paragraph state that the earliest laws were established to ensure cooperation in the building and use of irrigation dams and canals. These laws came before laws for housing, limiting surplus goods, governing, commerce, and education. Options (1), (2), (4), and (5) do not apply to the question.

4. (Evaluation) **(2) cooperation** All of the cultural developments described rely on cooperation among members of the society. Therefore, options (1), (3), and (5) are incorrect. There is not enough evidence for option (4).

5. (Evaluation) **(3) human life** The high fines of clearly valuable animals supports this conclusion. There is no evidence of attitudes toward options (1) and (2). Option (4) is incorrect because money plays no part in the transactions. Option (5) is incorrect because there is mention of raiding.

6. (Evaluation) **(5) organization** All the details described would require a high degree of organization. Option (1) is incorrect because, although armies are mentioned, there is no reference to a preoccupation with war. Options (2) and (4) are incorrect because the information refers more to institutions than to individual behavior. The degree of civilization makes option (3) incorrect.

LESSON 17 Evaluation Skill: Beliefs and Values–Recognizing Their Role

This skill helps you to recognize how beliefs and values function in people's lives.

You have read about how people make assumptions and have opinions based on facts. People also have beliefs that are based on their cultural values and experiences. A **belief** is an idea that a person thinks is true.

You read in Lesson 16 that cultural values influence how people behave. Beliefs do the same thing. A type of belief that is found all over the world is connected with religion. This kind of belief is often called **faith**, a trust in something that cannot be proven. People often organize their lives around their religious beliefs. Groups such as the Amish reject most modern conveniences because of their deep beliefs. Religious beliefs, when taken to an extreme, can even cause wars.

Beliefs that are based on other cultural values take many different forms. Some are positive, some are negative. Whatever beliefs an individual holds usually affect the way that person acts. For example, until recently most dolls had pinkish skin and blonde hair. Young black girls who played with those dolls often came to believe that light skin and hair were desirable. So, for a number of years, a large percent of the cosmetics manufactured for the black community consisted of products that were supposed to lighten a dark complexion and tint and straighten hair.

Another example of how beliefs affect our everyday lives can be seen in a belief based on the American values of success and hard work. Many individuals have come to believe that if they work hard enough they can achieve any goal they set for themselves. The result of this is that a number of people have left what seem to be safe but boring jobs and struck out on their own. Many of the small businesses formed in this way do not succeed, but the important thing is that people have taken actions based on their beliefs and values.

When trying to identify beliefs, think about what could have influenced a person's or a group's action.

Practicing Evaluation

Read the following information.

Over the years, many people have told of experiences similar to the ones recorded below.

"The summer before last (1965), my daughter and I were looking out the back door here and we noticed a silver object coming up very slowly over the hill. It was just sundown so we couldn't really see how large it was. It had red, blue, green, and white lights which kept blinking on and off, and it hovered directly between the huge tree and the power lines. It would hover there for about forty minutes each time we saw it. We both saw this object go through the same act ten nights in a row."

"My husband said that about three years ago, he and some of his fraternity brothers drove to Florida for spring vacation. They drove straight through from Muncie to Fort Lauderdale, with each boy taking a turn driving. On the way down at about three o'clock in the morning, one of them saw a lighted saucer-shaped object flying a little above and directly behind the car. He was really afraid, as there were no other cars on the road at that time of night, and he told the others. He said they were all simply petrified. They went faster and faster until they were going about one-hundred-and-twenty miles per hour, but the thing stayed with them. He said this went on for about ten minutes, and then the thing finally disappeared. He said all the boys saw it and will swear it's true."

Questions 1 and 2 refer to the information. Circle the best answer for each question.

1. The people who had these experiences probably share a belief in

(1) electricity
(2) family values
(3) the power of suggestion
(4) UFOs
(5) scientific proof

2. The speakers provide evidence for their beliefs by

(1) giving exact descriptions of the objects
(2) saying that the experience was shared by at least two people
(3) referring to scientific evidence
(4) describing the physical effects of the experience
(5) telling about official reactions

To check your answers, turn to page 236.

Topic 17: Individual and Group Behavior

People do not just behave as they please. Their actions and attitudes are the products of both their own personalities and cultural influences. The values and beliefs of large and small groups and of other individuals can influence the way a person thinks and acts.

A group is two or more people who have regular interaction and who identify, or feel something in common, with each other. Humans have probably always lived in groups. A group can protect an individual from dangers that come from other people, or from natural disasters. A group also allows people to share the responsibility for providing all the basic needs of life, such as food, shelter, and clothing.

Everyone associates with many groups. The first group anyone joins is the family. The family group gives love and support and teaches the basic values of the culture. The family group is where a person learns to become a social human being. A child who is isolated from the caring of a family grows up to be less aware of responsibility and cooperation than other people. As people grow older, they get involved with play groups, friends, schoolmates, work groups, and hobby groups—such as people who are all interested in racing or who all collect baseball cards. These groups influence how the individual will act in various situations.

Sociologists have discovered that people often act differently in groups than they do when they are alone. For example, a single woman who spends much of her time at home working on carpentry projects and tinkering with her car might go out for the evening with friends. Instead of wearing her jeans and t-shirt, she dresses in a silky blouse and long flowing skirt. People also will act differently with one group than they do when they are with another group. A supervisor at a factory might be very strict and distant with his crew but be casual and relaxed when out with his buddies.

Exercises

Questions 1 to 3 refer to the preceding information. Circle the best answer for each question.

1. A doctor, a lawyer, an auto mechanic, a salesclerk, and a potter have been meeting every Friday night for ten years to play a friendly game of cards. They sometimes talk about their work but do not feel bothered by the differences in their occupations. These people probably share the belief that

    (1) gambling is necessary
    (2) friends are more important than money
    (3) they have to get away from their spouses
    (4) money makes all the difference
    (5) some people are better than others

2. According to the information, groups affect an individual's behavior. This effect probably occurs because

    (1) individuals have no real personality
    (2) people react to other people's opinions
    (3) groups practice mind-control
    (4) all people are essentially lonely
    (5) sociologists say it does

3. Ed is having trouble fitting in with the people he has met since leaving his hometown. The best explanation for this is that

    (1) he is not good at fitting in
    (2) big cities are hard to live in
    (3) he has not yet met people with common interests
    (4) he has no social skills
    (5) he gets along well with everyone

To check your answers, turn to page 236.

Reviewing Lesson 17

Read the following paragraphs.

Can a cat be the mother of rabbits? Sure, if she wants to she can, answers Vivian Gussin Paley, teacher and author of *Mollie is Three: Growing Up in School*. In Paley's preschool classroom, such imagination is valued highly. Three-year-old Mollie and her classmates play out their thoughts and feelings under the supportive and unobtrusive direction of their teacher, who realizes that "the strongest incentives a preschool classroom can offer are friendship and fantasy."

Fantasy play, Paley believes, is a way for children to share and connect with others, to begin making sense of the real world. It is an outlet for expression, and provides a channel for uncomfortable emotions such as sadness, fear, and jealousy. Fredrick, for example, works through feelings surrounding a frightening near-drowning episode: "The Incredible Hulk jumps into some water and he gets his head wet. . . . I'm the Hulk. . . . I can swim fast. . . . And then I'm home."

Questions 1 and 2 refer to the paragraphs. Circle the best answer for each question.

1. According to the paragraphs, a child who pretends something is real

   (1) is learning to deal with the real world
   (2) should be discouraged
   (3) has a serious problem with adjustment
   (4) will never understand real emotions
   (5) is too young to go to school

2. The information in the paragraphs provides evidence that fantasy play

   (1) is limited to children
   (2) has a positive social role
   (3) comes from watching TV cartoons
   (4) has no role in the classroom
   (5) has nothing to do with emotion

Look at the following cartoon.

"Are you sure you won't quit after a year or two to get married?"

Questions 3 and 4 refer to the cartoon. Circle the best answer for each question.

3. The cartoonist is poking fun at an argument often used by corporations for not hiring a certain minority group. What is that argument?

(1) Men quit work to get married.
(2) Teenagers quit work to get married.
(3) Women quit work to get married.
(4) Men quit work to have children.
(5) Women quit work to have children.

4. Affirmative-action programs were begun by the government to make sure that companies would increase the number of minority groups, such as women, blacks, Hispanics, and the handicapped in their employ. The government probably took this action because of evidence that company executives believed that

(1) all people deserved a chance
(2) minorities would be good employees
(3) minorities were not reliable employees
(4) women were more responsible than men
(5) the handicapped were dedicated workers

Read the following paragraph.

Psychologists and folklorists have studied joking behavior and have come to the conclusion that jokes often serve as a way to criticize something the joker does not agree with.

Question 5 refers to the paragraph. Circle the best answer.

5. People who tell political jokes probably

(1) are firm believers in the political system
(2) believe that politicians are inefficient
(3) agree with all politicians
(4) are folklorists
(5) study joking behavior

To check your answers, turn to page 237.

Answers and Explanations

1. (Evaluation) **(4) UFOs** The stories indicate believed sightings of unexplainable objects in the sky. Option (1) might be suggested by the lights in each story, but is not the belief indicated. There is no support for options (2), (3), or (5).

2. (Evaluation) **(2) saying that the experience was shared by at least two people** A second observer helps to document the occurrence. The speakers do not give the information stated in options (1), (3), (4), or (5).

1. (Evaluation) **(2) friends are more important than money** As they have been meeting for so long and are comfortable together, the differences in their income do not seem to matter. There is no indication that the people play cards for money, so option (1) is incorrect. There is no support for option (3). Options (4) and (5) are the opposite of what is shown by their relationship.

2. (Analysis) **(2) people react to other people's opinions** As humans, we care about the opinions of our friends and associates, so what they expect will influence us. Option (1) is not true. There is no evidence of option (3). Option (4) might be the reason people join groups but not why groups affect behavior. Option (5) is incorrect because sociologists do not determine human behavior, they only study it.

3. (Evaluation) **(3) he has not yet met people with common interests** It is difficult to fit in with a group that does not share your interests. Option (1) is a circular argument that explains nothing. Option (2) is a red herring that introduces a topic that has nothing to do with Ed himself. Option (4) is a hasty generalization because there is no information about his social skills. Option (5) is a self-contradiction; if he gets along well, he should have little trouble fitting in.

1. (Comprehension) **(1) is learning to deal with the real world** This idea is stated in the second paragraph. Options (2), (3), and (4) are the opposite of what is suggested in the paragraphs. Option (5) has no support.

2. (Evaluation) **(2) has a positive social role** The classroom experience is positive and can be applied to all ages. There is no suggestion of options (1) or (3). Options (4) and (5) are the opposite of what is suggested in the paragraphs.

3. (Evaluation) **(3) Women quit work to get married.** This is correct based on the caption. The role reversal here works so that the woman asks the man the question women have often been asked: "Are you going to quit to get married?" The argument often used by corporations is not that men quit work to get married, but that women quit work to get married; therefore, option (1) is incorrect. Option (2) is incorrect because there is no clear indication that a teenager is involved. Options (4) and (5) are incorrect because there is no reference to having children in the caption.

4. (Evaluation) **(3) minorities were not reliable employees** The most likely reason a company executive would not hire an individual would be the belief that that person would be unreliable, even though, in this case, the judgment was often made on the basis of prejudice rather than the individual's qualifications. Therefore, options (1) and (2) are incorrect. Option (4) is the opposite of the belief. There is no support for option (5).

5. (Evaluation) **(2) believe that politicians are inefficient** Telling political jokes most likely indicates a negative belief. Therefore, options (1) and (3) are incorrect. Options (4) and (5) refer to behavioral scientists, not to the joke teller.

Review: Behavioral Science

The following items will help you review the evaluation skills of this unit and other skills from the book. You will also get further information about what happens in the behavioral sciences.

Directions: Choose the best answer to each item.

Items 1 to 4 refer to the following information.

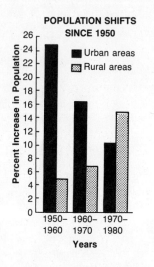

Americans have always been mobile people. From English settlements on the East Coast to pioneer towns in the West, America, which had begun as a rural nation, became predominantly urban from the 1800s to the first half of the 1900s.

While some people were moving to cities, others began moving into suburbs. After World War II the suburbs mushroomed. During the 1960s the population of suburbs increased by 27%, while the population of cities grew by only 6%. By 1970 more Americans lived in suburbs than in cities and rural areas.

Suburbs continued to grow in the 1970s, but a smaller proportion of the population lived in them. In the 1980s suburbs continued to grow but at an even slower rate than in the 1970s. Despite problems associated with living in big cities, there is evidence that the population of cities is once again growing. American cities may be on the threshold of a rebirth as a new generation of urban pioneers reclaims its land.

1. You can infer from the information that the money we spend on maintaining American roads is evidence of the high value we place on

   (1) building things
   (2) mobility
   (3) suburbs
   (4) rural areas
   (5) cities

2. The writer suggests that the trend of population shifts in the 1990s may be

   (1) a continuation of suburban growth
   (2) a general population decline
   (3) to rural areas
   (4) toward living in cities
   (5) along the Western frontier

3. Urban pioneers are best described as people who

   (1) move to the suburbs
   (2) move back to the cities
   (3) live in the West
   (4) continue to live in cities
   (5) live on ranches

4. According to the graph, the general trend of the population shift since 1950

   (1) has increased in urban areas
   (2) has increased in rural areas
   (3) has decreased in rural areas
   (4) increased most after 1970
   (5) is the same for urban and rural areas

Items 5 and 6 refer to the following paragraph.

Anthropologists and other behavioral scientists see culture as having two main parts: material culture and nonmaterial culture. This division serves as the basis for discussion of cultural change. Material culture consists of the tools, artifacts, and other objects that a culture produces. Nonmaterial culture includes the ways members of a society think and how they do things.

5. Which is the best example of nonmaterial culture?

(1) pollution
(2) a car
(3) Native American baskets
(4) clothing styles
(5) courtship behavior

6. Which is the best example of material culture?

(1) adobe ovens for baking
(2) religious practices
(3) Hinduism
(4) marriage
(5) first-hand observations

Items 7 and 8 are based on the following paragraph.

An unusual but fascinating study of cultural patterns was carried out by anthropologist Hortense Powdermaker. Her personal interest in movies led her to do fieldwork in Hollywood for a year. Powdermaker thought that the social structure in the film-making town influenced the content of the movies made there. She found, among other things, a self-imposed moral code and a constantly changing population of artists and businesspeople.

7. Which word reflects an opinion expressed in the paragraph?

(1) fascinating
(2) personal
(3) social
(4) self-imposed
(5) changing

8. A group of anthropologists objected to Powdermaker's study on the grounds that the proper focus for study is in nonwestern cultures. Which argument would have been a convincing one for them to use?

(1) She would either fail to meet the proper people or would get too involved in the movie scene.
(2) Hollywood types are just a bunch of self-interested actors.
(3) It is difficult to make an objective study of one's own culture.
(4) Studying filmmakers is not important because movie audiences are interested in the glamorous stars.
(5) There are no cultural patterns in Hollywood.

To check your answers, turn to pages 244 and 245.

Items 9 and 10 are based on the following map.

CULTURAL AREAS IN THE AMERICAS BEFORE THE ARRIVAL OF EUROPEANS

ARCTIC

SUBARCTIC
WEST
(Athapaeken)

COAST

SUBARCTIC
NORTHEAST
(Algonquin)

PLATEAU

GREAT BASIN

PLAINS

PRAIRIE

CALIFORNIA

SOUTHEAST

N
W   E
S

BAJA
CALIFORNIA

SOUTHWEST

NORTHEAST
MEXICO

MESO-AMERICA

9. According to the map, some Native American cultural areas are named after

(1) tribes
(2) famous chieftains
(3) objects
(4) geographical features
(5) rivers

10. When Europeans first arrived in the Americas, many of them thought that the natives were uncivilized savages. According to the map, which was a fact at that time?

(1) Native Americans had many distinct societies.
(2) Native Americans were very disorganized.
(3) Native Americans had cultures but no governments.
(4) European cultures were better than Native American cultures.
(5) The eastern Native American cultures were superior to the ones in the West.

Items 11 to 13 refer to the following table.

A FOLKLORIST'S COLLECTION OF BELIEFS ABOUT THE WEATHER

Urban	**Rural**
John Smith (two beliefs)	Joe Green (eleven beliefs)
red sky in morning (rain)	red sky in morning (rain)
ground hog appears Feb. 2 (early spring)	birds roosting in middle of day (rain)
	cows rolling over in the dirt (rain)
Ellen Freeman (seven beliefs)	cuckoos making lots of noise (rain)
arthritis acting up (rain)	arthritis acting up (rain)
birds roosting in middle of the day (rain)	salt placed on onion peels will predict rainy months
cats claw up furniture (rain)	fish settling near bottom of lake in early fall (cold winter)
persimmon seed shaped like spoon (mild winter) fork (cold winter)	the shape of a persimmon seed will tell you if the winter will be mild or severe
if the geese fly early and in tight formation (winter will be cold)	thickness of the breastbone of a wild goose killed in early fall will predict mild or severe winter
fish swimming deep in water in fall (cold winter)	a warm Christmas (rich harvest)
if January first is warm (the whole month of January will be warm)	persimmon seed shaped like spoon (wet summer, good crops); shaped like fork (dry summer and crop failures)

11. Which can be concluded from the information?

   (1) Urban people have no beliefs about the weather.

   (2) Rural people have no beliefs about the weather.

   (3) Both urban and rural people have beliefs about the weather.

   (4) Urban beliefs are based on facts.

   (5) Rural beliefs are based on facts.

12. What is true about causes and effects in these beliefs?

   (1) The action of fish causes cold winters.

   (2) The action of birds causes rain.

   (3) Red morning skies cause rain.

   (4) Fruit shapes affect the weather.

   (5) None of the beliefs involve causes.

13. Which proverb is most similar to the beliefs given in the information?

   (1) April showers bring May flowers.

   (2) Every cloud has a silver lining.

   (3) An apple a day keeps the doctor away.

   (4) A bird in the hand is worth two in the bush.

   (5) If March comes in like a lion, it goes out like a lamb.

To check your answers, turn to page 245.

Items 14 and 15 refer to the following cartoon.

"Of *course* I need to wear a top. How *else*
do you expect me to keep an aura of mystery?"

14. The cartoonist is suggesting that cultural values about women's roles are

   (1) taught early in childhood
   (2) mysterious
   (3) have nothing to do with children
   (4) wrong
   (5) changing

15. What makes this cartoon funny is the contrast between

   (1) the two children
   (2) the cultural value and the immaturity of the girl
   (3) the cultural value and the beach scene
   (4) the clothes each child is wearing
   (5) the adults and children

Item 16 refers to the following paragraph.

     The self-image of a child comes from how that child was raised. Even intelligent and physically able children may think of themselves as stupid and clumsy if they are brought up by uncaring or abusive parents. People who constantly underrate their own abilities often were heavily criticized as children. On the other hand, some people have much too high an opinion of themselves. These people probably had parents who admired them and praised them even when they did things poorly. A healthy self-image is a balance between the two. If we are realistic about our strengths and weaknesses, we know that we are good at some things and not so good at others.

16. Which of the following is true about the effects of child-raising according to the paragraph?

   (1) A child's intellectual and physical abilities determine a child's self-image.
   (2) The parents' attitude toward a child determines a child's self-image.
   (3) Overpraising a child is better than overcriticizing a child.
   (4) Overcriticizing a child is better than overpraising a child.
   (5) Parents always criticize a child's poor performance.

Items 17 to 20 refer to the following information.

Many people worry, or are anxious, about what happens in their lives. Psychologists have classified the main ways people try to avoid anxiety.

1. displacement—blaming one's own frustration on someone or something else that really did not cause the problem
2. projection—believing that someone else has the problem or bad habit that is actually one's own
3. rationalization—pretending that something else is the real reason for failing to do something important
4. reaction formation—acting in a way that is the opposite of how one feels or believes
5. repression—painful or disturbing memories involuntarily stored in the unconscious mind

17. A young member of a street gang is arrested for vandalism. When asked why he destroyed public property, he answers that it is all his father's fault for dying in the war. The boy's answer is an example of

(1) displacement
(2) projection
(3) rationalization
(4) reaction formation
(5) repression

18. Many adults who were abused as children do not remember long periods of their childhoods. They are using

(1) displacement
(2) projection
(3) rationalization
(4) reaction formation
(5) repression

19. Davy Bloch is afraid of doctors. Davy's friends have urged him to have a check-up to find out the cause of his constant stomach pains, but Davy says he just has not been able to find the time. Davy's answer is an example of

(1) displacement
(2) projection
(3) rationalization
(4) reaction formation
(5) repression

20. Mike O'Leary broke off his engagement to Anne Pallas. Anne still loves Mike, but when she runs into him, she acts as if they are almost strangers. Anne's attitude is an example of

(1) displacement
(2) projection
(3) rationalization
(4) reaction formation
(5) repression

To check your answers, turn to pages 245 and 246.

Answers and Explanations

1. (Evaluation) **(2) mobility** The paragraph states that Americans have always been a mobile people. You can infer, therefore, that the roads are kept in good shape so that people can travel easily. There is no support for option (1). Options (3), (4), and (5) support option (2) in that they refer to the points between which people travel.

2. (Comprehension) **(4) toward living in cities** The writer states that the population of cities is growing again. Therefore, options (1) and (3) are incorrect. There is no support for option (2). Option (5) refers to the area mentioned in the first paragraph.

3. (Comprehension) **(2) move back to the cities** The people who reclaim the cities are parallel to the pioneers who once conquered the West. The key adjective is urban. Therefore, options (1), (3), and (5) are incorrect. Option (4) is incorrect because those people are not pioneers.

4. (Comprehension) **(2) has increased in rural areas** The graph shows that the population has steadily shifted from urban to rural areas. The population has increased, not decreased in rural areas since 1950, so options (1) and (3) are incorrect. The graph does not indicate a great increase after 1970, so option (4) is incorrect. The graph does not remain equally divided between urban and rural areas, so option (5) is incorrect.

5. (Application) **(5) courtship behavior** Courting is a behavior, not a material item. Options (1), (2), (3), and (4) all refer to material things.

6. (Application) **(1) adobe ovens for baking** Ovens are material objects that are used to produce things. Options (2), (3), and (4) are aspects of nonmaterial culture. Option (5) is something we do.

7. (Analysis) **(1) fascinating** This word expresses a judgment about the study. Options (2), (3), (4), and (5) refer to facts.

8. (Evaluation) **(3) It is difficult to make an objective study of one's own culture.** Such an argument is based on the idea that an observer would not always see important cultural patterns because she was too familiar with them. Option (1) is an either-or error that ignores other possibilities. Option (2) is based on a stereotype. Option (4) is a red herring that leads to an unrelated idea; her concern was with the social structure of Hollywood, not with audience interest. Option (5) is an unfounded hasty generalization.

9. (Comprehension) **(4) geographical features** Examples are Plateau and Plains. Another naming technique is directional. Options (1), (2), (3), and (5) have no support.

10. (Analysis) **(1) Native Americans had many distinct societies.** A cultural area map must be based on clearly functioning social groups. There is no evidence of the opinion in option (2). There is no information about government given on the map, so option (3) is incorrect. No support is given for the opinions in options (4) and (5).

11. (Comprehension) **(3) Both urban and rural people have beliefs about the weather.** As both columns contain beliefs, option (3) is a valid conclusion; therefore, options (1) and (2) are incorrect. Options (4) and (5) are incorrect because factual bases are not indicated for any of the information.

12. (Analysis) **(5) None of the beliefs involve causes.** The beliefs concern prediction, not cause, of certain types of weather. Therefore, options (1), (2), (3), and (4) are incorrect.

13. (Application) **(5) If March comes in like a lion, it goes out like a lamb.** This proverb predicts weather based on a sign, as do the beliefs. Options (1) and (2) are not really weather proverbs. Options (3) and (4) have nothing to do with weather.

14. (Evaluation) **(1) taught early in childhood** Even little girls act according to valued behavior for women. Therefore, option (3) is incorrect. Option (2) is incorrect because the value is not mysterious. Option (4) is incorrect because the cartoonist is not judging whether the value is right or wrong. There is no contrast of values, so option (5) is incorrect.

15. (Evaluation) **(2) the cultural value and the immaturity of the girl** Although women are expected to hide their charms in order to be alluring, the little girl has not grown up enough to have anything to hide. Options (1), (3), and (4) provide no real contrast. Option (5) is much too general.

16. (Analysis) **(2) The parents' attitude toward a child determines a child's self-image.** Self-image is seriously affected by how the parents act toward the child, according to the paragraph. Option (1) is the opposite of what is suggested. Options (3) and (4) are incorrect because neither attitude results in a healthy self-image. Option (5) is incorrect because it is not an effect of child-raising.

17. (Application) **(1) displacement** The boy is angry that his father is not around, but the father's death did not cause his behavior. The definitions in options (2), (3), (4), and (5) do not deal with blaming one's actions on someone else.

18. (Application) **(5) repression** By forgetting what happened, these adults do not have to face the pain of their pasts. Options (1), (2), (3), and (4) do not deal with forgetting events to avoid pain.

19. (Application) **(3) rationalization** Davy's excuse is not the real reason he hasn't had a check-up; he is afraid, not busy. Options (1), (2), (4), and (5) do not apply to using something else as an excuse for inaction.

20. (Application) **(4) reaction formation** Anne is acting the opposite of how she feels. Options (1), (2), (3), and (5) are incorrect because they do not deal with acting the opposite of how one feels.

Use the chart below to identify your strengths and weaknesses in each reading skill area in the Behavioral Science unit.

Circle the number of each item that you answered correctly on the review.

Skill	Questions	Lesson(s) for Review
Comprehension	2, 3, 4, 9, 11	1, 2, 3, 5
Analysis	7, 10, 12, 16	9, 10, 12
Application	5, 6, 13, 17, 18, 19, 20	14
Evaluation	1, 8, 14, 15	13, 15, 16, 17

If you answered 18 or more items correctly, congratulations! You are ready to go on to the next section. If you answered 17 or fewer items correctly, determine which areas are most difficult for you. Then go back and review the lessons for those areas.

POSTTEST

Social Studies

Directions

The Social Studies Posttest is intended to measure your knowledge of general social studies concepts.

This posttest consists of multiple-choice questions that are based on short readings, graphs, maps, charts, and diagrams. Study the information given and then answer the question(s) that follow. Refer to the information as often as necessary in answering the questions.

You should spend no more than 45 minutes answering the questions on this test. Work carefully, but do not spend too much time on any one question.

Record your answers to the questions on the separate answer sheets provided on pages 261 or 262. Be sure that all requested information is properly recorded on the answer sheet. You may make extra copies of the answer sheets. To record your answers, mark the numbered space on the answer sheet beside the number that corresponds to the question on the posttest.

Example:

Early pioneers of the western frontier looked to settle on land that had adequate access to game and fowl.

To ensure access to food, many early pioneers settled on land near

(1) rivers
(2) grasslands
(3) forests
(4) glaciers
(5) oceans   ① ② ● ④ ⑤

The correct answer is <u>forests</u>; therefore, answer space 3 should be marked on the answer sheet.

Do not make any stray or unnecessary marks on the answer sheet. If you change an answer, erase your first mark completely. Mark only one answer space for each question. Multiple answers will be scored as incorrect. Do not fold or crease your answer sheet.

Posttest

Directions: Choose the best answer to each item.

Items 1 and 2 refer to the following paragraphs.

As geographers, we are interested in the relationship of people to the planet Earth—in the ways that people and the land act on each other. We are always concerned that people do not care enough about the delicacy of the earth or the changes in the Earth's environment that occur as a result of our ignorance or selfishness. We see people as temporary caretakers of their Earth home.

We also wish to draw attention to change. We can be certain that planet Earth, its people, environments, and institutions, will change. Beyond our lives, beyond those of our great-grandchildren, mountains will erode away, lakes will disappear, continents will drift. Today's rich neighborhoods are tomorrow's slums. Today's great industries are tomorrow's relics.

1. Which statement best expresses the main idea of the second paragraph?

- (1) Mountains will erode.
- (2) Lakes will disappear.
- (3) Today's industries are tomorrow's relics.
- (4) The Earth is constantly changing.
- (5) The continents will drift.

2. Which of the following do the paragraphs identify as a cause of changes in the Earth's environment?

- (1) people's actions
- (2) large industries
- (3) rich neighborhoods
- (4) geographers
- (5) the other planets

Item 3 refers to the following graph.

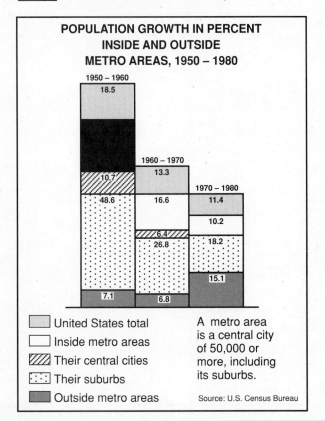

POPULATION GROWTH IN PERCENT INSIDE AND OUTSIDE METRO AREAS, 1950 – 1980

1950 – 1960: 18.5, 10.7, 48.6, 7.1
1960 – 1970: 13.3, 16.6, 6.4, 26.8, 6.8
1970 – 1980: 11.4, 10.2, 18.2, 15.1

- United States total
- Inside metro areas
- Their central cities
- Their suburbs
- Outside metro areas

A metro area is a central city of 50,000 or more, including its suburbs.

Source: U.S. Census Bureau

3. U.S. Census Bureau figures show that our central cities have very nearly stopped growing. Which evidence in the graph best supports this?

- (1) Between 1950 and 1960 the suburbs grew by 48.6 percent.
- (2) Between 1960 and 1970 the suburbs grew by only 26.8 percent.
- (3) The percentage of central cities' growth declined in the 1960s, then no longer appears as an item in the graph in the 1970s.
- (4) The graph shows total United States population growth declining to only 11.4 percent between 1970 and 1980.
- (5) The population outside metro areas grew more than twice as fast between 1970 and 1980 as it did between 1960 and 1970.

Items 4 and 5 refer to the following information.

Many theories and principles explain how people learn. Five of these are described below.

1. <u>positive transfer</u>—earlier learning makes the learning of new skills easier.
2. <u>negative transfer</u>—earlier learning interferes with the learning of new skills.
3. <u>cognitive dissonance</u>—new facts do not agree with earlier learning and are ignored.
4. <u>cognitive consonance</u>—new facts agree with earlier learning and are accepted.
5. <u>reinforcement</u>—learning that is rewarded through self-satisfaction or by social approval will be repeated.

The following questions describe or relate to one of the five principles described above. Choose the principle that would most likely apply.

4. A confirmed smoker sees a newspaper headline saying "American Medical Association Study Denies that Smoking is Linked to Early Death." Because of the article she decides to continue to smoke cigarettes. This is an example of which principle?

(1) positive transfer
(2) negative transfer
(3) cognitive dissonance
(4) cognitive consonance
(5) reinforcement

5. A teacher awards a gold star to the class for every ten minutes of quiet working. For ten gold stars the class will have an extra ten minutes of recess time. This is an example of which theory?

(1) positive transfer
(2) negative transfer
(3) cognitive dissonance
(4) cognitive consonance
(5) reinforcement

Items 6 and 7 refer to the following map.

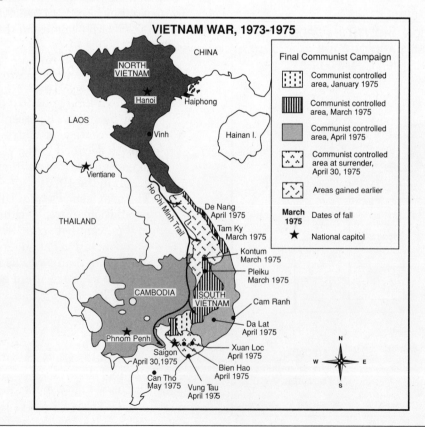

6. Which statement is clearly supported by the map?

(1) Vietnam was once governed by France.
(2) A war of independence resulted in the country's division into Communist North and non-Communist South Vietnam.
(3) By early 1973, the United States had withdrawn its forces.
(4) The South Vietnamese government fell in 1975, and the country became unified under Communist rule.
(5) Vietnam has had difficulty rebuilding its war-shattered economy.

7. Which of the following statements is <u>not</u> a fact based on the map?

(1) The capital of North Vietnam was Hanoi.
(2) The Ho Chi Minh Trail, the Communist supply route from the north, ran through Laos and Cambodia.
(3) Saigon fell to Communist forces in the spring of 1975.
(4) By war's end, the Communists also controlled most of Cambodia.
(5) South Vietnam fell because the United States pulled out its forces in 1973.

Item 8 refers to the following paragraph.

A potato blight in Ireland led to the great famine of 1846-1847. Nearly one million people died during the famine and another two million were forced to emigrate. About 1.5 million of them came to the United States.

8. Which of the following best explains why many Irish immigrants came to America?

(1) overcrowding in Ireland
(2) the need for economic survival
(3) a desire for religious freedom
(4) a desire for political freedom
(5) free farmland in the United States

Item 9 refers to the following maps.

9. Which statement is <u>not</u> a fact that can be verified on the map?

(1) The North Korean invasion of South Korea began in June 1950.
(2) June 1950 was probably chosen as an invasion date because the United States had just pulled its World War II troops out of Korea.
(3) North Korean troops drove south almost to the city of Pusan.
(4) Some United Nations forces landed at Inchon.
(5) Beginning in September 1950, United Nations forces drove into North Korea.

Item 10 refers to the following quotation.

"The time has come for the Congress of the United States to join with the executive and judicial branches in making it clear to all that race has no place in American life or law."
—President John F. Kennedy

10. Which of the following most likely resulted from President Kennedy's plea to Congress?

(1) the Peace Corps
(2) the Trade Expansion Act
(3) aid to Latin America with the Alliance for Progress
(4) increased aid to education
(5) the Civil Rights Act of 1964

Item 11 refers to the following paragraph.

For almost 50 years, AT&T, America's giant—and only—phone company, was an "authorized monopoly," a status that guaranteed it a fair profit in return for providing phone service to all who wanted it. In the 1970s, several lawsuits accused AT&T of abuse of monopoly. And in 1981, a federal judge ruled that the company had violated the antitrust laws. Rather than fight the case further, AT&T accepted the breakup of the company.

11. Which of the following was the most likely result of the AT&T breakup?

(1) AT&T became an "authorized monopoly."
(2) Lawsuits charged AT&T with abusing its monopoly status.
(3) Competing companies entered the telephone market.
(4) AT&T protested against the antitrust laws.
(5) The price of long-distance phone service increased.

Item 12 refers to the following paragraph.

Price-fixing is the formal or informal agreement among a group of sellers to set a certain price for an item they all produce, thus avoiding competition. Price-fixing without government approval is usually illegal.

12. Which of the following most likely results from price-fixing?

(1) lower profits for the seller
(2) lower prices for consumers
(3) higher prices for consumers
(4) an improved product
(5) too many items on the market

Items 13 and 14 refer to the following information.

The main purpose of the European Community (EC), also known as the Common Market, is to make trade easier between EC nations and to better compete with non-member nations.

13. To encourage easier trade, EC nations most likely make agreements on all of the following except

(1) prices of agricultural products
(2) tariffs, or taxes, on imported goods
(3) free movement of workers between nations
(4) wage policy
(5) placement of troops for the common defense

14. EC members probably believe most strongly in the value of

(1) communism
(2) nationalism
(3) a free-market economy
(4) economic austerity
(5) colonialism

Item 15 refers to the following paragraph.

The Census Bureau, usually associated with counting people, began counting robots in 1984. That year, the bureau found that about 75 companies shipped 5,535 complete robots, valued at more than $300 million. By 1986, sales of industrial robots had risen to $500 million.

15. The author implies that industrial robots

(1) cost more than they used to
(2) are becoming more common
(3) can increase labor costs
(4) are made by only 75 companies
(5) help create jobs

Item 16 refers to the following quotation.

"The truth is, we've got advantages over the Japanese in every car we make—but nobody knows it! . . . I think America's getting an inferiority complex about Japan: 'Everything from Japan is perfect, everything from America is lousy.' . . . Americans just don't understand the quality of our cars. We gotta get people to wake up to the truth."
—Lee Iacocca, Chairman, Chrysler Corporation

16. If the speaker's view is correct, which of the following would best help American auto makers sell more cars?

   (1) better technology
   (2) better quality cars
   (3) lower car prices
   (4) better advertising and marketing
   (5) higher wages for auto workers

Items 17 and 18 refer to the following paragraphs.

   Several federal agencies exist to protect consumers against fraud and dangerous products or practices. The Food and Drug Administration (FDA) tries to prevent the sale of dangerous foods, drugs, and cosmetics. The Federal Aviation Administration (FAA) sees to the safety of air travelers. The Federal Trade Commission (FTC) protects consumers from false or misleading advertising.
   Recently, the FTC, along with the attorneys general of several states, launched an investigation into the environmental claims of certain products: diapers said to decompose in landfills, "biodegradable" plastic bags, and "ozone friendly" hairsprays, to name just a few.

17. Which of the following is an example of a situation that the FTC would investigate?

   (1) an eyeliner that causes allergic reactions
   (2) defects in a brand of pacemaker
   (3) deaths from a new drug
   (4) inadequate training of air traffic controllers
   (5) a TV commercial claiming that one breakfast cereal prevents heart disease

18. The existence of agencies like those described in the paragraphs suggests that the U.S. government places a high value on

   (1) minority rights
   (2) states' rights
   (3) citizens' safety
   (4) individual responsibility
   (5) free speech

Item 19 refers to the following information.

   After World War II, all of Eastern Europe, with the exception of Yugoslavia, came under Soviet domination, and the people of Eastern Europe were subjected to rule by Communist dictatorships. Beginning in 1989, a rapid growth of popular pro-democracy protest began bringing those governments down.

19. If this trend continues, all of the following might be expected in Eastern Europe except

   (1) open political debate
   (2) multiple political parties
   (3) free elections
   (4) freer travel across borders
   (5) absolute power by a single party

Item 20 is based on the following information.

The Preamble to the Constitution of the United States says:

"We the people of the United States, in order to form a more perfect Union, establish justice, insure domestic tranquility, provide for the common defense, promote the general welfare, and secure the blessings of liberty to ourselves and our posterity, do ordain and establish this Constitution for the United States of America."

20. According to the Preamble, the writers of the Constitution had a desire for all of the following except

(1) a single, united nation
(2) a system of laws
(3) the conquest of foreign nations
(4) individual liberty
(5) peace

Items 21 and 22 are based on the chart.

21. Representative A introduces a bill to lower price supports for milk. Representative B, as congressman from a dairy state, would like the bill changed. During which process can Representative B first influence this bill?

(1) House committee hearings
(2) the House vote on the bill
(3) Senate committee hearings
(4) debate in the Senate
(5) conference committee discussions

22. A bill may fail to become law in all of the following ways except

(1) rejection by a House committee
(2) being voted down in the House
(3) rejection by Senate committee
(4) being voted down in both houses
(5) being signed by the president

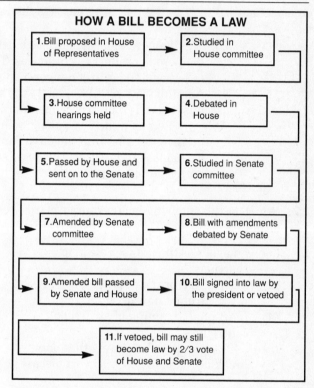

HOW A BILL BECOMES A LAW

1. Bill proposed in House of Representatives
2. Studied in House committee
3. House committee hearings held
4. Debated in House
5. Passed by House and sent on to the Senate
6. Studied in Senate committee
7. Amended by Senate committee
8. Bill with amendments debated by Senate
9. Amended bill passed by Senate and House
10. Bill signed into law by the president or vetoed
11. If vetoed, bill may still become law by 2/3 vote of House and Senate

Items 23 and 24 refer to the following information.

The First Amendment to the U.S. Constitution says that Congress shall make no law about an establishment of religion, or prohibiting the free practice of religion; or reducing the freedom of speech or of the press; or the right of the people to assemble peaceably, and to request that the government listen to their complaints.

23. This amendment supports which of the following rights?

(1) marching in support of legalized abortion
(2) voting by all qualified citizens in presidential elections
(3) receiving a trial by jury
(4) traveling freely between states
(5) owning a gun

24. By the addition of the First Amendment to the Constitution, the writers demonstrated that they placed a high value on

(1) a free-market economy
(2) the powers of Congress
(3) representative democracy
(4) the rights of individual citizens
(5) the division between federal and state governments

Items 25 and 26 refer to the following paragraph.

A <u>referendum</u> is a direct vote by the people to accept or reject a law proposed or already passed by a state legislature. Some states also allow an <u>initiative</u>, in which citizens can, by petition, propose new laws and submit them to a vote of the people.

25. Which of the following is an example of an initiative?

(1) The U.S. Congress votes to accept the president's nominee to the Supreme Court.

(2) The voters of Wilson County elect a new coroner.

(3) The people vote to reject a proposed amendment to the state constitution.

(4) Citizens petition the state to allow a vote to require handgun registration.

(5) The state asks its citizens to approve a one percent increase in the state income tax.

26. Both the referendum and the initiative allow people to

(1) bypass their representatives and directly affect legislation

(2) vote directly to repeal state laws

(3) impeach state legislators for corruption

(4) repeal federal laws

(5) propose state laws

Items 27 and 28 refer to the following graph.

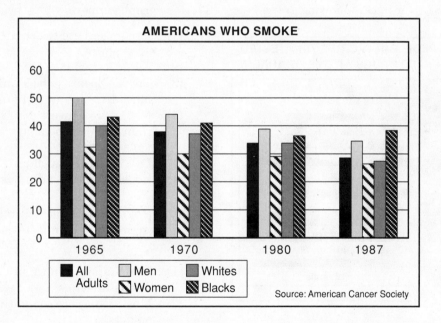

AMERICANS WHO SMOKE

Legend: All Adults | Men | Whites | Women | Blacks

Source: American Cancer Society

27. According to the data in the graph, smoking in the United States has

(1) decreased in the population as a whole

(2) increased across all categories

(3) increased only among black females

(4) become less popular among men than women

(5) become illegal in many public places

28. County Hospital starts a health screening program for the early detection of lung and throat cancer and of heart disease. Which group would benefit most from this program?

(1) women

(2) whites

(3) men

(4) blacks

(5) children between 7 and 14 years of age

Items 29 and 30 refer to the following information.

Does a violent childhood create a violent adult? University of Washington researcher Elise Lake, after questioning 237 prison inmates about their early exposure to violence, found that spanking, by itself, does not cause a child to become a violent adult. However, severe punishment (punching, kicking, or hitting with an object) can. Eighty-seven percent of the inmates who had committed violent offenses suffered abuse before they were 12 years old.

Simply observing harsh violence also can turn a child into a violent adult—if the observed violence is between the parents. If the violence is between a child's sibling and a parent, there is little effect on the observer's later adult behavior, nor is there an effect if the violence is between the child's siblings.

29. Adult violent behavior could be caused by all of these childhood experiences <u>except</u>

   (1)   punishment by being hit with an object
   (2)   punishment by being punched
   (3)   punishment by spanking
   (4)   punishment by being kicked
   (5)   seeing violence between parents

30. The largest percentage of those who had committed violence as adults had

   (1)   committed violence as children
   (2)   committed violence as parents
   (3)   never been abused as children
   (4)   been severely punished before age 12
   (5)   observed violence between a parent and a brother or sister

Items 31 and 32 refer to the following graph.

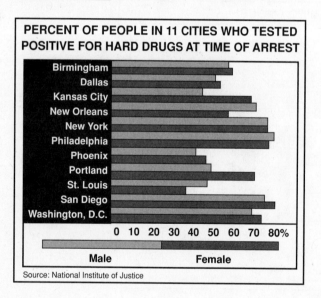

PERCENT OF PEOPLE IN 11 CITIES WHO TESTED POSITIVE FOR HARD DRUGS AT TIME OF ARREST

Birmingham, Dallas, Kansas City, New Orleans, New York, Philadelphia, Phoenix, Portland, St. Louis, San Diego, Washington, D.C.

0 10 20 30 40 50 60 70 80%

Male   Female

Source: National Institute of Justice

31. The graph supports which hypothesis?

   (1)   Drug users are the only victims of drug abuse.
   (2)   Addicts steal money to buy drugs.
   (3)   There appears to be a link between hard-drug use and criminal behavior.
   (4)   Male drug abusers are more likely than female drug abusers to commit violent crimes.
   (5)   Law enforcement officials see no relationship between drug use and crime.

32. Which of the following is a statement of opinion, rather than a fact based on the graph?

   (1)   The statistics shown are from 11 large American cities.
   (2)   Most crimes are committed by drug addicts.
   (3)   In New York, more than 70 percent of those arrested tested positive for hard drugs.
   (4)   In San Diego, more women than men tested positive for hard drugs at their time of arrest.
   (5)   In many cities, more women than men tested positive for hard drugs at their time of arrest.

Answers and Explanations

1. (Comprehension) **(4) The Earth is constantly changing.** In the second sentence of paragraph two, the author says that we can be sure that the Earth will change. Options (1), (2), (3), and (5) are examples of the kinds of changes that the author is talking about.

2. (Analysis) **(1) people's actions** In paragraph one, the author states that people do not care enough about "changes in the Earth's environment that occur as a result of our ignorance or selfishness." Options (2) and (5) may be responsible for changes in the Earth's environment, but they are not identified as such in the paragraphs. There is no information given to indicate that options (3) and (4) affect the environment.

3. (Evaluation) **(3) The percentage of central cities' growth declined in the 1960s, then no longer appears as an item in the graph in the 1970s.** The lined areas in the graph shows the growth of central cities. These areas show a decline in the growth rate between 1960 and 1970. The lined area disappears from the 1970-1980 graph, indicating that there was no growth in our central cities during these years. Options (1), (2), (4), and (5) are true according to the graph, but do not provide evidence that our central cities have very nearly stopped growing.

4. (Analysis) **(4) cognitive consonance** The smoker finds information that agrees with her prior learning and accepts that information. Therefore, options (1), (2), (3), and (5) are incorrect.

5. (Application) **(5) reinforcement** The teacher is using rewards to encourage positive behavior. Therefore, options (1), (2), (3), and (4) are incorrect.

6. (Evaluation) **(4) The South Vietnamese government fell in 1975, and the country became unified under Communist rule.** The map shows many South Vietnamese cities, including the capital, falling to the Communists in the spring of 1975. It also shows most of South Vietnam under Communist control by this time. This evidence supports only option (4). Options (1), (2), (3), and (5) may or may not be true, but they are not supported by information in the map.

7. (Analysis) **(5) South Vietnam fell because the United States pulled out its forces in 1973.** Option (5) is only an opinion. There is no evidence in the map to indicate that United States' withdrawal led to the fall of South Vietnam to the Communists. Options (1), (2), (3), and (4) are facts that can be demonstrated on the map.

8. (Comprehension) **(2) the need for economic survival** The paragraph implies that these people left Ireland for the United States in order to avoid starvation. In other words, they were seeking to survive economically. Option (1) is unlikely, since the paragraph states that almost one million people died during the famine. Options (3) and (4) are not discussed in the paragraph. Although option (5) is possible, no information indicates that free farmland was available in the United States.

9. (Analysis) **(2) June 1950 was probably chosen as an invasion date because the United States had just pulled its World War II troops out of Korea.** The word probably marks this as an opinion. Options (1), (3), (4), and (5) are statements of fact that can be supported or verified by the information in the map.

10. (Application) **(5) the Civil Rights Act of 1964** The subject of President Kennedy's speech was race. The Civil Rights Act of 1964 is the only option mentioned that dealt directly with race, making racial discrimination illegal in voting, education, public facilities, and federal assistance programs. Therefore, options (1), (2), (3), and (4) are incorrect.

11. (Analysis) **(3) Competing companies entered the telephone market.** By giving up its monopoly—its total control—over phone service, AT&T gave other companies a chance to sell phone service. Options (1), (2), and (4) were causes leading to the breakup. Option (5) is incorrect because there is not enough information on which to base a conclusion about costs.

12. (Analysis) **(3) higher prices for consumers** When sellers fix a price, they are likely to set it as high as they think customers will pay, in order to make as much profit as possible. One way sellers get consumers to buy their product rather than the competitor's is to lower the price. But there is no competition in a price-fixing situation, so the price charged buyers is likely to stay high, ruling out options (1) and (2). Option (4) is unlikely, since an improved product would result from customers' requests or from a situation where several sellers are competing for business. Option (5) is incorrect because one could not expect sellers who fix prices to produce more than they can sell.

13. (Analysis) **(5) placement of troops for the common defense** Options (1), (2), (3), and (4) are economic issues. Since the Common Market is an economic organization, it most likely deals with these matters. The Common Market is not a defense group, and there is no information in the paragraph or map that implies that option (5) is an issue that would be discussed by EC members.

14. (Evaluation) **(3) a free-market economy** A look at the map shows that the EC is made up of several European nations. The western democracies tend to have free-market economies, making option (1) unlikely. The fact that the EC is trying to increase trade through international cooperation rules out options (2) and (4). Option (5) is not an issue.

15. (Comprehension) **(2) are becoming more common** In two years, the sales of robots increased from $300 million to $500 million. This suggests that industrial robots are becoming more common. There is nothing in the paragraph to indicate that options (1), (3), (4), and (5) are true.

16. (Application) **(4) better advertising and marketing** Mr. Iacocca says that Americans do not know how good American cars are and that they must be told. He seems to suggest that if only auto makers could get their message across, Americans would buy more domestic, rather than Japanese, cars. Options (1) and (2) are incorrect because Iacocca seems to believe that American car makers are making high-quality cars. There is no mention of car prices or wages, ruling out options (3) and (5).

17. (Application) **(5) a TV commercial claiming that one breakfast cereal prevents heart disease** The last sentence of paragraph one states that it is the FTC's job to "protect consumers from false or misleading advertising." Only option (5) involves advertising. According to the information, options (1), (2), and (3) appear to be examples of problems that would concern the FDA. Option (4) is the FAA's area.

18. (Evaluation) **(3) citizens' safety** There is no information in the paragraphs to indicate that options (1), (2), and (5) are addressed by the agencies mentioned. Option (4) might be of concern to the FDA, the FAA, and the FTC, but they are less important to government regulatory agencies than is consumer safety.

19. (Application) **(5) absolute power by a single party** The information discusses pro-democracy protests against Communist dictatorships. Free debate, elections among two or more political parties, and the freedom to cross borders—things mentioned in options (1), (2), (3), and (4)—are typical of democratic governments. Option (5) is typical of a Communist government and is inconsistent with the move toward a democratic system.

20. (Comprehension) **(3) the conquest of foreign nations** The Preamble states that the Constitution was established in order to achieve those things described in options (1), (2), (4), and (5). There is mention of providing for national defense, but that cannot be interpreted as conquering other nations, option (3), making this the only idea not expressed in the Preamble.

21. (Application) **(1) House committee hearings** According to the diagram, the first hearings would be held by a House committee; Representative B could first influence the bill there. Options (2) and (5) describe stages in the process that take place after the committee hearings. Options (3) and (4) are incorrect because they refer to the Senate, not to the House of Representatives.

22. (Analysis) **(5) being signed by the president** According to the diagram, a bill becomes law when it is signed by the president (or when the president's veto is overridden by two-thirds of both houses). Options (1), (2), (3), and (4) describe ways a bill fails to become a law.

23. (Application) **(1) marching in support of legalized abortion** The First Amendment guarantees people the right to assemble, or gather, peaceably. As long as a march or demonstration is not violent, it is protected. Options (2), (3), (4), and (5) are not issues dealt with by the First Amendment.

24. (Evaluation) **(4) the rights of individual citizens** This amendment guarantees people the freedom to worship as they choose, to speak and publish freely, and to assemble and petition, or request, that the government hear their complaints. This is a statement of the rights of individual citizens. Options (1), (2), (3), and (5) are covered in other parts of the Constitution.

25. (Application) **(4) Citizens petition the state to allow a vote to require handgun registration.** This fits the definition of an initiative given in the paragraph. Options (1) and (2) are not related to either referendum or initiative. Options (3) and (5) are both examples of a referendum.

26. (Analysis) **(1) bypass their representatives and directly affect legislation** Only the referendum allows voters to repeal state laws, ruling out option (2). Only the initiative allows voters to propose state laws, ruling out option (5). And neither process is related to options (3) or (4).

27. (Comprehension) **(1) decreased in the population as a whole** Between 1965 and 1987, the percent of smokers decreased steadily in all categories except one. The percent of black smokers decreased between 1965 and 1980 but then increased slightly between 1980 and 1987. However, the overall message of the graph is that there was a smaller percent of smokers in 1987 than there was in 1965, making options (2), (3), (4), and (5) incorrect.

28. (Application) **(4) blacks** Smoking has been shown to cause cancer and heart disease. The graph shows that blacks have a higher percentage of smokers than any other group. Other groups would clearly benefit from the screening program, but blacks would benefit most, making option (4) the best answer. Options (1), (2), (3), and (5) are not the best answers based on the information in the graph.

29. (Analysis) **(3) punishment by spanking** The first paragraph states that "spanking, by itself, does not cause a child to become a violent adult." It goes on to say that severe punishments, such as those noted in options (1), (2), and (4), could. Option (5), observing harsh violence between parents, is mentioned in the second paragraph as contributing to violent adult behavior.

30. (Comprehension) **(4) been severely punished before age 12** The first paragraph states that 87% of those who committed violence as adults had suffered abuse before age 12.

31. (Evaluation) **(3) There appears to be a link between hard-drug use and criminal behavior.** From the statistics in the graph, it does appear that many people who commit crimes are drug users. Option (1) is contradicted by the data. There are not enough data to support options (2), (4), or (5).

32. (Analysis) **(2) Most crimes are committed by drug addicts.** First, these statistics are for only 11 cities; statistics for other cities might suggest little relationship between crime and drug use. Second, those arrested could be one-time drug users, not addicts. Third, not all who commit crimes are arrested. Therefore, there is not enough evidence in the graph to either prove or disprove the statement that most crimes are committed by drug addicts. It is an opinion, whereas options (1), (3), (4), and (5) are facts that are illustrated in the graph.

POSTTEST Correlation Chart

Social Studies

The chart below will help you determine the strengths and weaknesses in the four skill areas and in the content areas of geography, history, economics, political science, and behavioral science.

Directions

Circle the number of each item that you answered correctly on the Posttest. Count the number of items you answered correctly in each column. Write the amount in the Total Correct space for each column. (For example, if you answered 5 comprehension items correctly, place the number 5 in the blank before *out of 6.*) Complete this process for the remaining columns.

Count the number of items you answered correctly in each row. Write that amount in the Total Correct space for each row. (For example, in the Geography row, write the number correct in the blank before *out of 4.*) Complete this process for the remaining rows. Bold-face items indicate that the question refers to a map, chart, table, or graph.

Cognitive Skills/Content	Comprehension	Analysis	Application	Evaluation	Total Correct
Geography (*pages 26-63*)	1	2	5	**3**	____ out of 4
History (*pages 64-127*)	8	**7, 9**	10	**6**	____ out of 5
Economics (*pages 128-167*)	15	11, 12, **13**	16, 17	**14**, 18	____ out of 8
Political Science (*pages 168-217*)	20	**22**, 26	**19, 21**, 23, 25	24	____ out of 8
Behavioral Science (*pages 218-247*)	**27**, 30	4, 29, **32**	**28**	**31**	____ out of 7
Total Correct	____ out of 6	____ out of 11	____ out of 9	____ out of 6	total correct:____out of 32 1-25: need more review 26-32: Congratulations! You're Ready

If you answered fewer than 26 questions correctly, determine which areas are hardest for you. Go back to the *Steck-Vaughn GED Social Studies* book and review the content in those areas. In the parentheses under the item type heading, the page numbers tell you where you can find specific instruction about that area of social studies in the *Steck-Vaughn GED Social Studies* book.

Tests of General Educational Development

TEST _____

TEST TAKEN AT _____

TEST NUMBER

TEST ANSWERS   DO NOT MARK IN YOUR TEST BOOKLET

Fill in the circle corresponding to your answer for each question. Erase cleanly.

① ② ③ ④ ⑤

1 ① ② ③ ④ ⑤	19 ① ② ③ ④ ⑤	36 ① ② ③ ④ ⑤	54 ① ② ③ ④ ⑤
2 ① ② ③ ④ ⑤	20 ① ② ③ ④ ⑤	37 ① ② ③ ④ ⑤	55 ① ② ③ ④ ⑤
3 ① ② ③ ④ ⑤	21 ① ② ③ ④ ⑤	38 ① ② ③ ④ ⑤	56 ① ② ③ ④ ⑤
4 ① ② ③ ④ ⑤	22 ① ② ③ ④ ⑤	39 ① ② ③ ④ ⑤	57 ① ② ③ ④ ⑤
5 ① ② ③ ④ ⑤	23 ① ② ③ ④ ⑤	40 ① ② ③ ④ ⑤	58 ① ② ③ ④ ⑤
6 ① ② ③ ④ ⑤	24 ① ② ③ ④ ⑤	41 ① ② ③ ④ ⑤	59 ① ② ③ ④ ⑤
7 ① ② ③ ④ ⑤	25 ① ② ③ ④ ⑤	42 ① ② ③ ④ ⑤	60 ① ② ③ ④ ⑤
8 ① ② ③ ④ ⑤	26 ① ② ③ ④ ⑤	43 ① ② ③ ④ ⑤	61 ① ② ③ ④ ⑤
9 ① ② ③ ④ ⑤	27 ① ② ③ ④ ⑤	44 ① ② ③ ④ ⑤	62 ① ② ③ ④ ⑤
10 ① ② ③ ④ ⑤	28 ① ② ③ ④ ⑤	45 ① ② ③ ④ ⑤	63 ① ② ③ ④ ⑤
11 ① ② ③ ④ ⑤	29 ① ② ③ ④ ⑤	46 ① ② ③ ④ ⑤	64 ① ② ③ ④ ⑤
12 ① ② ③ ④ ⑤	30 ① ② ③ ④ ⑤	47 ① ② ③ ④ ⑤	65 ① ② ③ ④ ⑤
13 ① ② ③ ④ ⑤	31 ① ② ③ ④ ⑤	48 ① ② ③ ④ ⑤	66 ① ② ③ ④ ⑤
14 ① ② ③ ④ ⑤	32 ① ② ③ ④ ⑤	49 ① ② ③ ④ ⑤	67 ① ② ③ ④ ⑤
15 ① ② ③ ④ ⑤	33 ① ② ③ ④ ⑤	50 ① ② ③ ④ ⑤	68 ① ② ③ ④ ⑤
16 ① ② ③ ④ ⑤	34 ① ② ③ ④ ⑤	51 ① ② ③ ④ ⑤	69 ① ② ③ ④ ⑤
17 ① ② ③ ④ ⑤	35 ① ② ③ ④ ⑤	52 ① ② ③ ④ ⑤	70 ① ② ③ ④ ⑤
18 ① ② ③ ④ ⑤		53 ① ② ③ ④ ⑤	

Tests of General Educational Development

TEST _____

TEST TAKEN AT _____

TEST NUMBER

TEST ANSWERS   **DO NOT MARK IN YOUR TEST BOOKLET**

Fill in the circle corresponding to your answer for each question.
Erase cleanly.

① ② ③ ④ ⑤

1 ① ② ③ ④ ⑤	19 ① ② ③ ④ ⑤	36 ① ② ③ ④ ⑤	54 ① ② ③ ④ ⑤
2 ① ② ③ ④ ⑤	20 ① ② ③ ④ ⑤	37 ① ② ③ ④ ⑤	55 ① ② ③ ④ ⑤
3 ① ② ③ ④ ⑤	21 ① ② ③ ④ ⑤	38 ① ② ③ ④ ⑤	56 ① ② ③ ④ ⑤
4 ① ② ③ ④ ⑤	22 ① ② ③ ④ ⑤	39 ① ② ③ ④ ⑤	57 ① ② ③ ④ ⑤
5 ① ② ③ ④ ⑤	23 ① ② ③ ④ ⑤	40 ① ② ③ ④ ⑤	58 ① ② ③ ④ ⑤
6 ① ② ③ ④ ⑤	24 ① ② ③ ④ ⑤	41 ① ② ③ ④ ⑤	59 ① ② ③ ④ ⑤
7 ① ② ③ ④ ⑤	25 ① ② ③ ④ ⑤	42 ① ② ③ ④ ⑤	60 ① ② ③ ④ ⑤
8 ① ② ③ ④ ⑤	26 ① ② ③ ④ ⑤	43 ① ② ③ ④ ⑤	61 ① ② ③ ④ ⑤
9 ① ② ③ ④ ⑤	27 ① ② ③ ④ ⑤	44 ① ② ③ ④ ⑤	62 ① ② ③ ④ ⑤
10 ① ② ③ ④ ⑤	28 ① ② ③ ④ ⑤	45 ① ② ③ ④ ⑤	63 ① ② ③ ④ ⑤
11 ① ② ③ ④ ⑤	29 ① ② ③ ④ ⑤	46 ① ② ③ ④ ⑤	64 ① ② ③ ④ ⑤
12 ① ② ③ ④ ⑤	30 ① ② ③ ④ ⑤	47 ① ② ③ ④ ⑤	65 ① ② ③ ④ ⑤
13 ① ② ③ ④ ⑤	31 ① ② ③ ④ ⑤	48 ① ② ③ ④ ⑤	66 ① ② ③ ④ ⑤
14 ① ② ③ ④ ⑤	32 ① ② ③ ④ ⑤	49 ① ② ③ ④ ⑤	67 ① ② ③ ④ ⑤
15 ① ② ③ ④ ⑤	33 ① ② ③ ④ ⑤	50 ① ② ③ ④ ⑤	68 ① ② ③ ④ ⑤
16 ① ② ③ ④ ⑤	34 ① ② ③ ④ ⑤	51 ① ② ③ ④ ⑤	69 ① ② ③ ④ ⑤
17 ① ② ③ ④ ⑤	35 ① ② ③ ④ ⑤	52 ① ② ③ ④ ⑤	70 ① ② ③ ④ ⑤
18 ① ② ③ ④ ⑤		53 ① ② ③ ④ ⑤	

Permission is granted to reproduce this form for student use.

Social Studies

Directions

The Social Studies GED Simulated Test is intended to measure your knowledge of general social studies concepts.

The test consists of multiple-choice questions that are based on short readings, graphs, maps, charts, and diagrams. Study the information given and then answer the question(s) that follow. Refer back to the information as often as necessary in answering the questions.

You should spend no more than 85 minutes answering the questions on this test. Work carefully, but do not spend too much time on any one question.

Record your answers to the questions on the separate answer sheets provided on pages 261 and 262. Be sure that all requested information is properly recorded on the answer sheet. You may make extra copies of the answer sheets. To record your answers, mark the numbered space on the answer sheet beside the number that corresponds to the question on the test.

Example: Early pioneers of the western frontier looked to settle on land that had adequate access to game and fowl.

To ensure access to food, many early pioneers settled on land near

(1)   rivers
(2)   grasslands
(3)   forests
(4)   glaciers
(5)   oceans   ① ② ● ④ ⑤

The correct answer is <u>forests</u>; therefore, answer space 3 should be marked on the answer sheet.

Do not make any stray or unnecessary marks on the answer sheet. If you change an answer, erase your first mark completely. Mark only one answer space for each question. Multiple answers will be scored as incorrect. Do not fold or crease your answer sheet.

GED Social Studies—Simulated Test

Directions: Choose the best answer to each item.

Items 1 to 3 refer to the following paragraphs.

In defining economic systems, it is important to determine who owns the means of production (factories, businesses, etc.) and who, as a result, makes most economic decisions.

Under capitalism, private persons own most businesses, and individual producers and consumers decide what to produce, how to produce it, and for whom it should be produced. To earn more money, producers use their resources to manufacture goods that consumers want. Consumers tell producers what they want when they buy certain goods in the marketplace. Under capitalism, government plays a very small role in economic decision-making: it regulates more than controls.

Under socialism, the government owns more of the natural and industrial resources, especially large-scale resources such as steel mills and utilities, so government makes most of the important economic decisions. Under socialism, government sets goals for the society as a whole and controls the economy to try to reach those goals. Scandinavia and many European countries have socialist economies. But they differ greatly from each other in the degree to which their governments own businesses and make economic policy.

1. Which is not an effect of capitalism?

   (1) Consumers influence prices by buying or not buying products.
   (2) Government controls the price of water and electricity.
   (3) Producers make as much profit as they can.
   (4) Producers make more of an item when consumers demand it.
   (5) Individuals buy factories.

2. What is most likely to happen in a socialist economy?

   (1) The owner of a textile mill decides to sell stock in his company.
   (2) National Motor Works makes air bags standard equipment on all its cars because drivers want air bags.
   (3) A dairy farmer sells his milk to the bottler who offers the highest price.
   (4) Government planners ask the nation's farmers to produce 10 percent more wheat this year.
   (5) A railroad drops its unprofitable passenger service between two small cities.

3. Which generalization is supported by the paragraphs?

   (1) There are no poor people in capitalist countries.
   (2) Everyone has a job in socialist countries.
   (3) Self-interest is the motive that drives most socialists.
   (4) The United States is the world's leading capitalist economy.
   (5) Many modern economies have both capitalist and socialist elements.

Item 4 refers to the following paragraph.

In Canada, police officers stop cars every night at roadblocks to examine drivers for signs of drinking. People do not seem to mind, and most say they are grateful. In 1988, the Supreme Court of Canada ruled that roadside stops by police looking for drunk drivers were not an invasion of the rights of drivers who were not drinking. In the United States, police would need probable cause, a good reason to be suspicious, in order to stop a particular driver.

4. According to the paragraph, which is more highly valued by Canadians than by Americans?

   (1) individual rights
   (2) public safety
   (3) police control
   (4) free speech
   (5) trial by jury

"A politician in this country must be the man of a party," wrote John Quincy Adams in 1802. Just five years after George Washington left office, political parties were a fact of American life. Also a fact, then as now, was the dominance of two major parties. Today it is Republicans versus Democrats; in the past it was Republicans challenging Federalists, and Democrats against Whigs. Third parties appeared as early as 1832. Populist, Prohibition, Socialist, Progressive—these and many other third parties have backed presidential candidates, some as well-known as Theodore Roosevelt. But no third-party candidate has ever been elected. Since 1860, fewer than one vote in 20 has been cast for a third-party presidential candidate. It may be the power of the major parties' machinery— their organization and money—that keeps them on top. Or perhaps voters are hesitant to vote for a person, or a party, that they see as having little chance of winning.

5. Which statement about the paragraph appears to be the best summary?

   (1) Because third parties get so few votes, the United States remains a two-party system.
   (2) Third parties have always existed in the American political system.
   (3) Third parties have failed to offer popular candidates for president.
   (4) American voters are either Democrats or Republicans.
   (5) Because third parties get so few votes, the Republican and Democratic parties have always been dominant.

6. The writer of the paragraph has the opinion that

   (1) a politician in this country must be a man of the party
   (2) third parties appeared in 1832
   (3) since 1860, fewer than one vote in 20 has been cast for third-party candidates
   (4) voters possibly hesitate to vote for someone they think cannot win
   (5) Theodore Roosevelt once ran as a third-party candidate for president

For more than 50 years, between 1892 and 1943, Ellis Island in New York Harbor was the major United States' immigration station. More than 12 million arrivals were examined and recorded there, often having their names Americanized or changed entirely. Today, Ellis Island is a national historic site.

7. From the information above, it can be inferred that

   (1) the United States is no longer accepting immigrants
   (2) immigrants are no longer received and processed in New York
   (3) the United States is populated largely by immigrants and their descendants
   (4) immigration policy now favors people with professional skills
   (5) no more immigrants were accepted after World War II

8. What does the cartoon imply about the homeless?

   (1) There are more homeless people than we can count.
   (2) There are fewer homeless people than previously thought.
   (3) Government is helping the homeless.
   (4) The homeless will be counted but not helped.
   (5) As soon as the homeless are counted, they will get government help.

Items 9 to 11 are based on the following information.

Item 12 refers to the following cartoon.

The Sixth Amendment to the United States Constitution says, in part, that a person accused of a crime

> "shall enjoy the right to a speedy and public trial, by an impartial jury of the state and district wherein the crime shall have been committed . . . and to be informed of the nature and cause of the accusation; to be confronted with the witnesses against him; . . . and to have the assistance of counsel for his defense."

BLONDIE

9. According to the information, which situation is prohibited by the Sixth Amendment?

    (1) Someone is accused of a crime.
    (2) A home is searched by police who have no warrant.
    (3) Arrested for murder, the accused is denied bail.
    (4) A person is jailed for a year before being brought to trial.
    (5) A person is tried twice for the same crime.

10. Which Supreme Court decision most likely resulted from a case that was appealed as a violation of the Sixth Amendment?

    (1) Freedom of speech does not extend to words that would create a clear and present danger to others.
    (2) Police officers must inform suspects of their rights before questioning them.
    (3) If the accused in a criminal case cannot afford a lawyer, the court will appoint one.
    (4) Evidence obtained in an illegal search cannot be used in a criminal trial.
    (5) Each legislative district in a state must have approximately the same number of voters.

11. The Sixth Amendment affirms belief in the

    (1) protection of accused people
    (2) supremacy of federal over state government
    (3) rights of minorities
    (4) right of citizens to petition the government
    (5) powers of the presidency

12. A social scientist might use this cartoon to illustrate which concept?

    (1) peer groups—informal groups of approximately the same ages and interests
    (2) phobias—unreasonable fears
    (3) sex roles—the beliefs, attitudes, and behaviors expected of a man or a woman
    (4) prejudice—strong emotional opposition to members of a group
    (5) introversion—a tendency to keep to oneself

Items 13 and 14 refer to the following table.

TEMPERATURE TABLE

CITIES	LENGTH OF RECORD	JANUARY MAXIMUM	JANUARY MINIMUM	APRIL MAXIMUM	APRIL MINIMUM	JULY MAXIMUM	JULY MINIMUM	OCTOBER MAXIMUM	OCTOBER MINIMUM	EXTREME MAXIMUM	EXTREME MINIMUM
	YEAR	°F	°F	°F	°F	°F	°F	°F	°F	°F	°F
...mark, N. D.	30	20	0	55	32	86	58	59	34	114	-45
...se, Idaho	30	36	22	63	37	91	59	65	38	112	-28
...wnsville, Tex.	30	71	52	82	66	93	76	85	67	104	12
...ffalo, N. Y.	30	31	18	53	34	80	59	60	41	99	-21
...eyenne, Wyo.	30	37	14	56	30	85	55	63	32	100	-38
...icago, Ill.	30	33	19	57	41	84	67	63	47	105	-23
...s Moines, Ia.	30	29	11	59	38	87	65	66	43	110	-30
...dge City, Ks.	30	42	20	66	41	93	68	71	46	109	-26
...Paso, Tex.	30	56	30	78	49	95	69	79	50	109	-8
...lianapolis, Ind.	30	37	21	61	40	86	64	67	44	107	-25
...cksonville, Fla.	30	67	45	80	58	92	73	80	62	105	10
...nsas City, Mo.	30	40	23	66	46	92	71	72	49	113	-22
...s Vegas, Nev.	30	54	32	78	51	104	76	80	53	117	8
...s Angeles, Ca.	30	64	45	67	52	76	62	73	57	110	23
...uisville, Ky.	30	44	27	66	43	89	67	70	46	107	-20
...ami, Fla.	30	76	58	83	66	89	75	85	71	100	28
...nneapolis, Mn.	30	22	2	56	33	84	61	61	37	108	-34

13. Which is not a fact based on the table?

(1) The temperature record covers a period of 30 years.
(2) The table shows the highest and lowest temperatures recorded at each city during a 30-year period.
(3) Bismark is the coldest city in North Dakota.
(4) Buffalo is the only city not to have recorded a high temperature of at least 100° F in the 30-year period.
(5) In Indianapolis, the average daily temperatures in January are between 37° and 21° F.

14. Based on the table, which city would have the largest tourist industry offering people a warm winter vacation?

(1) Bismark
(2) Chicago
(3) Des Moines
(4) Kansas City
(5) Miami

Items 15 and 16 refer to the following paragraphs.

In 1974, Congress passed the Equal Credit Opportunity Act (ECOA). This act bans any discrimination based on sex or marital status in the granting of credit.

Before this act, a married woman could get credit only if her husband's credit was good. A credit card had to be issued in the husband's name. When a woman divorced, she usually had no credit history and was often denied credit because of it.

Since passage of the ECOA, a lender may not ask about marital status unless the borrower

(1) is applying jointly with a spouse,
(2) is letting a spouse use the account, or
(3) lives in a community-property state.

Nor may a lender ask about alimony, child support, or separate maintenance, unless the borrower is depending on those to repay the loan.

The lender must issue the card or account in the name of the applicant and give the reasons if credit is denied.

15. Before the Equal Credit Opportunity Act, lenders were able to give or deny credit based on which assumption?

(1) Many women work.
(2) Women are good credit risks.
(3) Single men earn more than single women.
(4) Married people are better credit risks than single people.
(5) Married women are economically dependent on their husbands.

16. By passing the Equal Credit Opportunity Act, Congress recognized the value of

(1) marriage
(2) children
(3) economic fairness
(4) equal educational opportunity
(5) women in the work force

Items 17 and 18 are based on the following graphs.

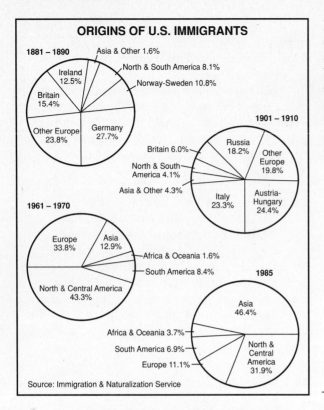

ORIGINS OF U.S. IMMIGRANTS

1881 – 1890
- Asia & Other 1.6%
- North & South America 8.1%
- Norway-Sweden 10.8%
- Ireland 12.5%
- Britain 15.4%
- Germany 27.7%
- Other Europe 23.8%

1901 – 1910
- Russia 18.2%
- Other Europe 19.8%
- Britain 6.0%
- North & South America 4.1%
- Asia & Other 4.3%
- Italy 23.3%
- Austria-Hungary 24.4%

1961 – 1970
- Europe 33.8%
- Asia 12.9%
- Africa & Oceania 1.6%
- South America 8.4%
- North & Central America 43.3%

1985
- Asia 46.4%
- Africa & Oceania 3.7%
- South America 6.9%
- Europe 11.1%
- North & Central America 31.9%

Source: Immigration & Naturalization Service

17. According to the information, which would most likely be found in the United States?

(1) many schools teaching English as a second language
(2) a low standard of living among newly arrived immigrants
(3) a concentration of Latin American immigrants in the Midwest
(4) pressure to allow more immigrants from Asia and Latin America
(5) more immigrants settling in rural areas than in cities

18. Which conclusion is best supported by information in the graphs?

(1) Each year, the United States allows about 20,000 immigrants from each country.
(2) There is a growing racial, ethnic, and cultural diversity in the United States.
(3) The American population is becoming older.
(4) Most immigrants to the United States work at unskilled, low-paying jobs.
(5) There is increasing political pressure to allow more Europeans into the United States.

Item 19 refers to the following paragraph.

Secretary of Health and Human Services, Dr. Louis W. Sullivan spoke out against the plan of one tobacco company to test-market a new cigarette, called Uptown, aimed primarily at blacks. Dr. Sullivan, who is black, said: "At a time when our people desperately need the message of health promotion, Uptown's message is more disease, more suffering, and more death for a group already bearing more than its share of smoking-related illness and mortality."

19. From the paragraph, it can be inferred that

(1) smoking will become illegal in the near future
(2) test-marketing encourages children to begin smoking
(3) as a group, blacks have a high percentage of smokers
(4) as a group, smokers are no more inclined to disease than nonsmokers
(5) cigarette ads are not allowed on television

Item 20 is based on the following advertisement.

20. Which applicant is best qualified for one of the jobs described in the ad?

(1) Brenda has done some lawn and yard maintenance.
(2) Glen graduated with honors from high school.
(3) Bob has done some roofing, but he does not have a driver's license.
(4) Pedro has worked as a carpenter for three years and has his own tools and car.
(5) Jan would like to work with his hands, has a car, and lives in the south suburbs.

Items 21 to 23 refer to the following paragraphs.

In 1787, delegates from 12 states met to write the Constitution of the United States. Among the issues they faced was how many representatives each state should have in the new legislature.

The Virginia Plan, introduced by Edmund Randolph, proposed a legislature of two houses. Members of the first house were to be elected by the people. Members of the second house were to be elected by members of the first house. States would be represented in proportion to their populations.

States with small populations were naturally worried. Their alternative was the New Jersey Plan, introduced by William Paterson. It proposed that each state have an equal voice in the legislature and that each state elect an equal number of representatives.

Delegates remained split on the issue for months. At last, a committee was formed that worked out the final compromise. Congress would be made up of two houses. Each state would elect two representatives to the Senate. States would elect representatives to the House of Representatives in proportion to their population.

21. Which idea underlies the final compromise made by the writers of the Constitution?

(1) Government should be by consent of the people.
(2) A weak central government was best.
(3) Representatives should be property owners.
(4) Voters must be white, male property owners.
(5) States should not have their own legislatures.

22. Under this plan for representation, if Maine loses population, it will be represented in Congress by

(1) fewer senators
(2) fewer representatives
(3) fewer state senators
(4) more representatives
(5) more senators, to make up for losing representatives

23. Which most likely resulted from the decision on representation?

(1) Congress's power to impeach the president
(2) the census, a regular count of the population
(3) the lifetime appointment of Supreme Court judges
(4) the two-thirds vote needed to override a president's veto
(5) making the president commander-in chief of the armed forces

Items 24 and 25 refer to the following graph.

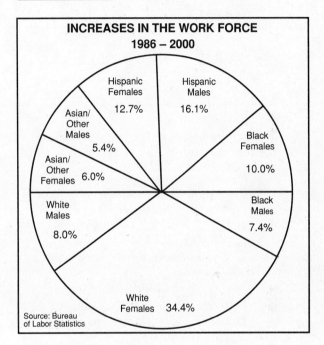

INCREASES IN THE WORK FORCE
1986 – 2000

Hispanic Females 12.7%
Hispanic Males 16.1%
Asian/Other Males 5.4%
Asian/Other Females 6.0%
White Males 8.0%
Black Females 10.0%
Black Males 7.4%
White Females 34.4%

Source: Bureau of Labor Statistics

24. According to the graph, what is a likely cause of the increases in the work force?

(1) a lower divorce rate
(2) a higher birthrate
(3) a higher percentage of immigrants from Asia
(4) fewer white women going to college
(5) more job opportunities for women

25. Based on the graph, one can conclude that there will soon be legislation dealing with

(1) restricting Asian immigrants
(2) more vocational training in high schools
(3) child care programs
(4) a lower minimum wage
(5) an increase in income tax

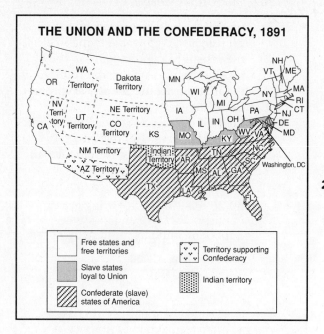

THE UNION AND THE CONFEDERACY, 1891

Legend:
- Free states and free territories
- Slave states loyal to Union
- Confederate (slave) states of America
- Territory supporting Confederacy
- Indian territory

26. Which information in the map best supports the fact that slavery was not the only issue of the Civil War?

(1) Texas and the Arizona Territory supported the Confederacy.
(2) Indian Territory was not yet the state of Oklahoma.
(3) The nation's capital was located in a slave state.
(4) Slavery existed in the border states between the Confederacy and the Union, but these states remained loyal to the Union.
(5) There were 18 free and 15 slave states in 1861.

27. Which is a statement of opinion rather than a statement of fact according to the map?

(1) By 1861, Texas had become a state.
(2) By 1861, Kansas had become a state.
(3) Kansas entered the Union as a free, or anti-slave, state.
(4) The Confederate states were in the South, the Union states in the North.
(5) The border states probably remained in the Union because most of their populations believed slavery was wrong.

"We are determined to enforce the law, to make our streets and neighborhoods safe. . . . We won't have safe neighborhoods unless we are tough on drug criminals, much tougher than we are now. Sometimes that means tougher penalties, but more often it just means punishment that is sure and swift."

—President George Bush

28. Based on the quotation, which would the president most likely support?

(1) legalizing marijuana use
(2) more treatment programs for drug addicts
(3) mandatory jail terms for convicted drug dealers
(4) decreased federal funds for the Drug Enforcement Agency
(5) fewer police

29. Which assumption appears to be behind President Bush's statement?

(1) All criminals take drugs.
(2) Drugs contribute to crime.
(3) Judges are too hard on drug addicts.
(4) Drug addicts can be treated medically.
(5) There are not enough prisons to hold all of the country's drug criminals.

Items 30 to 32 refer to the following paragraph.

The most common animals in the Arctic and subarctic are reindeer and caribou, and vast herds of them roam the arctic pastures. But lemmings and voles compete with caribou and reindeer for the arctic grass. A single pair of these mouselike creatures may have more than a hundred descendants a year. Their number reaches a high point every three or four years. This cycle in the lemming and vole populations affects other animals and people. Snowy owls and other birds, together with foxes, eat the creatures. The birds fly north in great numbers when there are many lemmings and voles to eat. The foxes raise large families because of the abundant food supplies. Then the Eskimos can trap more foxes and sell their furs. But the lemmings and voles use up the grasses as their numbers increase, and this forces the caribou to move away. The whole cycle begins again as the grasses grow once again, and the lemmings and voles increase.

30. Which statement is the best summary of the paragraph?

(1) Lemming and vole populations reach a high point every three or four years.
(2) Snowy owls, other birds, and foxes eat lemmings and voles.
(3) Foxes raise large families because of the abundant food supply.
(4) The lemming and vole population cycles affect other animals and people.
(5) Lemmings and voles compete with caribou and reindeer for the arctic grasses.

31. What might Eskimos do in years when the lemmings and voles are most plentiful?

(1) live by trapping
(2) turn to fishing
(3) hunt more caribou
(4) move to better grassland
(5) move to subarctic regions

32. A geographer might use this information to illustrate which concept?

(1) urbanization—the process by which the proportion of people living in cities increases
(2) mixed farming—using crop rotation and mixed land use for conservation and higher crop yields
(3) ecosystem—an ecological community, the relationship of living things to each other and their environment
(4) acculturation—the ways in which people become accustomed to a new environment
(5) domestication—the adaptation of plants and animals to human use

Item 33 is based on the following information.

Long hours and low wages were some of the results of the industrialization of America—and some of the reasons for the growth of labor unions. The first national union was organized in 1866, but unions were not made legal until 1914. And not until the late 1930s did unions get the full legal right to organize and negotiate contracts. Union membership reached its highest point in 1945, representing 35.5 percent of the nation's workers. Membership began to fall in the 1960s as jobs were lost in industry. Overall, union membership has continued to fall in recent years.

UNION MEMBERSHIP IN THE UNITED STATES

Percent of total workers

1981–82 statistics not available.   Source: U.S. Bureau of Labor Statistics

33. Which statement from the information is best illustrated by the graph?

(1) Long hours and low wages were some of the results of the industrialization of America.
(2) The first national union was organized in 1866.
(3) Unions were made legal in 1914.
(4) Membership began to fall in the 1960s as jobs were lost in industry.
(5) Union membership has continued to fall in recent years.

Item 34 refers to the following information.

Before 1971, citizens of the United States had to be at least 21 years old to vote. In 1971, the states ratified the Twenty-sixth Amendment to the U.S. Constitution. It says: "The rights of citizens of the United States who are eighteen years of age or older, to vote shall not be denied or abridged by the United States or any state on account of age."

34. The Twenty-sixth Amendment extended the vote to all of the following <u>except</u>

(1) an 18-year-old male citizen
(2) a 19-year-old female citizen
(3) a 20-year-old citizen living in Texas
(4) a 19-year-old recently naturalized citizen
(5) an 18-year-old noncitizen

Item 35 refers to the following map.

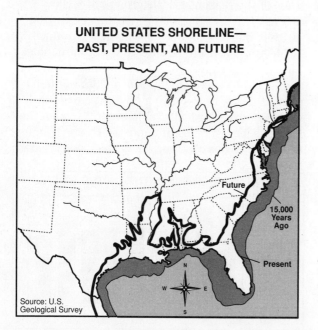

35. Based on the information in the map, which is most likely to happen?

(1) The average temperature of North America will become cooler.
(2) Present-day coastal cities of the eastern United States will disappear.
(3) The population of the United States will decrease.
(4) The population of the United States will increase a great deal.
(5) America's West Coast will experience severe earthquakes.

Items 36 and 37 are based on the following information.

The proposed Clean Air Act of 1990 attacks three major air pollution problems: smog, acid rain, and the toxic and cancer-causing particle emissions of industry. The proposed federal bill requires

(1) cars that burn cleaner gas and control tailpipe emissions,
(2) use of low-sulphur coal in place of dangerous high-sulphur coal,
(3) installation of the latest technology to reduce industrial emissions, and
(4) shutting down plants that do not comply with the regulations.

The government estimates the cost to consumers at $21.5 billion a year. But environmentalists estimate that citizens will save $40 billion each year in health-care costs.

36. What is a likely result if this act becomes law?

(1) Health insurance costs will rise.
(2) Gasoline costs will come down.
(3) Automobile operating costs will rise.
(4) Electricity costs will remain stable.
(5) There will be more jobs for coal miners.

37. According to the information, legislators in favor of the Clean Air Act place the highest priority on

(1) protecting jobs
(2) states' rights
(3) citizens' health
(4) the free-market economy
(5) the national defense

Items 38 to 40 refer to the following article.

Writer John J. O'Connor spent two weeks in 1989 watching television commercials aimed at children. Here is part of what he found:

"Considering the feminist gains of the past couple of decades, for instance, it is little less than astonishing to discover the rampant sexist stereotypes in the bulk of commercials. Boys still get to play sports and be charmingly rowdy; girls play with dolls that look like "Charlie's Angels" rejects and that can be bought with such added-cost extras as nail polish, makeup, perfume and, of course, cool blond hair.

The message: little girls must be prepared for a life of buying clothes and cosmetics and all those other wonderful things that will make them irresistibly alluring objects. Life, it seems, is a look."

38. Based on the article, what is the probable meaning of "sexist stereotypes"?

   (1)   an idea of what is appropriate for younger, as opposed to older, people
   (2)   a limited, traditional idea about how a male or female should act
   (3)   the belief that one race is superior to another
   (4)   one's position in society
   (5)   a common mental disorder

39. If one accepts O'Connor's opinion about TV advertising, it can be inferred that one effect of commercials aimed at children is to

   (1)   create rowdiness
   (2)   sell perfumes and cosmetics
   (3)   reinforce sexist values and attitudes
   (4)   correct stereotypes
   (5)   teach smart shopping

40. The writer believes that most commercials aimed at children teach girls to value

   (1)   intelligence
   (2)   attractiveness
   (3)   responsibility
   (4)   hard work
   (5)   competitiveness

Item 41 is based on the following paragraph.

On becoming president of the Soviet Union in 1988, Mikhail Gorbachev attempted to change Soviet society and revive its stagnant economy with the application of glasnost and perestroika, defined in the West as "openness" and "reform."

41. An example of glasnost would be

   (1)   a military buildup
   (2)   a crackdown on anti-government demonstrations
   (3)   allowing freedom of the press
   (4)   writing a new Soviet constitution
   (5)   stopping the emigration of Soviet Jews

Item 42 refers to the following graphs.

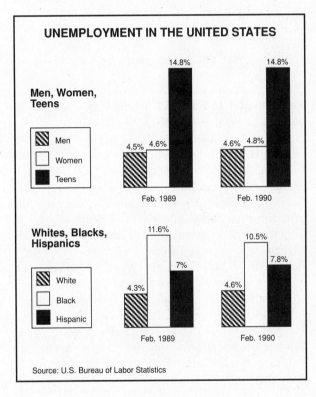

UNEMPLOYMENT IN THE UNITED STATES

Men, Women, Teens
Men / Women / Teens
Feb. 1989: 4.5% 4.6% 14.8%
Feb. 1990: 4.6% 4.8% 14.8%

Whites, Blacks, Hispanics
White / Black / Hispanic
Feb. 1989: 4.3% 11.6% 7%
Feb. 1990: 4.6% 10.5% 7.8%

Source: U.S. Bureau of Labor Statistics

42. What is the most likely explanation for the figures in the graphs?

   (1)   few job skills and little work experience among teens
   (2)   a smaller proportion of blacks than whites in the population
   (3)   a large number of Hispanic immigrants
   (4)   more women staying home to have children
   (5)   white males losing jobs to women, blacks, and Hispanics

Item 43 refers to the following paragraph.

To become a functioning member of a society, a person must learn the beliefs, values, and standards acceptable to that society. One way a person learns is through peer groups. These are informal groups of people, usually of about the same age and having similar interests. A church, a school class, an Army platoon are all examples of peer groups. Peer groups can exert considerable pressure on an individual to look and act in a certain way.

43. Usually a person successfully learns the values and standards of a peer group. As a result, that person is likely to have a sense of

    (1)   belonging
    (2)   individuality
    (3)   alienation
    (4)   inferiority
    (5)   hostility

Items 44 and 45 refer to the following paragraph.

In the 1932 presidential election, Franklin D. Roosevelt won a landslide victory with his promise of a "New Deal" for a United States suffering from a severe economic depression. His program included public works, welfare legislation, and aid to agriculture. Almost as important as his programs was his confident, personal style. Continuing a practice begun when he was governor of New York, Roosevelt broadcast a number of "fireside chats" over the radio in which he spoke to the people as a neighbor who had just dropped by for a talk. These "chats" were designed to keep the public informed and to reassure them that government was acting in their interests.

44. The purpose of Roosevelt's "fireside chats" was to

    (1)   persuade the public to support legislation
    (2)   win votes in the 1932 presidential election
    (3)   recruit people into public works programs
    (4)   tell the people that government was working for them
    (5)   inform government about what people wanted

45. It is the writer's opinion that

    (1)   Franklin D. Roosevelt was once governor of New York
    (2)   Roosevelt was elected president in 1932
    (3)   Roosevelt promised the country a "New Deal"
    (4)   Roosevelt's confident, personal style was almost as important as his programs
    (5)   Roosevelt gave a number of "fireside chats" over the radio

Items 46 to 48 refer to the following information.

Taxes are paid to all levels of government in order to support the services they provide. Listed below are five types of taxes followed by a brief description.

    (1)   Income tax—People with an income above a certain level pay an income tax to the federal government based on their income. Many states also require payment of an income tax.
    (2)   Social Security tax—People whose income falls within a certain range pay social security tax to the federal government. The money is used to support retired workers as well as widows, widowers, and children.
    (3)   Sales tax—Sales tax varies from state to state. Some states do not have sales tax. These taxes are added to the prices of goods when you buy them. Sales tax is usually paid to the state.
    (4)   Excise tax—Manufacturers of certain goods, such as liquor and cigarettes, pay the federal government an excise tax. Manufacturers then add the amount of the excise tax to the price of the goods.
    (5)   Property tax—A person who owns land, buildings, or other property pays a property tax. This tax is usually paid to local and county governments to support local services.

The following statements describe or relate to one of the five taxes described above. Choose the tax that would most likely apply.

46. A town needs to raise money to build a new school. The residents of the town voted for and approved the budget for this project. The tax that would most likely be increased is the

(1) income tax
(2) Social Security tax
(3) sales tax
(4) excise tax
(5) property tax

47. Taxes can be classified in two categories: direct taxes and indirect taxes. When you pay direct taxes, you know the amount you are paying. Indirect taxes are built into a larger price, and the exact amount of the tax is not known to the buyer. All of the taxes listed below are examples of direct taxes except the

(1) income tax
(2) Social Security tax
(3) sales tax
(4) excise tax
(5) property tax

48. Myra had to pay $400 in taxes on a used car she bought. This is an example of a(n)

(1) income tax
(2) Social Security tax
(3) sales tax
(4) excise tax
(5) property tax

Item 49 refers to the following paragraph.

When President Dwight Eisenhower became convinced that Fidel Castro was allied with the Soviet Union, he put in motion a plan to overthrow Castro's government. John F. Kennedy inherited the plan when he became president, and shortly after his inauguration, he launched the disastrous Bay of Pigs invasion. On April 17, 1961, 1,500 Cuban exiles, trained and equipped by the United States, landed at the Bay of Pigs on Cuba's southern coast. Every member of the invasion force was quickly killed or captured. Kennedy at first denied U.S. involvement, but soon accepted responsibility.

49. What was the most likely reason for trying to overthrow Castro?

(1) anti-Communist sentiment among Americans
(2) anti-Cuban sentiment among Americans
(3) pressure from Cuban exiles
(4) President Kennedy's fear that Cuba would invade the United States
(5) President Eisenhower's alliance with the Soviet Union

Items 50 to 52 refer to the following information.

The highest official in state government is the governor. The governor's executive powers include enforcing state laws and heading the National Guard and the state police forces. Listed below are other executive officers that exist in most states. These officials are either appointed by the governor or elected by the people.

(1) lieutenant governor—serves as governor when the governor is out of the state. Becomes governor if the elected governor leaves office before his or her term is up.

(2) attorney general—legal officer who advises the governor on matters of law and represents the state in important court cases.

(3) secretary of state—the chief clerk of the state who keeps the documents of the state and records all official actions taken by the state government.

(4) comptroller—the chief financial officer of the state who keeps track of the accounts of those who collect and spend state money. The comptroller makes sure that state money is being spent legally.

(5) treasurer—receives and keeps state money and maintains accurate records of all money received and spent. The treasurer can only pay out money on checks written by the comptroller.

50. In some states, most of the above officials are elected by the people. The best reason for this would be to

(1) give more people a chance to run for office
(2) make sure the governor does not have too much power
(3) make sure all minority groups are represented
(4) make sure the governor does not spend too much money
(5) get more people interested in voting

51. The state treasurer receives a check requesting that an unusually large sum of money be paid out. Which course of action would the treasurer most likely choose?

(1) call the governor for his approval
(2) pay out the money
(3) look for the attorney general's signature
(4) look for the comptroller's signature
(5) ask the secretary of state to record the transaction

52. Kim is looking for a job in which she can use her accounting skills and her knowledge of the legal system. She should apply for a job with the

(1) lieutenant governor
(2) attorney general
(3) secretary of state
(4) comptroller
(5) treasurer

Item 53 refers to the following paragraph.

Today about 5.6 million American children under 15 years of age live in homes without a father. Only one-third of those children receive financial support from their fathers. According to one child advocacy group, only 23 percent of the child support due in 1987 was actually paid. In 1988, Congress passed a bill to correct this problem. When the law is in full effect in 1994, payments will automatically be taken out of the paycheck of the parent who is ordered to pay child support.

53. What is the most likely effect of the 1988 law?

(1) There will be more divorces.
(2) More women will join the work force.
(3) More men will gain custody of their children.
(4) Fewer children not living with their fathers will live in poverty.
(5) The law will be repealed because fathers will be unable to afford the child support payments.

Items 54 to 56 refer to the following map.

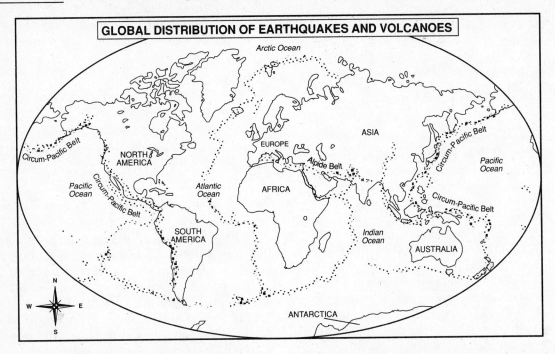

GLOBAL DISTRIBUTION OF EARTHQUAKES AND VOLCANOES

54. According to the map, in which region would you expect an increased use of earthquake-resistant architecture?

  (1) northern Africa
  (2) the eastern coast of South America
  (3) the western coast of the United States
  (4) northern Europe
  (5) Australia

55. All of the following statements are true. Which one is supported by evidence in the map?

  (1) There are an estimated one million earthquakes a year, but most are so minor that they are not noticed.
  (2) Volcanic eruptions cannot be accurately predicted.
  (3) There are about 500 active volcanoes, 20 or 30 of which erupt each year.
  (4) Soils from volcanic rocks are extremely fertile.
  (5) Compared to dry land, the ocean floor is thin and easily pierced by the underlying hot molten rock.

56. Which statement is an opinion rather than a fact according to the map?

  (1) A large earthquake will occur along the west coast of the United States.
  (2) There have been large concentrations of volcano and earthquake activity in the Pacific Ocean.
  (3) Large concentrations of volcano and earthquake activity have been recorded in Central America.
  (4) There have been few recorded earthquakes or volcanoes in the Great Lakes region of the United States.
  (5) More earthquakes or volcanoes occur in the oceans than on the land.

Items 57 to 59 refer to the following information.

The United States took part in the following programs to help rebuild Europe after World War II. All, except for the Marshall Plan, continue to help develop the economies of the underdeveloped nations of the world.

(1) Marshall Plan—supplied food and equipment to European countries
(2) Point Four Program—helps foreign countries gain the technical knowledge needed to develop their own resources and industries
(3) International Bank for Reconstruction and Development—lends money to countries or individuals to develop economically-sound projects
(4) International Monetary Fund—stabilizes the world currency exchange rates through international cooperation
(5) Military Aid—given to countries allied with the United States

The following questions refer to one of the five programs described above. Choose the program that would most likely apply.

57. A small African country asks the United States for economic assistance to start a fish-farming cooperative. Which program will provide this assistance?

(1) Marshall Plan
(2) Point Four Program
(3) International Bank for Reconstruction and Development
(4) International Monetary Fund
(5) Military Aid

58. A private investor in Bangladesh has developed a financial plan for a factory. The plan has identified buyers of the finished product and sellers for the raw materials. The person cannot get a loan from a Bangladesh bank. Where could he get a loan?

(1) Marshall Plan
(2) Point Four Program
(3) International Bank for Reconstruction and Development
(4) International Monetary Fund
(5) Military Aid

59. In response to the invasion of Kuwait by Iraq, the United States sent troops to Kuwait's neighbor, Saudi Arabia. Under which program could U.S. aid to the Saudis be justified?

(1) Marshall Plan
(2) Point Four Program
(3) International Bank for Reconstruction and Development
(4) International Monetary Fund
(5) Military Aid

Item 60 refers to the following paragraph.

A worldwide survey conducted in 1988 by the United Nations found no evidence that capital punishment was a deterrent to crime. In addition, innocent people have been, and no doubt will continue to be, executed by mistake. Yet the United States, alone among the Western democracies, maintains an active death sentence, with public opinion polls showing that 79 percent of Americans favor the death penalty.

60. According to the paragraph, Americans appear to place the highest value on

(1) mercy
(2) human life
(3) punishment
(4) democratic principles
(5) protection of the innocent

Items 61 and 62 refer to the following information.

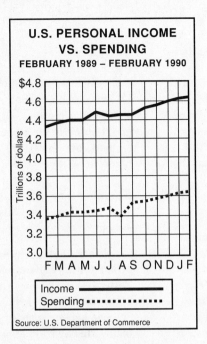

U.S. PERSONAL INCOME VS. SPENDING
FEBRUARY 1989 – FEBRUARY 1990

Trillions of dollars — vertical axis: $4.8, 4.6, 4.4, 4.2, 4.0, 3.8, 3.6, 3.4, 3.2, 3.0

Horizontal axis: F M A M J J A S O N D J F

Income ——
Spending ··········

Source: U.S. Department of Commerce

Between February 1989 and February 1990, American incomes increased more rapidly than did American spending, resulting in an increase in savings.

61. According to the information above, the effect of an increase in income together with a greater increase in spending would be

(1) less income
(2) lower spending
(3) less savings
(4) more savings
(5) higher prices

62. Which supports the idea that Americans do not always increase spending when they have an increase in income?

(1) In February 1989, Americans earned more than $4.3 trillion.
(2) In February 1989, Americans spent $3.4 trillion.
(3) Between December 1989 and January 1990, American incomes and spending both increased.
(4) In August 1989, American incomes went up slightly, but spending dropped considerably.
(5) Americans saved approximately the same amount of money in February, March, and April of 1989.

Item 63 refers to the following paragraph.

The Earth's outer shell consists of moving plates, some of which carry the continents. As some plates move apart and collide with continental plates, the material gets crushed up into mountain chains. The Himalayas were formed by the collision of continental plates. The Andes were formed by a collision between a continental and an oceanic plate.

63. Based on the paragraph, one can conclude that the Earth's surface is

(1) unchanging
(2) constantly being reformed
(3) mostly covered by water
(4) set in motion by earthquakes
(5) gradually being smoothed by erosion

Item 64 refers to the following paragraph.

The main units of local government include counties, townships, municipalities (villages, towns, and cities), and special districts. Special districts usually govern a single service, such as parks or flood control, in a geographical area.

64. According to the information, all of the following are responsibilities of local government except

(1) redesigning and rebuilding a dangerous intersection of a U.S. highway
(2) installing street lights in the village of Wayne
(3) providing ambulance service to the Tri-City area
(4) taxing the users of a county airport
(5) funding School District 303

Answers and Explanations

1. (Analysis) **(2) Government controls the price of water and electricity.** In paragraph three the author explains that under socialism, government owns more businesses and makes the economic decisions. Option (2), then, is a more likely effect of socialism. Options (1), (3), (4), and (5) would be effects of capitalism as explained in paragraph one.

2. (Application) **(4) Government planners ask the nation's farmers to produce 10 percent more wheat this year.** Options (1), (2), (3), and (5) show private persons or groups owning businesses, responding to consumers and to prices, and seeking profits. These are characteristics of capitalism. A government directive to producers, option (4), is more characteristic of a socialist economy.

3. (Comprehension) **(5) Many modern economies have both capitalist and socialist elements.** The article says that private persons own "most" businesses under capitalism, and that government owns "more" businesses under socialism. Ownership and control are not total in either case. The article's last sentence also points out that socialist economies differ greatly from each other in amounts of government ownership and control. This supports option (5), ruling out options (1), (2), (3), and (4).

4. (Evaluation) **(2) public safety** In this situation, individuals are giving up whatever right they may have to travel freely in order to guard the public as a whole against drunk drivers, ruling out option (1). Police control, option (3), is not the issue, since it appears that the public supports their actions. Options (4) and (5) are not issues in this situation.

5. (Comprehension) **(1) Because third parties get so few votes, the United States remains a two-party system.** Only option (1) summarizes the information. Option (2) is only one detail from the article. Options (3), (4), and (5) are untrue, according to the information.

6. (Analysis) **(4) voters possibly hesitate to vote for someone they think cannot win** This is offered as a possible explanation; it is the writer's opinion. Option (1) was the opinion of John Quincy Adams. Options (2), (3), and (5) are facts; they could be checked independently.

7. (Comprehension) **(3) the United States is populated largely by immigrants and their descendants** The fact that more than 12 million immigrants passed through Ellis Island in a 50-year period strongly suggests that the United States has a large immigrant population. The information will not support options (1), (2), (4), and (5).

8. (Comprehension) **(4) The homeless will be counted but not helped.** In the cartoon, the homeless man is being counted for the first time. This rules out options (1) and (2). Nothing in the cartoon supports option (3). That the homeless will now become "statistics," only numbers, suggests that they will be filed away and forgotten. This rules out option (5).

9. (Application) **(4) A person is jailed for a year before being brought to trial.** The Sixth Amendment insures an accused person "a speedy trial." This appears to prohibit the situation described in option (4). Option (1) is ruled out because the Sixth Amendment concerns what happens <u>after</u> a person is accused of a crime. The Sixth Amendment does not deal with the issues in options (2), (3), and (5).

10. (Application) **(3) If the accused in a criminal case cannot afford a lawyer, the court will appoint one.** The Sixth Amendment says that a person accused of a crime has the right "to have the assistance of counsel for his defense." In 1963, the Supreme Court ruled that if a person could not afford a lawyer, one had to be provided by the state. The issues in options (1), (2), (4), and (5) are not addressed by the Sixth Amendment.

11. (Evaluation) **(1) protection of accused people** The Sixth Amendment outlines those things that must be done to protect people accused of crimes. The amendment naturally protects the rights of minorities, option (3), when they are accused of crimes, but this is not the best answer. The Sixth Amendment does not address the issues in options (2), (4), and (5).

12. (Application) **(3) sex roles— the beliefs, attitudes, and behaviors expected of a man or a woman** The joke concerns whether it is appropriate for a man to do housework. The subject of the cartoon is sex roles, ruling out options (1), (2), (4), and (5).

13. (Analysis) **(3) Bismark is the coldest city in North Dakota.** Nothing in the table allows you to compare Bismark's temperatures with those of any other North Dakota city. Options (1), (2), (4), and (5) can be verified by information in the table.

14. (Application) **(5) Miami** According to the table, Miami has the warmest January temperatures, between 76° and 58° F, of any of the cities listed. This is likely to attract people looking for warm weather in winter. Options (1), (2), (3), and (4) are cities where the average temperature in January was 40° and lower.

15. (Analysis) **(5) Married women are economically dependent on their husbands.** Lenders treated women as if they had no money of their own. If lenders had assumed option (1) or (2), they would have most likely given women credit. Options (3) and (4) do not explain why married women would be denied credit.

16. (Evaluation) **(3) economic fairness** The law says that it is unfair to deny a person credit based on sex or marital status. This rules out options (1) and (2). Options (4) and (5) are not related to the question of marital status.

17. (Application) **(1) many schools teaching English as a second language** The graphs do show a large proportion of immigrants from non-English speaking parts of the world. Nothing in the graphs supports options (2), (3), or (5). Option (4) is unlikely since, as the graphs show, a large proportion of immigrants to the United States are now Asians and Latin Americans.

18. (Evaluation) **(2) There is a growing racial, ethnic, and cultural diversity in the United States.** The graphs show that in the past most immigrants were white Europeans. Their descendants now populate the United States. Today, there are growing numbers of Asian and Latin American immigrants. This supports the idea that there is a growing diversity in the country's racial, ethnic, and cultural makeup. No evidence is given in the graphs that supports options (1), (3), (4), or (5).

19. (Comprehension) **(3) as a group, blacks have a high percentage of smokers** Dr. Sullivan described blacks as "a group already bearing more than its share of smoking-related illness" and death. This suggests that a high percentage of blacks smoke. The information does not support options (1), (2), (4), or (5).

20. (Application) **(4) Pedro has worked as a carpenter for three years and has his own tools and car.** He has one year less experience than is required, but Pedro meets more of the job requirements (experience, tools, car) than the applicants in options (1), (2), (3), and (5).

21. (Analysis) **(1) Government should be by consent of the people.** Whether or not the people would elect their representatives was never an issue throughout the delegates' discussions. The disagreement was only about how many should be elected from each state. There is no information in the article that supports options (2), (3), (4), and (5).

22. (Application) **(2) fewer representatives** States elect representatives to the House of Representatives in proportion to their population. If a state loses population, it elects fewer representatives, ruling out option (4). Options (1) and (5) are incorrect because they involve senators, and the article says that each state would elect two senators, regardless of its size. Option (3) can be ruled out because it describes state, not federal, government.

23. (Application) **(2) the census, a regular count of the population** To insure that the population is accurately represented, the delegates established the government census, a count of the people every ten years. Options (1), (3), (4), and (5) are not related to the system of states' representation.

24. (Analysis) **(5) more job opportunities for women** According to the graph, women will make up more than 60 percent of all new workers. Options (1), (2), and (4) would more likely keep women out of the work force. Option (3) is not relevant to the increase in women workers.

25. (Application) **(3) child care programs** With so many women going to work, their children will have to be cared for by others. It is likely that working mothers will be asking for child care programs. There is no information in the graphs to support options (1), (2), (4), or (5).

26. (Evaluation) **(4) Slavery existed in the border states between the Confederacy and the Union, but these states remained loyal to the Union.** This is direct evidence that there were considerations other than slavery in a state's decision to support the Union or the Confederacy. Options (1), (2), (3), and (5) may or may not be true, but they do not support the fact that slavery was not the only issue of the Civil War.

27. (Analysis) **(5) The border states probably remained in the Union because most of their populations believed slavery was wrong.** This is an opinion that cannot be proved by reference to the map. Options (1), (2), (3), and (4) are facts based on the map.

28. (Application) **(3) mandatory jail terms for convicted drug dealers** The president says we must be tough on drug criminals. "Sometimes," he says, "that means tougher penalties." This supports option (3). Being "tougher" would rule out options (1), (4), and (5). He says nothing about treatment for drug addicts, ruling out option (2).

29. (Analysis) **(2) Drugs contribute to crime.** The president seems to assume that there is a relationship between drugs and crime stating that the country will not have safe streets and neighborhoods until we are "tougher on drug criminals." Option (1) is incorrect because the quotation discusses only drug criminals and does not indicate that all criminals take drugs. Option (3) is incorrect because according to the president, the opposite is true. Options (4) and (5) are not issues discussed in the quotation.

30. (Analysis) **(4) The lemming and vole population cycles affect other animals and people.** Options (1), (2), (3), and (5) are details that support the main idea of the paragraph.

31. (Comprehension) **(1) live by trapping** The article explains that when there are many lemmings and voles, foxes have plenty to eat and so raise more young. You can infer that Eskimos can then trap more foxes for their fur. Options (2) and (4) describe actions that Eskimos probably take when the lemming and vole populations are low. Option (3) is incorrect because the article states that the caribou move away when the lemming and vole populations are high. Option (5) is unlikely because the first sentence says that this situation exists in both the Arctic and the subarctic.

32. (Application) **(3) ecosystem—an ecological community, the relationship of living things to each other and their environment** The paragraph describes how several animals affect each other, their environment, and the people who live there. The article does not deal with people in cities or with farming, ruling out options (1) and (2). It does not show people getting used to a new environment or adapting plants and animals to their use, ruling out options (4) and (5).

33. (Evaluation) **(5) Union membership has continued to fall in recent years.** The graph records union membership between 1979 and 1989 and shows it falling throughout that period. The graph suggests nothing about hours or wages, ruling out option (1). It shows nothing about union history, so options (2) and (3) are incorrect. The graph does not record membership in the 1960s, so it cannot illustrate option (4).

34. (Application) **(5) an 18-year-old noncitizen** The Twenty-sixth Amendment extended the vote to all citizens between 18 and 21 years old. It did not give the vote to noncitizens, option (5). The amendment does not distinguish between male, female, or naturalized citizens, nor does it exclude any of these groups. This rules out options (1), (2), and (4). The amendment says that this right shall not be abridged or denied by any state, ruling out option (3).

35. (Analysis) **(2) Present-day coastal cities of the eastern United States will disappear.** The map shows the United States' eastern and Gulf of Mexico shorelines. Today's shoreline, according to the map, will be under water in the future. So today's east coast cities will be under water. Nothing on the map suggests temperature changes or earthquakes, ruling out options (1) and (5). A changing shoreline will not necessarily affect the growth of population, so options (3) and (4) are incorrect.

36. (Analysis) **(3) Automobile operating costs will rise.** Cars will need new technology to help control their emissions and burn cleaner gas. Auto makers will probably pass these costs on to consumers. If health costs go down, this law will not be the cause of a rise in health insurance costs, thus ruling out option (1). Cleaner gas will have to be made and/or blended, so option (2) is incorrect. Electric generating plants burning high-sulphur coal will need new technology, ruling out option (4). If less high-sulphur coal is used, some miners will lose their jobs, so option (5) is incorrect.

37. (Evaluation) **(3) citizens' health** It is implied in the first paragraph that polluted air is unhealthful. This law might result in a loss of jobs, ruling out option (1). These are federal standards, so option (2) is incorrect. Government controls are being put on industry, ruling out option (4). National defense, option (5), is not an issue here.

38. (Comprehension) **(2) a limited, traditional idea about how a male or female should act** The writer describes how commercials show boys behaving in one way and girls in another. And his description of what is offered in the commercials as appropriate behavior for girls is "limited and traditional." There is no information in the article to indicate that the term "sexist stereotype" is related to age, race, social position, or mental health, ruling out options (1), (3), (4), and (5).

39. (Analysis) **(3) reinforce sexist values and attitudes** The writer says that boys and girls are shown behaving in only certain limited ways "in the bulk of commercials." If children are shown repeatedly that only certain behaviors and attitudes are appropriate, they will believe that they can only act and think in those ways. If O'Connor is correct, one can infer that this is a likely effect of these commercials. Options (1) and (2) may or may not be true, but neither is given by the writer as an effect of TV advertising. Option (4) is the opposite of the writer's opinion. There is no evidence to support option (5).

40. (Evaluation) **(2) attractiveness** In the last paragraph, the writer says that little girls are being prepared for a life of buying things that will make them "irresistibly alluring objects," or in other words, attractive. There is nothing in the article to indicate that the writer believes commercials teach the values in options (1), (3), (4), or (5).

41. (Application) **(3) allowing freedom of the press** Glasnost means "openness," implying more freedom of expression. Option (1) is not related to social reform. Options (2) and (5) are incorrect because they are examples of attempts to prohibit freedom of expression and movement. Option (4) is an example of reform.

42. (Analysis) **(1) few job skills and little work experience among teens** Of the groups included in the graphs, teens have the highest rate of unemployment. Since they are young, it is reasonable to think that they have fewer work skills and less work experience than adults, and that this would cause their higher unemployment. The proportions of blacks and the numbers of Hispanic immigrants are not reflected in these unemployment figures, ruling out options (2) and (3). Female unemployment is relatively low, suggesting the opposite of option (4). White males have the lowest unemployment of all groups, so option (5) is incorrect.

43. (Analysis) **(1) belonging** A person who learns the values and standards of the group is likely to be accepted into the group. Being accepted should give one a sense of belonging. A sense of individuality, option (2), is likely to be much less important among members of a group. Alienation, option (3), is the opposite of belonging. Inferiority and hostility, options (4) and (5), are not likely to result from being accepted or welcomed into a group.

44. (Comprehension) **(4) tell the people that government was working for them** The last sentence of the paragraph says that the fireside chats "were designed to keep the public informed and to reassure them that government was acting in their interests." The chats probably did help persuade people to support legislation, option (1), but this was not their main, or their stated, purpose. Roosevelt won the 1932 presidential election, so option (2) is incorrect. Nothing in the paragraph hints that the fireside chats were used for options (3) or (5).

45. (Analysis) **(4) Roosevelt's confident, personal style was almost as important as his programs** It is the writer's opinion that Roosevelt's personality was as important as his legislation. There is no way to prove such a statement. Options (1), (2), (3), and (5) are facts that can be proven.

46. (Application) **(5) property tax** Since it was a local decision to build the new school, the funds would be raised through an increase in property taxes. The taxes listed in options (1), (2), (3), and (4) are all paid to the state or federal governments and could not be used to fund the project.

47. (Analysis) **(4) excise tax** This tax is paid by the manufacturer and included in the price of the goods, so one has no way of knowing the exact amount of the tax. In options (1), (2), (3), and (5), the exact amount of tax is known.

48. (Comprehension) **(3) sales tax** She paid a tax on something she purchased; therefore, it is a sales tax, option (3). Options (1) and (2) are not correct because they have nothing to do with a purchase. There is no information in the passage to support options (4) and (5) since they are not taxes that would be paid on the sale of an automobile.

49. (Comprehension) **(1) anti-Communist sentiment among Americans** President Eisenhower decided to overthrow Castro when he became convinced that Castro was allied with the Soviets. In other words, Eisenhower decided that Castro was a Communist. Anti-communism has been a major attitude in American foreign policy since 1945. Nothing in the paragraph suggests there was anti-Cuban feeling, option (2), or pressure from Cuban exiles, option (3). Nor does the paragraph say that Kennedy feared a Cuban invasion of the United States, option (4). Eisenhower was not allied with the Soviet Union, ruling out option (5).

50. (Comprehension) **(2) make sure the governor does not have too much power** If the governor can appoint officials to key positions, he or she may be tempted to choose people who will support his or her policies. Nothing in the information presented addresses options (1), (3), and (5). Option (4) may be true, but it would result from an abuse of power mentioned in option (2).

51. (Analysis) **(4) look for the comptroller's signature** The comptroller is the only person who can authorize withdrawals from the state treasury. Therefore, option (2) cannot be the first course of action. The officials in options (1), (3), and (5) are not involved in this financial transaction.

52. (Evaluation) **(4) comptroller** Option (4) is the only office in which accounting skills and knowledge of the legal system are needed. Options (1) and (3) do not list these as part of their functions. Option (2) suggests that knowledge of the law is needed, but it does not mention anything about accounting. Option (5) suggests that accounting skills are needed, but it does not mention anything about law.

53. (Analysis) **(4) Fewer children not living with their fathers will live in poverty.** More support money should go to children when the law is in force, so fewer children will be poor. The information does not give support for the law resulting in more divorces, more women going to work, or more men gaining custody of their children, so options (1), (2), and (3) are incorrect. Nothing in the paragraph suggests that fathers will be unable to afford the payments, ruling out option (5).

54. (Application) **(3) the western coast of the United States** The map shows that the western coast of the United States has a higher concentration of earthquakes and volcanoes than northern Africa, option (1); eastern South America, option (2); northern Europe, option (4); or Australia, option (5).

55. (Evaluation) **(5) Compared to dry land, the ocean floor is thin and easily pierced by the underlying hot molten rock.** The map shows far more volcanoes and earthquakes occurring in oceans than on land, giving support to option (5). The map suggests nothing about "unnoticed" earthquakes, ruling out option (1). It gives no information about predicting volcanoes, so option (2) is incorrect. One cannot tell from the map how many active volcanoes there are, ruling out option (3). Nor can one tell anything about volcanic soils from the map, ruling out option (4).

56. (Analysis) **(1) A large earthquake will occur along the west coast of the United States.** This is an area of many earthquakes and volcanoes, according to the map, so it seems possible that an earthquake will occur in that area, but we cannot be certain. Therefore, this is an opinion. It is a fact that the map shows earthquake and volcano concentrations in the Pacific Ocean, option (2), and in Central America, option (3). It is also a fact that the map shows few earthquakes and volcanoes around the Great Lakes, option (4), and shows more earthquakes and volcanoes in the oceans than on land, option (5).

57. (Analysis) **(2) Point Four Program** This program provides the technical assistance to begin the fish-farming cooperative. Options (1), (3), (4), and (5) are not related to providing technical assistance.

58. (Application) **(3) International Bank for Reconstruction and Development** Individuals who need money for projects can get loans from this bank if the financial plan is sound. Options (1), (2), (4), and (5) do not deal with financial assistance.

59. (Analysis) **(5) Military Aid** The passage says that military aid is given to allies. Saudi Arabia is an ally of both the United States and Kuwait. Options (1), (2), (3), and (4) do not provide funds for military purposes.

60. (Evaluation) **(3) punishment** If Americans valued either mercy or human life most highly, options (1) and (2), they would not execute people. There is no evidence in the paragraph to support option (4). Since the paragraph states that innocent people are executed, option (5) is incorrect. This leaves punishment, option (3), as the most valued.

61. (Analysis) **(3) less savings** Savings is the difference between income and spending. If income increases but spending also increases, savings would decrease, ruling out option (4). Options (1) and (2) are the opposite of what is stated. Income, spending, and savings would have no obvious effect on prices, so option (5) is incorrect.

62. (Evaluation) **(4) In August 1989, American incomes went up slightly, but spending dropped considerably.** This shows that Americans do not always increase spending as their incomes increase, thus supporting the idea. Options (1) and (2) do not show a relationship between spending and income. Option (3) supports the opposite idea that Americans do increase spending as income increases. Option (5) deals more with amounts of savings than with the relationship between income and spending.

63. (Comprehension) **(2) constantly being reformed** The Earth's plates are said to be "moving" and "colliding" to form mountain chains. This suggests that the Earth's surface is being constantly changed, supporting option (2) and ruling out option (1). Option (4) is not mentioned. The paragraph does not say how much of the Earth is ocean, so option (3) is incorrect. Nor does the paragraph mention erosion, ruling out option (5).

64. (Application) **(1) redesigning and rebuilding a dangerous intersection of a U.S. highway** The letters U.S. suggest that this is part of the federal highway system, so the federal government would be responsible for it. Also, the size and complexity of such a job suggest that a larger unit of government, at least as large as the state, would probably handle it. Option (2) could be handled by the municipality. Option (4) would be handled by the county. Options (3) and (5) appear to be special district matters.

SIMULATED GED TEST Correlation Chart

Social Studies

The chart below will help you determine your strengths and weaknesses in the four skill areas and in the content areas of geography, history, economics, political science, and behavioral science.

Directions

Circle the number of each item that you answered correctly on the Simulated Test. Count the number of items you answered correctly in each column and row. Write the amount in the Total Correct space for each category. (For example, if you answered 10 comprehension items correctly, place the number 10 in the blank before *out of 12*). Complete this process for the remaining columns and rows.

Count the number of items you answered correctly. Write that amount in the overall Total Correct space. Boldface items indicate that the question refers to a map, chart, table, or graph.

Cognitive Skills/Content	Comprehension	Analysis	Application	Evaluation	Total Correct
Geography *(pages 26-63)*	31, 63	**13**, 30, **35, 56**	14, 32, **54**	55	____ out of 10
History *(pages 64-127)*	44, 49	**27**, 45		26	____ out of 5
Economics *(pages 128-167)*	3, 48	1, **24**, 36,**42,** 47,53, 57,**61**	2, **25**, 41, 46	**33**, 37, **62**	____ out of 17
Political Science *(pages 168-217)*	5, 7, **8**	6, 21, 59	9, 10, **17**, 22, 23, 28, 34, 58, 64	4, 11, **18**, 60	____ out of 19
Behavioral Science *(pages 218-247)*	19, 38, 50	15, 29, 39, 43, 51	**12**, 20	16, 40, 52	____ out of 13
Total Correct	____ out of 12	____ out of 22	____ out of 18	____ out of 12	total correct:___out of 64 1-51: need more review 52-64: Congratulations! You're Ready

If you answered fewer than 52 questions correctly, determine which areas are hardest for you. Go back to the *Steck-Vaughn GED Social Studies* book and review the content in those areas. In the parentheses under the item type heading, the page numbers tell you where you can find specific instruction about that area of social studies in the *Steck-Vaughn Social Studies* book.

GLOSSARY

abolitionist a person who wanted to do away with slavery in the United States

Amendments corrections or alterations to the United States Constitution

anthropology the study of the physical and social development of human beings over the centuries

anthropologist someone who studies anthropology

Anti-Federalists a historic U.S. political party that wanted to make changes to the Constitution before its adoption

arms race competition beginning in the 1950s between the United States and the Soviet Union to develop nuclear weapons

Articles of Confederation the first U.S. constitution (1781–89); established a confederation of sovereign states. Under the Articles, the Congress had very little power.

assume to believe something is true without having proof of it

assumption something believed to be true without actual proof

authoritarian government a government that advocates obedience to political powers as opposed to encouraging personal liberty

barter economy a system in which goods and services are exchanged for other goods and services, rather than paid for with money

belief an idea that a person thinks is true

black codes a system of employment in Southern states after the Civil War that treated blacks as second-class citizens

bureaucracy a system of government handled by departments headed by bureau chiefs, emphasizing movement by routine and conservative action

capital the manmade things that are used in production

capital gains tax a national tax on the money made from the sale of property not included in the owner's business

capitalism the private or corporate owner-ship of goods and means of production

cause the reason something happens

centralized government a governing body controlled by the greatest political power gathered at one point

checks and balances the limitations placed on all branches of government, giving each branch the right to amend the actions of another

circular argument restates an idea in different words without giving any new supporting information

civil disobedience a form of non-violent protest against unjust laws or conditions

collective bargaining negotiation between management and union leaders on terms for employee contracts

colonization a country sends people to establish its own political, cultural, and economic controls in a previously unsettled area

colony an area or a country that is under the political or economic control of another country with people of the controlling country living in that area

Commander-in-Chief a military officer of the highest command; in the U.S., the president

communism a system of government in which the state owns the means of production and plans the economy of the nation

compass rose a special sign, usually a circle with lines or points, that shows direction on a map

Confederate States of America a group of seven Southern states that seceded from the Union in 1861

consumption the way goods and services are used by people

continent a major landmass, one of seven on the Earth

cost-push inflation higher prices caused by a push for higher wages; also called the wage-price spiral

cultural regions areas of the world with similar physical, economic, historical, and political backgrounds

culture the knowledge, beliefs, arts, morals, laws, and customs of members of a society

demand-pull inflation higher prices caused by a demand for goods that are in short supply

democracy a centralized government in which the process of government is carried on by the people

democrat a member of the Democratic party which is one of the two major political parties in the U.S.

Democratic-Republican party the historic U.S. political party headed by Thomas Jefferson, which was opposed to the Federalists

Department of Housing and Urban Development a government office that provides funding for rental housing for low-income families, the handicapped, and the elderly; it also provides funds for rehabilitating urban areas

depression a severe reduction or slowing of business activity and cash flow

displacement the act of blaming one's own frustration on someone or something else that really did not cause the problem

distribution the way in which the total income of a society is divided

draw a conclusion to look at the facts about an idea and make a decision based on those facts

ecology the balance between nature and humanity

effect an outcome; that which happens as a result of some occurrence

either-or error sets up only two choices when others actually exist

elevation the measurement of the height of land above sea level

Emancipation Proclamation a statement by President Abraham Lincoln announcing that all slaves were to be regarded as free citizens

environmentalists people that advocate the care of the animal and plant life of the world

ethnology a branch of anthropology that studies the processes leading to the unique social life of a particular society at a particular time

expansion a cycle in which business activity increases until it reaches a peak

exporting selling goods to another country

fact a statement about something that has actually happened or actually exists

faith trust in something that cannot be proven

Federal Reserve System (FRS) the central banking authority in the U.S. established by Congress in 1913. The FRS supervises commercial banks by checking on accounts and controlling interest rates.

Federalists an early U.S. political party that supported the Constitution and a strong central government

folklore the study of a society's beliefs and traditions

folklorist someone who studies folklore

Food Stamp Program a federal assistance program that issues food stamps to individuals and families having serious financial difficulties

foreign aid money, goods, and services given by one country to another

foreign policy a way in which a country chooses to deal with other nations

fossil fuel combustible matter like natural gas or petroleum formed from the remains of prehistoric plant and animal life

free enterprise the openly competitive market of a capitalist economy which operates by supply and demand

funnel to concentrate, steer, or push in a certain direction

geography the science of studying the Earth's climate, populations, resources, and countries

Gettysburg Address an 1863 speech by President Abraham Lincoln dedicating a national cemetery at Gettysburg, Pennsylvania, and stressing the importance of a unified nation

Good Neighbor Policy a policy that supported the right of Latin American countries to develop their own governmental systems

goods material items made and used by people

government the person or people who administrate and control public policy in a society

graph a drawing that shows how one quantity depends on or changes with another. The four types of graphs are pictographs, line graphs, bar graphs, and pie graphs.

Gross National Product (GNP) the total monetary value of goods and services produced and sold in a country during one year

group two or more people who have regular interaction and who feel something in common with each other

hasty generalization a broad statement based on inadequate evidence

immigration people moving from one country to permanently settle in another country

implication an idea that is not stated directly but is only suggested

importing buying goods from another country

industrialization the process of becoming developed by mechanized industry

Industrial Revolution the time during the 19th century when machines replaced much of the hand labor

inference a type of decision based upon assumptions

inflation a continuing rise in the prices of goods and services

interest rate the percentage paid for the use of borrowed money

isolationism a political policy of separation from other countries

Jim Crow laws discriminatory laws created to separate blacks and whites

labor the human effort involved in making goods or providing services

laissez-faire French for "to leave alone;" the belief that government should interfere as little as possible in the economy

land the natural resources of the Earth; the part of the earth above the water

latitude the distance of a place from the equator

legal authority based upon and permitted by law

legend a list or chart of symbols that explains the information that can be found in a map

legitimate power the basis of a stable government with a leader who has the authority to make decisions that the people will follow

lobbyist a person who tries to influence the voting of those in government

main idea the most important, central theme

map a line drawing of a specific area; a representation of the Earth showing relative size and position

Marshall Plan the plan that helped war-torn Europe to rebuild its economies after the destruction of World War II

mass political participation political activism by a wide and large group, rather than by a small or an elite group

material culture the tools, artifacts, and other objects that a culture produces

Mayflower Compact a key document in American history, stating that the English settlers would form a government and would obey any laws or regulations that would be established by that government at a later time

Medicare an organization that pays some or all medical costs for a U.S. citizen of 65 or over who has worked long enough to qualify for Social Security benefits

monetary economy a system by which goods and services are paid for with money

monopoly a company with exclusive ownership of a product, trade, or use of a business

Monroe Doctrine a foreign-policy statement issued by President James Monroe in 1823 that warned European countries that further interference by those countries in U.S. affairs would no longer be tolerated

muckrake to search for and expose corruption

National Republican party a political party that formed when the Democratic-Republican party split during the presidency of John Quincy Adams

natural resources materials we use that are supplied by nature

New Deal President Franklin Roosevelt's plan to pull the nation out of the depths of an economic crisis

New Frontier President John F. Kennedy's 1960s challenge to fulfill national goals in economic development, civil rights, and space exploration

nonmaterial culture the ways members of a society think and how they do things

ocean a large body of salt water

Open Door Policy a policy that encouraged trade between the U.S. and China and any other interested nations

opinion one person's thoughts or judgments about something he or she has heard, seen, or read

oversimplification two events incorrectly linked as cause and effect

physical features major areas of the Earth's surface that can be seen and observed

platform the policies supported by a political party or candidate

Plessy v. Ferguson a Supreme Court case in which the court ruled that segregation was legal as long as "separate but equal" facilities were provided for blacks

policy a method or plan that helps people take care of their affairs

politicians people who make the decisions about how cities, states, and countries are run

politics the part of government that deals with policy making; the processes used in government

production the creation of goods and services

profit the difference between how much production costs and how much the consumer pays

projection the act of believing that someone else has the problem or bad habit that is actually one's own

propaganda ways in which people try to influence other people's decisions

proprietary colony a colony that was granted to an individual or group by the British government. The owner of the colony selected a governor to rule over the colonists.

psychologist a person who practices psychology

psychology the study of the emotions and behavioral characteristics of individuals and society as a whole

rationalization the act of pretending that something else is the real reason for failing to do something important

reactionary a person who opposes change

reaction formation behavior that is opposite to how one feels or believes

Reaganomics President Ronald Reagan's 1980s plan to curb federal spending in order to reduce huge budget deficits

rebate a refund of part of the purchase price

recession a period when production declines and people have less money

Reconstruction the period of rebuilding the cities, schools, farms, and railroads in the Southern states after the Civil War

red herring propaganda that switches the reader's attention from a relevant political issue to an unrelated issue that appeals to the emotions

region a specific area of the Earth

regulatory commission a commission created by Congress that makes rules and comes to decisions that affect banking, transportation, labor unions, communications, and certain corporations. Regulatory commissions also help to settle disputes between opposing parties.

Republican a member of the Republican party, one of the two major political parties in the U.S.

royal colony a colony with a governor chosen by the King of England

scalawag a white Southern Republican during Reconstruction after the Civil War

scale a ratio between two sets of distance measurements on a map

secede to withdraw from an organization or a federation. Preceding the Civil War, the Southern states seceded from the Union.

segregation separation or withdrawal from a group due to religious or racial differences

self-contradiction two ideas that contradict each other and are used together in an attempt to support an argument

self-governing colony a colony in which the people elected their own governor and members of the legislature

services work that does not produce material items

settle to move to a new place to live

slavery a practice in which a person is owned by and forced to work for another person

socialism a system in which the state owns all the major means of production and plans the economy for the good of all, but encourages competition among small businesses

Social Security a federal insurance plan that pays benefits to retired persons or their spouses, based on their income while working

sociologist someone who studies sociology

sociology the study of human social behavior, especially the relationship between individuals or small groups and society as a whole

special interests groups that band together to seek advantages or make demands upon society

stereotype a biased image of the characteristics of a group of people

stock market the marketplace where securities, stocks, and bonds are traded

subtropical bordering the geographical regions of the tropical zone

summary a short, accurate account of the main points in a spoken or written work

supporting details extra facts that help to explain the main idea

table the arrangement of information in rows and columns

tariff a tax on imported goods; a way of regulating trade by reducing competition from foreign products

topic sentence one sentence that tells the reader what a paragraph or article is about

totalitarian government a centralized government that does not tolerate opposing political opinions

truce a suspension of hostilities for a certain period of time

Truman Doctrine a doctrine issued in 1947 that stated that the U.S. would help any government that requested support against Communist influence

Underground Railroad safe houses across the country for runaway slaves

unemployment insurance weekly cash benefits to workers who have lost their jobs involuntarily

union a workers' organization whose purpose is to advance its members' interests with respect to working conditions, wages, and benefits

values the goals and ideals that make life meaningful for people

Veteran's Administration an organization that gives people who have served in the armed forces money for education, job training, and hospital care, as well as special rates for housing loans and life insurance

Watergate a political scandal caused by high-level coverups leading to the resignation of President Richard Nixon in 1974

waterway a route or passage for water

ACKNOWLEDGMENTS

Grateful acknowledgment is made to the following authors, agents, and publishers for permission to use copyrighted materials.

The *Akron Beacon Journal* for capital gains cartoon by Bok. Reprinted by permission of the *Akron Beacon Journal*. (p. 212)

Chip Bok for capital gains cartoon. Reprinted by permission of the cartoonist. (p. 212)

Cartoon Features Syndicate for cartoon captioned "Made in Hong Kong! Made in Hong Kong! How can we compete with their cheap labor?" from *Can Board Chairmen Get the Measles?* edited by Charles Preston. (p. 163) For cartoon by Wyatt from *Can Board Chairmen Get the Measles?* edited by Charles Preston. (p. 235) Both reprinted by permission of Cartoon Features Syndicate.

Creators Syndicate for cartoon by Mike Luckovich. Copyright © 1989 by Mike Luckovich. Used with permission of Mike Luckovich and Creators Syndicate. (p. 122) For cartoon by Doug Marlette. Copyright © 1989 by Doug Marlette. Used with permission of Doug Marlette and Creators Syndicate. (p. 205)

Gale Research Company for excerpt from *The Weather Almanac*, edited by James A. Ruffner and Frank E. Bair. Gale Research Company, 1987. Reprinted by permission of the publisher. (p. 267)

Indiana University for excerpt from *A Basic Guide to Fieldwork for Beginning Students* by Folklore Publications Group. Reprinted by permission of the Folklore Institute, 504 N. Fess, Bloomington, Indiana 47405. (p. 241)

The *Indianapolis News* for cartoon by Barnett. Copyright © 1989 by Barnett. Reprinted by permission of the *Indianapolis News*. (p. 154)

John Jonik for his cartoon from *Psychology Today*, June 1989. Copyright © 1986 by John Jonik. Reprinted with permission of John Jonik. (p. 242)

King Features Syndicate for *Blondie* strip of March 24, 1990. Reprinted with special permission of King Features Syndicate, Inc. (p. 266)

Macmillan Publishing Company for adapted excerpt from *Geography: An Introductory Perspective* by Robert E. Norris and Keith D. Harries. Copyright © 1982 by Bell & Howell Company. Reprinted by permission of the publisher. (p. 249)

Meredith Corporation for excerpt from "Is Your Child Hyperactive?" in *Better Homes and Gardens*, April 1989. Copyright 1989 Meredith Corporation. All rights reserved. (p. 20)

National Solid Wastes Management Association for map of U.S. landfill capacity. Reprinted by permission of National Solid Wastes Management Association. (p. 211)

The New York Times for excerpt from "What Are Commercials Selling to Children?" by John J. O'Connor, June 6, 1989. Copyright © 1989 by The New York Times Company. Reprinted by permission. (p. 273)

Newsweek magazine for "Rather Astronomical" table from "Harvest of Red Ink" by Rich Thomas in *Newsweek*, September 18, 1989. (p. 197) For excerpt from "Punish the Ambassador" by David Bank and Peter Leyden in *Newsweek*, October 23, 1989.

(p. 204) Reprinted by permission of *Newsweek* magazine.

PT Partners for excerpts from article entitled "Value of Make-Believe" from *Psychology Today*, June 1989. Reprinted with permission from *Psychology Today* magazine. Copyright 1986 PT Partners, L.P. (p. 234)

Public Gaming Research Institute, Inc. for table from *Handbook of Lottery Operations and Statistics*. Reprinted by permission of Public Gaming Research Institute, Inc. (p. 210)

Random House, Inc. for Figure 1 from *The American Profile Poster* by Stephen J. Rose. Copyright © 1986 by Social Graphics Co. Reprinted by permission of Pantheon Books, a division of Random House, Inc. (p. 160)

Richmond Times-Dispatch for cartoon by Brookins. Copyright © 1989. Reprinted by permission of the Richmond Times-Dispatch Newspapers, Inc. (p. 111)

United Media for cartoon by Rob Rogers. Copyright © United Features Syndicate. Reprinted by permission of UFS, Inc. (p. 265) For cartoon by Art and Chip Sansom. Copyright © 1990 by NEA, Inc. Reprinted by permission of UFS, Inc. (p. 83)

USA TODAY for excerpt from "Violence Begets Violence" from *USA TODAY MAGAZINE*, December 1989. Reprinted in *USA TODAY* by the Society for the Advancement of Education. (p. 256) For cartoon by Vietor entitled "Funny Business." Copyright 1989, *USA TODAY*. Reprinted with permission (p. 137) For excerpt from the weather map in *USA TODAY*, September 14, 1989. Copyright 1989, *USA TODAY*. Excerpted with permission. (p. 14) For snapshot entitled "Shrinking Federal Agencies" by

Suzy Parker. (p. 195) Copyright 1989, *USA TODAY*. Reprinted with permission.

The Wall Street Journal—Permission, Cartoon Features Syndicate for cartoon captioned, "We plan to bargain all night until an agreement is reached" from *Can Board Chairmen get the Measles?* edited by Charles Preston. (p. 145)

The Washington Post for Herblock's cartoon captioned "Help" from *The Herblock Gallery* (Simon and Schuster, 1968). Reprinted by permission of Herblock Cartoons and *The Washington Post*. (p. 53) For Herblock's cartoon captioned "Slums" from *The Herblock Gallery* (Simon and Schuster, 1968). Reprinted by permission of Herblock Cartoons and *The Washington Post*. (p. 60)

World Book Publishing for excerpt from an article on the Arctic adapted from *The World Book Encyclopedia*. Copyright © 1990 World Book, Inc. Reprinted by permission of the publisher. (p. 271)

Yale University Press for chart from *Who Votes?* by Raymond E. Wolfinger and Steven J. Rosenstone. Copyright © 1980 by Yale University Press. Reprinted by permission of the publisher. (p. 18)

Every effort has been made to trace the ownership of all copyrighted material, and necessary permissions have been secured. Should there prove to be any question regarding the use of any material, regret is here expressed for such error. Upon notification of any such oversight, proper acknowledgment will be made in future editions.

*Page numbers in parentheses indicate pages in the *Steck-Vaughn GED Social Studies Book*.

INDEX

A

abolitionists, 88

acid rain, 52

Adams, John Quincy, 182

adequacy of information, recognizing, 150

Agricultural Adjustment Act, 110

Alaska, 108

Allied powers, 108

Amendments, 120, 186

American exploration and colonization, 68–69

American Federation of Labor, 100

American political process, 182

American Revolution, 65, 78

Antarctica, 34

Anti-Federalists, 182

anxiety avoidance, 243

apartheid, 201

arms race, 112–113

Articles of Confederation, 80, 82

assumptions, recognizing, 130

authoritarian governments, 172–173, 176

automobile, fuel efficiency, 191

Axis powers, 108

B

banking, 196

bar graph, 48–49, 50, 54–55, 135

barter economies, 132

Battle of Gettysburg, 87, 92

behavior, individual and group, 232

beliefs and values, 230

Berlin Wall, 111

birth and death rates, U.S., 59

black codes, 119

Bush, President George, 162

business cycles, 135

businesses, organization of, 131

C

Canada, features of, 40

capital, defined, 128–129

capitalism, 151

cause and effect
analysis of, 140–141
identifying, 96–97

centralized government, 172

Charles, King of England, 117

checks and balances, 184

Chinese demonstration in 1989, 111

circular argument, 200

cities, problems of, 49

civil disobedience, 112–113

Civil War, 65, 87–88, 92

climate, factors determining, 58–59

collective bargaining, 142

colonization
of America, 68–69, 70–71
motives for, 67

colonize, defined, 65

Columbus, Christopher, 68, 116

communism, 151, 205

compass rose, 30–31

conclusions
distinguishing from supporting statements, 106
drawing, 48

Confederate States of America, 88

Connecticut, 71, 72–73

conservative, defined, 187

Constitution of the United States, 82, 175

consumer rights, 155

consumption, defined, 129

Continental Congress, 78

continents, defined, 26, 30
map of, 27

corporation, defined, 131

cost-push inflation, 159

Cuba, rebellion against Spain, 108

cultural regions, 30, 35

cultural values, 221

culture, defined, 26, 27, 222

S

Samali, 227
sanction, 201
scale, map, 30–31
segregation, 93
self-contradiction, 200
self-governing colonies, 73
Senate, 82
services, 128–129
settle, defined, 64–65
Seven Years War, 77
slavery, 88, 90
sludge, disposal of, 52
slums, 60
socialism, 151
Social Security Act, 110
Social Security program, 192
Soil Conservation Act, 110
South Carolina, 71
Southern colonies, 71–72
South Pole, 34
Soviet Union
    population of, 60
    and U.S. relationship, 65, 122
Spain, in the Americas, 67, 68–69
Stamp Act, 78
stereotypes, 180
summarizing ideas, 38
supporting details, determining, 38
supporting statements, 106

T

table, 27
    reading skills, 40
Taft-Hartley Act, 142
takeovers, 141
taxation, of colonies, 77–78
teenage unemployment, 146
territorial growth in U.S., 81
Texas, map of, 43
13 colonies, 71, 72
topic sentences, 38
totalitarian governments, 172–173, 176
Townsend Act, 78
transportation, importance of, 42
Treaty of Paris, 78

Truman Doctrine, 202
Tuskegee Institute, 102

U

Underground Railroad, 88
unemployment, 146, 162
Unemployment Insurance, 192
unions, 100, 142
United States
    birth and death rates, 59
    features of, 40
    history of, 64–127
    immigration to, 58, 101
    political process in, 182
    population of, 41
    waterways in, 42
    weather in, 44–45

V

values, recognizing, 220
Veterans Administration, 192
Vietnam War, 123
Virginia, 71

W

wage-price spiral, 158–159
War Between the States, 65, 87–88, 92
War of Independence, 78
Washington, Booker T., 102
Washington, George, 118, 182, 202
waste disposal, 52
water cycle, 54
Watergate, 112–113
water pollution, 54
waterways, 42
weather, in U.S., 44–45
Whitney, Eli, 98
"Wild West," 116
world cultural regions, 35
World War I, 108, 123
World War II, 108, 123